Tom

TOM PETTY

Essays on the Life and Work

Edited by Crystal D. Sands

McFarland & Company, Inc., Publishers
Jefferson, North Carolina

LIBRARY OF CONGRESS CATALOGUING-IN-PUBLICATION DATA

Names: Sands, Crystal.
Title: Tom Petty : essays on the life and work / edited by Crystal D. Sands.
Description: Jefferson, North Carolina : McFarland & Company, 2019 |
    Includes bibliographical references and index.
Identifiers: LCCN 2019009041 | ISBN 9781476675480 (paperback : acid
    free paper) ∞
Subjects: LCSH: Petty, Tom—Criticism and interpretation. | Rock
    music—United States—History and criticism.
Classification: LCC ML410.P3135 T66 2019 | DDC 782.42166092—dc23
LC record available at https://lccn.loc.gov/2019009041

ISBN (print) 978-1-4766-7548-0
ISBN (ebook) 978-1-4766-3608-5

BRITISH LIBRARY CATALOGUING DATA ARE AVAILABLE

The front cover image is of Tom Petty, 1989 (MCA Records/Photofest)

Printed in the United States of America

McFarland & Company, Inc., Publishers
  Box 611, Jefferson, North Carolina 28640
  www.mcfarlandpub.com

For my two favorite writers, Ron Sands and Tom Petty.
My soul is thankful for your words.—CS

Table of Contents

Introduction

CRYSTAL D. SANDS

When Tom Petty died on October 2, 2017, much of America was already in mourning over one of the largest mass shootings in our nation's history. As such, Tom Petty's death many not have garnered the media attention one might expect for one of our country's most talented and prolific storytellers. But, in the coming weeks and months, as Tom Petty fans from all walks of life began to process his death and the significant influence of his life and work, stories, fan groups, blog posts, art, and essays began to appear in an attempt to understand the importance of Tom Petty and his legacy.

Since Tom Petty's death, fans from all over the country have articulated how much losing him has impacted their lives, to many, much more so than they expected. Although many fans have struggled to come to terms with their grief, some have discovered that, quite simply, losing Tom Petty felt like they were losing a piece of themselves. Certainly, Petty's music spoke to his fans on a deeply personal level. There is something in his music that is general enough to appeal broadly and yet something so specific and deeply personal that any one of us may feel as if Petty was writing his songs with us in mind.

Mikael Wood from the *Los Angeles Times* writes, "[Tom Petty] was perhaps the quintessential American rock star, with an iconic shades-and-long-hair look, a nasal voice gloriously unsuited to any other genre and a seemingly bottomless bag of tunes that felt as though he'd written them to soundtrack the specifics of your life." Indeed, Petty's ability to make individual connections to such a diverse fan base are unique. With a career spanning forty years and a style that, at times, defied genre, Petty's career as a writer and musician is one that begs for deeper examination and analysis. As more and more people began to write and speak the words, "Tom Petty wrote the soundtrack to my life," I began to wonder what makes this so.

Although Petty's career was jumpstarted in the U.K., his body of work represents one that is quintessentially American—in our most romantic sense.

And though this collection includes essays from authors across the globe, the authors are primarily American, something that seems appropriate given Tom Petty's place in American music and cultural history.

The purpose of this collection is to explore the *why*, not *why* we lost Tom Petty when we did, but *why* he meant so much to so many of us. What gave him the broad appeal that would span generations, political affiliations, educational levels, and socioeconomic statuses? What makes an artist so well loved by so many? Why does his body of work speak to people on personal and philosophical levels? And in responding to these questions of *why*, this collection ultimately explores the diversity of Tom Petty's genius. While he was most certainly one of the most talented song writers and musicians our modern culture has known, he was more than this: He was, to many, an activist, a philosopher, a leader, a critic, and an example of a good human being. Interestingly and profoundly, Tom Petty was often exactly what we needed him to be—and this meant being diverse things to diverse groups of people. Petty, in his broad appeal, remains somewhat of an enigma to me and others. How could one person be so much and so many different things to so many people? One of the things this collection does is explore that enigma and give us much to consider about who Petty was, who he presented himself to be, and how he grew and changed with the times, with America, and as a human being who stood for something more.

Stephen Newton opens this collection with his essay entitled "No! in Thunder: American Wildflowers Reborn." In it, Newton explores a chain of musical and artistic and literary influences that begin with Melville and the American Romantics, are passed down, ultimately, to Tom Petty. Through his analysis, Newton engages the reader in questions about background and both acknowledged and unacknowledged influences we can see in a line of great artists, including writers and musicians, when we simply explore the contextualizations and connections. In as much as this essay situates Tom Petty among both literary and musical geniuses, Newton's exploration offers readers insight into Tom Petty's potential place in literary and musical history and culture.

In "Place, Race and Mutability: Everyman's Hillbilly Rhetoric," Mara Lee Grayson examines Tom Petty's appeal across such diverse audiences. She rhetorically investigates Tom Petty's songs, actions, and public statements to discern some of the personas Tom Petty developed and shared with his fans during his forty-year career. One of the most intriguing aspects of Grayson's study is her focus on the dichotomies Tom Petty presented and how he was able to effectively change, grow, and continually position himself as an important and powerful cultural and musical icon.

In the third essay in this collection, "Tom Petty's 'Magic' of Success and the Craft of a Writer," I investigate Tom Petty's music with a focus on his writing process. Using insight Petty gives into his writing process through interviews, I seek to better understand the writing process of such a rhetorically effective and commercially successful writer. Comparing Petty's process to other successful writers who have shared much of their process in print, including Stephen King and Elizabeth Gilbert, as well as writing process scholarship, I offer a study that can reveal ways in which Petty was consistent with successful writing process practices and unique to his own intuition. I offer readers insight into what a successful and effective writing process looks like and how Tom Petty's process can offer both students and teachers of writing insight into the ways in which hard work, support, and "magic" intersect to create lasting compositions.

In the fourth essay, "A Career in Review," Spencer Rowland follows my study of writing process with another examination of Petty's writing, only with a focus on his product. Rowland delves extensively into reviews of Tom Petty's album releases through his career. This thorough analysis provides readers with a lens through which to consider Tom Petty's success as an artist as seen through his album releases. In doing so, Rowland uses these album reviews, which span the decades of Tom Petty's career, to explore his influence on other artists and pop culture in general.

In a thoughtful examination of Petty's videography, "Psychedelic Strangeness: 'Don't Come Around Here No More' and Other Magical Music Videos," Tom Zlabinger examines another important aspect of Tom Petty's career and legacy—his music videos. With a focus on music videos that fit within the fantasy genre from "You Got Lucky" (1982) to "Walls" (1996), Zlabinger explores ways in which Tom Petty's music videos present a different perspective of Tom Petty as an artist. Through the examination of Petty's fantasy-oriented (and often "trippy") music videos, Zlabinger examines aspects of Petty's musical output enhanced with visions from beyond our world. Zlabinger asserts Petty's series of fantasy-oriented visions constitute a unique blend of music and fantasy, made possible by the medium of music videos.

In another examination of Petty's visual artistry, Lauren Alex O'Hagan offers a fascinating visual analysis of Tom Petty's tour t-shirt art. Her essay, "Running Down an American Dream: Tom Petty and the Tour T-Shirt," explores this often neglected aspect of Tom Petty's creativity and uses multimodal analysis to investigate three tour t-shirts from 1991 to 2003. O'Hagan's analysis demonstrates how Petty's design choices in these t-shirts were used to convey symbolic meaning about Petty's work, specifically the American Dream.

In keeping with visual themes and analysis, Megan Volpert explores Tom Petty's clothing choices in "Fashioning a Rock Star: Petty's Clothing Choices and Their Connections." Volpert examines the ways in which rock stars like Tom Petty use attire choices to establish ethos, which lends itself toward a philosophy of style meant to move audiences in certain ways. Iconic symbols of Tom Petty, including his top hat and velvet jackets are examined. Volpert also explores the ways in which Tom Petty's clothing reflect his musicianship and interest in and connection to other artists, including Stevie Nicks and Kurt Cobain.

In a shift toward cultural analysis, in the next essay in this collection "Contributing to Success: Tom Petty, the Heartbreakers and Baby Boomer Behavior," Rebecca A. Caton explores core values of the Baby Boomer generation and how these values can be seen in the success of Tom Petty and the Heartbreakers. Caton also offers important insight into the ways in which Tom Petty was able to take certain leadership qualities significant in the Baby Boomer generation to aid in his transition into an artist who would ultimately have appeal across many generations.

In "Pretty Woman, American Girl: The Female in American Popular Music, 1960–2000," Pamela P. O'Sullivan examines women's roles from the 1950s to recent decades and explores the ways in which Tom Petty's portrayal of women offers a different perspective. O'Sullivan argues that Petty's portrayal of women was never stereotypical and that he did more than many of his musical contemporaries by portraying women as more than objects. In her analysis, O'Sullivan studies the portrayal of women in American music through several decades and contends that Tom Petty offers a more complete, complex presentation of women in his work.

Alessandra Clayton Trindle follows with "Rebels, Refugees and American Girls: A Study of Tom Petty's Political Mojo," an engaging exploration of Tom Petty on a more personal level. By examining his music, his management style, his personal life, and political leanings, Trindle reveals patterns that offer some insight in Tom Petty and a life philosophy from him. She contends that Tom Petty's choices in music and in life reveal a person who was anti-authoritarian, rejecting capitalism in many ways.

In the next essay, "Something Good: An Exploration of the Issue of Cover Bands," Karen Friend explores the issue of tribute and cover bands among Tom Petty fans and what these bands contribute to Tom Petty's legacy. In conducting original interviews with both fans and members of tribute bands, Friend examines the tribute band phenomenon and puts it in context of Elvis Presley tributes, bringing the idea of the way artists influence future generations in different ways full circle.

In "Fears, Frustrations and Knowing How It Feels: The Emotional Signifiers of Tom Petty's Songs," Nate Bauer and Shye Gilad provide an in-depth analysis of Tom Petty's music in relation to his appeal to broad audiences. Bauer and Gilad use psychological and sociological theories to analyze themes and language in Petty's work that make his work so universally appealing.

The authors examine 20 songs for themes related to social belonging, esteem, and self-actualization. They make some interesting and profound connections between Petty's music and the economic conditions within American culture.

The final essay of this collection, "Peace and Petty: Music's Healing Power," by Shawn W. Murphy brings readers full circle with an analysis of the ways in which Tom Petty's music promotes healing during times of anguish, loss, and grief. Using psychology studies combined with personal accounts from Tom Petty fans, Murphy contends that music, specifically Tom Petty's music in this case, can be helpful to humans as we process and deal with difficult times in our lives, such as times of anxiety, divorce, death of a loved one—and even the death of Tom Petty himself. Readers who have struggled during difficult times and used music as a part of the healing process should find Murphy's study both fascinating and helpful.

Ultimately, this collection of essays is meant to offer an insightful analysis into some of the many facets of Tom Petty's talent, genius, and influence. When selecting writers for this collection, I aimed for analysis that is both meaningful and accessible to those who want to learn more about Tom Petty and the power of his presence in our culture as one of the most prolific and successful artists of our generation. While this kind of thoughtful analysis is a necessary component to understanding the cultural significance of Tom Petty's life and work, this collection goes even further to *honor* the cultural significance of Tom Petty's life and work.

No! in Thunder

American Wildflowers Reborn

Stephen Newton

"There is the grand truth about Nathaniel Hawthorne. He says No! in thunder; but the Devil himself cannot make him say *yes*."
—Herman Melville, Letter to Nathaniel Hawthorne, April 16, 1851

In this essay, I am going to explore ways that Tom Petty both exemplifies and expresses what I believe to be a longtime underground current in American culture, a stream that has both surfaced and submerged with a steady, churning regularity for the last 150 years, but which has rarely, if ever, been explicitly articulated in the context of the work of Mr. Petty. This line of connections, I want to argue, is in actual fact a tradition, but it does take a bit of explanation if one is going be so bold as to call it that, as the word tradition implies, at least most of the time, a kind of conscious intent in the creative process, a sense of belonging to a distinct, clearly defined lineage, and while this is demonstrably true with a few of the artists I am going to be writing about, when it comes to some of the most important ones, like the Beatles, The Traveling Wilburys, the Rolling Stones, and to a lesser degree Bob Dylan and the Byrds, the lines of influence and the distant demarcations of possible affinities become much more difficult to construe, however inarguably evident the sympathetic vibrations might be.

In an article in the online edition of *Rolling Stone Magazine*, published on November 14, 2002, journalist David Wild wrote the following:

The man who told the world "I Won't Back Down," "Don't Do Me Like That" and "Don't Come Around Here No More" doesn't need any assertiveness-training course. Tom Petty's determined, sometimes defiant attitude has collided with the music business throughout the years. For instance, in 1982 Petty recorded *Hard Promises* with the Heartbreakers, only to find that his then-record company had plans to use his name to initiate a new, higher $9.98 list price for albums. Petty withheld the tapes and threatened to retitle his record $8.98 in protest [Wild].

Mr. Petty stonewalled the corporations selling his concert tickets when they wanted to raise the ticket prices, at no little cost to his own career, at least in the short term. He stood up for his fans, for all of the people that had been supporting him, in the face of the corrupt, thieving suits, the minions of the corporate power players in the music business. His actions brought down a rain of criticism on Mr. Petty from the higher-ups in the string-pulling, puppet master business world, but in the midst of the storm, in the center of the downpour with lightning flashing all around him, Tom Petty said No! in thunder, in the same way that Herman Melville described Nathaniel Hawthorne.

But 150 years after Melville wrote his letter to Hawthorne, Tom Petty was using the rock and roll hammers of the gods—the Fender Stratocaster, Fender Esquire, Fender 12 String, and Fender Telecaster, the Gibson 335, Gibson Firebird, Gibson Flying V, and Gibson SG, the Rickenbacker 12 String, the Guild 12 String, the Ampeg Dan Armstrong Plexi, and the Gretsch Country Gentleman, as his warrior totems. Tom Petty was saying, in effect, that this ticket price inflation stops, and it stops here and now.

In the midst of a cataclysm, then, Tom Petty would not back down. You could stand him up at the gates of the inferno, and Tom Petty would still be standing there, holding up, perhaps, his sunburst 1964 Stratocaster, (which actually belonged to lead guitarist and co-songwriter Mike Campbell, but Tom played it in the Heartbreakers for decades) like Ahab holding up his burning harpoon in the lightning storm. Tom Petty was saying No! in the midst of the thunder, yes, but he was also saying No! thunderously, and he did this throughout his career.

In a chapter titled "The Candles" in *Moby Dick*, Herman Melville writes, "But dashing the rattling lightning links to the deck, and snatching the burning harpoon, Ahab waved it like a torch among them: swearing to transfix with it the first sailor that but cast loose a rope's end" (383). *The Pequod*, the whaling ship hunting Moby Dick, had been hit by a typhoon, and in the midst of flashes of lightning and flames at the tops of the three masts of the ship, and then at the end of Ahab's harpoon, Ahab goes on a kind of metaphysical rant—like Lear, perhaps, also in a storm—which is an expression of individual resistance in the face of the inscrutable, cosmically unknowable face of the infinite. "Oh! Thou clear spirit of clear fire, whom on these seas I as a Persian once did worship, till in the sacramental act so burned by thee, that to this hour I bear the scar; I now know thee, thou clear spirit, and I know that the right worship is defiance" (Melville 382). In *Call Me Ishmael* poet Charles

Olson argued that *King Lear* was an inspiration *for Moby Dick*. "It was Lear that had the deep creative impact. In *Moby Dick* the use is pervasive" (Olson 46).

Mr. Petty, then, was, in a sense, also creating a storm much like the typhoon that hit the Pequod, only he did it with his angry, rebellious actions, his bad boy attitude, his refusal, in fact, to back down, which, of course, his song of the same name says that he rather explicitly will not do, and it is precisely this kind of complex, distilled, intelligent, simultaneously raw and refined rebellion that is one of the hallmarks of not only Tom Petty's work, but also arguably of Walt Whitman, Henry David Thoreau, Ralph Waldo Emerson, Herman Melville, Ezra Pound, T.S. Eliot, Allen Ginsberg, Jack Kerouac, William S. Burroughs, Bob Dylan, the Beatles, and the Rolling Stones.

Is it too much of a reach to compare Ahab to Tom Petty when Tom is singing "I Won't Back Down," "Don't Do Me Like That," "I Don't Scare Easy," "You Don't Have To Live Like a Refugee," "You Don't Know How it Feels" or "Stop Dragging My Heart Around"? Some people might say that this is an absurd comparison, a reach that exceeds its grasp, but I want to argue that placing Tom Petty in this particular context, of mythic rebellious American literature, a world of the imagination where visions of the everyday are charged with the same electricity that ignites sparks and flames on the tip of a monomaniac's harpoon, creating fire that burns with an otherworldly heat, is precisely the place where we can perhaps begin to find some of the transhistorical metaphysics that inform the enduring truth of the music and ever-present, jagged, musically explosive presence of Tom Petty.

There are few people more closely identified with Tom Petty than Bob Dylan. Dylan was a huge influence on both Petty's singing and songwriting; Tom Petty and the Heartbreakers opened for Dylan, and were his backing band as well, during a tour of Australia in the mid-eighties. Dylan also, of course, along with George Harrison, Jeff Lynne, Tom Petty and Roy Orbison, was a member of the Traveling Wilburys. The following passage is from Bob Dylan's Nobel Prize for Literature acceptance speech, where he is describing Moby Dick and the influence that it had on his songwriting:

> Ahab's harpoon has been baptized in blood. Moby attacks Ahab's boat and destroys it. Next day, he sights Moby again. Boats are lowered again. Moby attacks Ahab's boat again. On the third day, another boat goes in. More religious allegory. He has risen. Moby attacks one more time, ramming the Pequod and sinking it. Ahab gets tangled up in the harpoon lines and is thrown out of his boat into a watery grave. Ishmael survives. He's in the sea floating on a coffin. And that's about it. That's the whole story. That theme and all that it implies would work its way into more than a few of my songs [Dylan].

In a sense, perhaps, we are all, always, "in the sea floating on a coffin" moving through our lives and doing whatever we can do, some days better than others, to help us make it through. It might be a commonplace thing to say that rock roll music can help people get through these hard times, but it might be that Tom Petty's music functions in precisely this way for his fans in ways that are more immediate and profound than that of many, even most, other rock and roll musicians, and it might also be true that part of this sympathetic response is due to the fact that Mr. Petty himself went through some very publicly acknowledged difficulties—he experienced child abuse when he was growing up, struggled with drug addiction, had gotten divorced, and dealt with the aforementioned entanglements with nefarious conscience-challenged capitalists who wanted to rip off his fans—but it might also be true that Tom Petty just had a knack for taking whatever hard luck life may have thrown at him and somehow, through an alchemical, transformational magic, injected that pain and heartache into songs that, while not being clearly autobiographical, nevertheless were informed by deep currents of both personal and cultural feeling that then were combined, merging in ways that made people identify with the music in mysterious, yet comforting, ways.

There are obviously times when one might be temporarily feeling bad, and then, through consuming some kind of art—listening to music, reading a novel or a poem, looking at a painting in a museum, watching a movie—one can somehow feel a little bit better, though it might well be that this happens in ways that are not really clear. Sometimes, of course, it is through a kind of catharsis, to use the Greek term originally derived from a word for cleansing. But one might also argue that it is because the music was forged precisely out of a crucible of pain and rage in Mr. Petty's life, his traumatic personal history. This cauldron of intersecting forces, one might argue, also produced the elusive, magical, slippery magician persona that enabled Tom Petty to remain firmly entrenched in American popular culture for forty years, a will o' the wisp that could disappear in the blink of an eye but who also always returned to center stage.

From Queequeg, Walt and Alice to Allen, Jack and Bob

Early in *Moby Dick*, Melville has a bizarrely comedic introduction to Queequeg, a tattooed, harpoon wielding South Sea cannibal whom Ishmael encounters at the Spouter Inn, and winds up sleeping with the night they meet in a strange kind of quasi-homoerotic-but-not-quite sort of honeymoon marriage bed. The next morning they have breakfast:

> But as for Queequeg—why, Queequeg sat there among them—at the head of the table, too, it so chanced; as cool as an icicle. To be sure I cannot say very much for his breeding. His greatest admirer could not have cordially justified his bringing his

harpoon into breakfast with him, and using it there without ceremony; reaching over the table with it, to the imminent jeopardy of many heads, and grappling the beefsteaks towards him. But that was certainly done very cooly by him, and everyone knows that in most people's estimation, to do anything cooly is to do it genteely [Melville 40].

To say that Tom Petty was cool is to perhaps understate the matter by a significant degree, at least for people of a certain age, but even there, I think that there are people across multiple age groups that would say that Tom Petty was pretty gosh darned chill. Coolness, or the state or condition of being cool, is a hard word or concept to define, although many people have tried, but if you look at the music video for "Don't Come Around Here No More" with Tom Petty playing the Mad Hatter in a surrealistic interpretation of *Alice's Adventures in Wonderland*, I think that most young people today, seeing this video from thirty years ago, would say the guy singing the song is an eminently cool dude. I could be wrong about that, of course, and it certainly would not be the first or last time, but I am around young people every day, at the university where I am an English professor, and I do not think that I am mistaken. I also would submit that the Mad Hatter is a mysterious trickster figure, magical and elusive, able to conjure up hallucinatory images, with Tom Petty as the Hatter acting as both ringmaster and wizard, effortlessly spinning a wondrous web of surrealistic chaos, but all the while, and perhaps most importantly, maintaining his cool. Tom Petty was always, and apparently also effortlessly, the most chill hombre in the room, but he was also always essentially a mystery, a cloud floating over a rainforest in the mist, which was a big part of the elusive, hippest cat on the block, and catnip to all of the kitties, vibe. Tom Petty in fact wore a top hat while he was backing up Bob Dylan, playing a blonde Gibson ES-335 vintage hollow body guitar, and as far as this old cowboy is concerned, it just does not get any cooler than that.

There is a clear line of influence and affection that runs from the authors of the American Renaissance to some of the central writers of the Beat Generation. Allen Ginsberg's debt to Walt Whitman is well documented, perhaps most clearly seen in his poem "In a Supermarket in California," but Ginsberg also paid tribute to Ezra Pound, visiting Pound in Rapallo, Italy in 1968, where Pound was receiving visitors but basically not talking, existing in a kind of existential isolation in his late life silent period. Dylan acknowledged Jack Kerouac in his memoir *Chronicles: Volume One* as being one of his major influences, one of his guiding lights. Dylan writes, "I suppose what I was looking for was what I read about in On The Road—looking for the great city, looking for the speed, the sound of it, looking for what Allen Ginsberg had called 'the hydrogen jukebox world'" (Dylan 235). On Dylan's 1975 Rolling Thunder Revue tour, which had a kind of expanded group of supporting musicians including Roger McGuinn from The Byrds, Dylan went to visit

Kerouac's grave in Lowell, Massachusetts, with Allen Ginsberg, who was also traveling with the tour. "In a cemetery outside Lowell, Dylan played guitar and Ginsberg played harmonium at Jack Kerouac's grave, improvising a song and a scene while the cameras rolled. Dylan read aloud a poem of Kerouac's from Ginsberg's copy of *Mexico City Blues* " (Epstein 234).

The connection of Dylan to Petty and the Beatles and the Wilburys is clear, but there are also other, less obvious, connections. Johnny Cash wrote the liner notes for Dylan's 1968 album *Nashville Skyline*, and Dylan appeared on *The Johnny Cash Show*, which was broadcast from the Ryman Auditorium, the original home of the Grand Ole Opry, in June 1969. Tom Petty sang harmony and played guitar, and The Heartbreakers were the band, for a Johnny Cash nineties album produced by Rick Rubin. On that album Tom sang a Merle Haggard song with Cash, "The Running Kind." Tom also played a cover version of "Lost Highway," a Hank Williams song, in a rehearsal that is on YouTube, and Dylan acknowledges Hank Williams as one of his biggest influences, along with Woody Guthrie. There is a clear connection, then, if one chooses to look for it and see it, from the Beats to both Whitman and Pound, and to Whitman through Pound. Pound also was one of the main editors and shapers of "The Waste Land," by T. S. Eliot, and there is a famous line in Dylan, in "Desolation Row," on Highway 61 Revisited, involving Ezra Pound and T. S. Eliot having an argument in a tower. The connections of Tom Petty and the writers of the American Renaissance, then, through the Beats, as well as through the early twentieth century high modernists, is not a frivolous reach. But it goes on and on, once you start teasing it out a little bit.

Dylan famously turned the Beatles on to marijuana in a hotel in NYC in 1964, a seminal cultural event which clearly had far reaching effects all over the world, and Tom Petty's connection to both the Beatles and Dylan has multiple levels, from the influence on his songwriting and singing, to his touring with Dylan, to the Traveling Wilburys, where both Dylan and George Harrison were members, to Petty's appearance at The Concert for George, the tribute to George Harrison in London after Harrison's death in 2001, to Petty's performance of "While My Guitar Gently Weeps" at The Rock and Roll Hall of Fame, and Petty's appearance along with Harrison, Eric Clapton, Neil Young, and a host of other luminaries, at the 30th Anniversary Concert celebrating Dylan's career at Madison Square garden in 1992.

These connections are not only influences that come from music on the radio, or through fan magazines or television. They can also be organized according to geography. Many of Tom Petty's artistic inspirations and relationships were centered in California, where he moved after leaving Florida, and stayed for forty years, when he was not on the road, and Merle Haggard was a kind of archetypal California singer-songwriter. Haggard led an authentically outlaw life, and he was always in a kind of liminal condition—an ex-con singing country, jazz, western swing, blues, rock and roll, yet all with a social conscience that would have been a par with James Agee and Walker Evans. "Irma Jackson," written and performed by Haggard, was the first interracial love song on a country album, and there is a strong connection to the openhearted Whitmanic vision here—although probably not consciously, but who knows. Haggard's family were Okies, the people who left Oklahoma, Texas, and Arkansas during the dust bowl, the struggling, impoverished field workers that Steinbeck and Woody Guthrie wrote about, and Guthrie, Ginsberg, and Kerouac were all significant influences on Dylan, who toured with Merle Haggard in 2005, where I saw them perform at the Beacon Theatre in Manhattan. Ginsberg and Kerouac, as well as Woody Guthrie, had also effaced the high-low distinction in American literature in their work, but Bob Dylan perhaps most influentially did it. Regarding Dylan, Joshua Clover writes, "His apotheosis is an index of perhaps the most singular fact concerning 'the literary' in the post—World War II era: the accelerating collapse of high and popular art into a seemingly homogenous sphere of 'culture'" (Clover 904–908).

That collapse had already been long-erased by Melville, who was an influence on Kerouac, and by James Joyce, also an influence on Kerouac and possibly on Dylan, who mentions reading James Joyce in one of his more recent songs, and then along comes Merle Haggard, an ex-con banty rooster honky-tonk singer with a punk attitude and killer chops, singing about executions and doomed men walking past his cell, about labor camps and interracial romance, about turning twenty-one in prison, and this was all happening at the same time that the Beats were writing and influencing the West Coast scene, with Neal Cassady, another San Quentin con at the same time that Haggard was there, who was the inspiration for Dean Moriarty, the always fast-moving American Adonis and primary driving force in Jack Kerouac's *On the Road*. Cassady went on to drive the psychedelic bus on its trip across the country commandeered by Ken Kesey, author of *One Flew Over the Cuckoo's Nest*. Kesey had held several psychedelic events in California in the mid–1960s, called Acid Tests, at a time when LSD was still legal, and the Grateful Dead were the house band, and Neal Cassady sometimes provided stream of continuous narration over the PA system for the electrified revelers. By February 1970, when I saw the Grateful Dead at the Fillmore East with the Allman Brothers, they played "Mama Tried," by Merle Haggard. Twenty five years after that, Tom Petty sang a Merle Haggard song on a Johnny Cash album—after touring as both opening act and backing band for Bob Dylan in the time in between, which the Grateful Dead did as well—and twenty years after that, Petty produced a record by Chris Hillman, who played bass and sang in the Byrds, one of the biggest influences on Petty of all of the Sixties bands. It is all part, I would argue, of the same weave.

It is perhaps also time to start considering the ways, then, that Tom Petty is part of some expanded literary and musical tradition, or web, or architecture, or firmament, one that includes Merle Haggard, Bob Dylan, Woody Guthrie, Jack Kerouac, Ezra Pound, the Beatles, Elvis, T.S. Eliot, Herman Melville, Mick Jagger, Hank Williams, Van Morrison, Keith Richards—famously a great friend of Gram Parsons—and Walt Whitman, a line of writers that sings the song of the self as lyric autobiography for the common people as well as for the intelligentsia, giving us all ways to interpret our lives and escape from and transcend our troubles while at the same time holding up a mirror to the times. These writers do not need us to say they are legitimate. We need them to keep us from becoming absurd.

Tom Petty produced Chris Hillman's 2017 Rounder Records album, *Bidin' My Time*, which had harmony vocals by David Crosby and Roger McGuinn. Hillman, McGuinn and Crosby were all original members of the Byrds. After Crosby left the Byrds he was replaced by Gram Parsons, who then went on to form the Flying Burrito Brothers with Hillman, before recording two solo albums with Emmy Lou Harris and part of Elvis's back-up band, notably James Burton on guitar, but also Glen D. Hardin on keyboards, Ronnie Tutt on drums, and Emory Gordy, Jr., on bass, all of whom toured with Elvis, for Parsons' second solo album, *The Return of the Grievous Angel*. Rick Grech from Blind Faith played bass on Parsons first solo album, GP, along with the other Elvis band musicians from the second solo record. Petty has long acknowledged the influence that Gram Parsons had on him when he was playing in Mudcrutch, and he famously told a story of seeing Elvis in person when Elvis came to Gainesville to film one of his eminently forgettable movies, an appearance that made a huge impression on Tom. Dylan mentions in *Chronicles* listening to Ricky Nelson on the radio when he first came to NYC, and how they were roughly the same age and had been shaped by many of the same things. James Burton played the hot lead guitar on Ricky Nelson's records, as well as on Merle Haggard's mid-sixties Bakersfield hits, and then went on to play with Gram and Elvis and Emmy Lou Harris in her Hot Band, after Gram Parsons 1973 death of a morphine overdose in a motel room near Joshua Tree National Park, in California.

The circle of life goes around and around. Both Tom Petty and Prince, the team that performed so transcendently at the Rock and Roll Hall of Fame Concert tribute to George Harrison, performing "While My Guitar Gently Weeps," were to die only a year apart, 2016 and 2017, both due to accidental fentanyl overdoses related to severe pain, perhaps caused by all of the years of hard touring. Fentanyl is an opioid, the same family of drugs that killed Janis Joplin, Jim Morrison, Tim Buckley, Mike Bloomfield, Paul Butterfield, Tim Hardin, Jesse Ed Davis, Lowell George, Danny Whitten, and, of course, Howie Epstein, long-time bass layer in the Heartbreakers, as well as multiple grunge musicians in later decades, and which also kept Jerry Garcia addicted for much of his adult life. It perhaps does not need to be pointed out that dying of an overdose is part of a long tradition for rock and roll and jazz musicians, and when coupled with deaths caused by years of hard living.

But one of the best ways to celebrate life, in the midst of our own ever-approaching mortality, is by singing along and dancing to a crackerjack, kick-ass rock and roll band. Sometimes the songs that can be the most mindless, forget your troubles and party, carpe diem and rock the night away, purely just plain old fun, are songs you remember fondly from your (perhaps) mis-spent youth. Tom Petty habitually covered songs like this in live performances, songs that many, if not most, people would consider garage band music, a kind of American primitive songbook of the barbaric yawp, raucous rockers that predated punk but shared a similar embrace of only the most rudimentary musical skills, a lack of anything even remotely approaching emotional complexity, at least lyrically, and only the most rudimentary songwriting ability. Many of these songs were part of the beach culture/frat party/Animal House ethos that Mr. Petty and the Heartbreakers came up with, in Florida in 1960s, songs Petty covered live, like "A Little Bit of Soul," "Psychotic Reaction" "Gloria," "Shout," and "Baby Please Don't Go." This is also a music, how-ever, where one can clearly see Tom Petty as both seer and shaman, channeling the halcyon years of his youth as refracted and reflected through the silver bullet performance of a band that was light years in skill levels beyond any of the original performers, some of whom, like the Byrds, had The Wrecking Crew, a crackerjack A-team of L.A. studio musicians, playing on the original tracks, rather than the musicians in the band.

Mr. Petty also performed covers of songs that were a little bit to harder the categorize, songs such as "So You Want to be a Rock 'n' Roll Star," "Don't Bring Me Down," "Bye Bye Johnny," "Carol," "Oh Well," "Ballad of Easy Rider," "Born in Chicago," "Willin'," "Image of Me," "Mystic Eyes," "Roll Over Beethoven," "Diddy Wah Diddy," "I'm a Man," "Friend of the Devil," "I Just Want to Make Love to You," and "Little Red Rooster," some of which, but by no means all, were AM radio hits, either by the original artists, or perhaps more frequently as cover versions, usually by British invasion bands, at a time when Tom Petty and the Heartbreakers were teenagers in Florida or when they were coming up in the seventies. Others were album tracks or B-sides, the flip side of a 45-rpm record, or single. These songs, however, could probably not be strictly or properly called garage band, proto punk rock, or beach party music, although these categories are, admittedly, rather dramat-ically permeable, at best, and almost all of these songs did share a kind of driven joy and hypnotic abandonment that also frequently characterized some of the more, shall we say, elementary songs. And make no mistake about it, garage band or Americana, channeled Celtic mysticism or teen rave up, protopunk or beach party hullabaloo, they all were songs that rocked the house, and rocked it hard.

A couple of things are consistent with these cover song performances, and these qualities did not really vary much at all in this regard, from gig to gig. One unchanging factor was that Tom Petty and the Heartbreakers were one of the truly great cover bands of all time, when they wanted to be, which was every night, actually, taking all of these songs and performing them in ways that, for the most part, the original performers could only have dreamt of achieving—a big statement, but one that I do not think most rock and roll musicians would argue with, especially if they watch live performance videos of Tom Petty and the Heartbreakers.

Dive Bars, Honky Tonks and Beachside Lounges

Wait—forget that. Rock and roll musicians, and jazz musicians, as well as blues and folk and bluegrass and heavy metal musicians, will argue about almost anything, if the internet guitar player discussion forums that I read are any indication. I would venture, however, that if any kind of rough consensus could ever be reached on these esoteric kinds of things, surely Tom Petty and the Heartbreakers are part of a very, very short list of the greatest all-time cover bands, perhaps only along with Bruce Springsteen and the E Street Band. There really is not anyone else that even comes close when it comes to performing covers of somewhat obscure hits from fifty years ago with consummate skill, cannonball ferocity, and a gospel fervor that brings the ethos, drama, lightning bolt crackling energy, and steam engine thunder, of that old time tent revival religion onto the rock and roll stage. I realize that this is the kind of statement that people argue about at closing time in dive bars, honky tonks, beachside lounges, and exclusive high-rise cafes, in much the same way that baseball fans used to eternally argue over Mickey Mantle versus Willie Mays, and I also realize that there is no clear cut definitive answer, but, for what it is worth, to quote an old Buffalo Springfield song, I stand by that statement.

On the 1985 *Pack Up the Plantation Tour*, Tom wore what came to be known as his space suit. It looks like it was perhaps made for a wizard cocktail lounge singer, or a transgalactic businessman, or a shaman CEO of an interdimensional corporation. The suit jacket and pants were covered with crescent moons and planets and there were rocket ships on the sleeves and legs. One can watch these performances easily on YouTube. Of course Tom and the Heartbreakers are playing seamlessly, expertly, crashing through any possible boundaries that might separate them from their audience, doing a kind of high-wire prismatic dance composed of precisely appropriate guitar tones and musical phrases—rhythms, patterns, licks, swells, growls, screeches, moans, and whistles, churning driving wheel low notes and hummingbird filigrees of sliding delicacy—which then are married to an equally sophisticated and refined phalanx of musical counterpoint from the drums, keyboards, second guitar, back-up singers, and, on the 1985 tour, horn section, to create a seamless blend of divinely heavenly racket, the likes of which has seldom been heard anywhere with this professionally exact, precise samurai sword delivery, all of which is offset by the floating, ethereal image of Tom Petty wearing a suit covered with planets and rockets.

But these moments, these performances on this 1985 tour, are also emblematic of a kind of deep and little recognized fellowship, and this is the second thing that is consistent with these cover versions. Tom Petty was, I want to argue, always a part of a somewhat elusive and perhaps even mysteriously vaporous tradition, one that supports, informs, and undergirds his music as a kind of invisible interior architecture, a celestial blueprint that threads through Tom Petty's music like silk through steel, and, in fact, I want to argue furthermore that there are really several traditions at work, one of which is really just the tradition of being in an artistic center, an inspirational nexus of forces of whiplash ferocity that drive an audience wild one moment and into swoons of passion the next, with all of it focused on the band of traveling wizards that have come to their town and who will be leaving after the show.

I listed off a bunch of guitars, earlier, when I was referring to Tom holding up his hammer of the gods sunburst 1964 Fender Stratocaster like Ahab's flaming harpoon, and this is another place where Tom Petty and Mike Campbell both, throughout their careers, have rather rigorously placed themselves within strictly defined parameters of rock and roll tradition. There have been exceptions, primarily with Mike playing Duesenberg guitars, which are a contemporary German brand, but for their entire careers Tom Petty and Mike Campbell have both played, pretty much exclusively, vintage American guitars and amplifiers, primarily from the 1960s, and, to a significantly lesser degree, some British guitars and amps.

Tom Petty and the Heartbreakers had a warehouse practice space in Los Angeles filled with guitars and amplifiers, and they were all vintage pieces, a veritable museum of mid-twentieth century guitar Americana, but as such it was also a temple of totems, of magical power amulets, keys to the kingdom, the tools of heroes, the shards and gathered treasures of one man's modern day Iliad and Odyssey, both siege and war and the attendant voyage home, the spear points, electricity, wire, wood, paint, tweed and vacuum tubes that shaped and sculpted the heartbreaking poetic diction of a boy from Gainesville who rocked the world, a clubhouse filled with magical resonance, with clouds of dreams, repeating through the years and sweetened by the driving rock of one of the finest bands the world has ever seen. Let the light-ning come. This man, and this band, will say No! in thunder while flames leap from their Fender and Gibson harpoons, and the sails fill with the wind of hound dog poetry and Florida hurricane power, with a Mudcrutch rhythm roiling and churning away under the Spanish moss hanging like wisps of green fog from the live oaks of Gainesville.

But there is also another way that Mr. Petty connects to some of the writers from 160 years ago, and it is one that also threads through many of the writers in this loosely construed tradition that passes from Melville and Whitman and Emerson and Thoreau, to Pound and Eliot, and on to Ginsberg and Kerouac and eventually on to Dylan and Harrison and Petty. That con-nection, I want to argue, is perhaps most clearly and lucidly exemplified in one of the most popular and representative songs in the entire Tom Petty and the Heartbreakers catalog, and which was the song that was the last one played at Mr. Petty's final concert, with the Heartbreakers, at the Hollywood Bowl. That song is "American Girl."

If any of Tom Petty's songs can be said to carry symbolic meaning, and perhaps even a kind of metaphysical weight, and which may be a kind of symbol in and of itself, it would be "American Girl." This song encapsulates so many ideas and themes in such a short yet charged space that it virtually explodes with meaning, radiating vectors of power and romantic yearning through both the lyrics and the music.

In one of his most famous and often quoted reviews, the rock critic Lester Bangs, who died in 1982 at age 33, of a drug overdose, writes, of Van Morrison's 1968 album, *Astral Weeks*:

> Astral Weeks, insofar as it can be pinned down, is a record about people stunned by life, completely overwhelmed, stalled in their skins, their ages and selves, paralyzed by the enormity of what in one vision they can comprehend. It is a precious and ter-rible gift, born of a terrible truth, because what they see is both infinitely beautiful and terminally horrifying: the unlimited human ability to create or destroy, accord-ing to whim. It's no Eastern or mystic or psychedelic vision of the emerald beyond, nor is it some Baudelairean perception of the beauty of sleaze and grotesquerie. Maybe what it boils down to is one moment's knowledge of the miracle of life, with its inevitable concomitant, a vertiginous glimpse of the capacity to be hurt, and the capacity to inflict that hurt" [Bangs 23–24].

He might as well of been writing about "American Girl."

At the final concert Tom begins the song with ringing chords played on the Fender electric twelve-string, a somewhat esoteric, but also both emi-nently practical, and simultaneously reverently historical, choice. Electric twelve-string guitars have a unique and instantly recognizable sound, like the guitar intro to "Mr. Tambourine Man" by the Byrds, or George Harrison's guitar on "You Can't Do That," "Ticket to Ride," and "If I Needed Someone," by the Beatles, all of which were played on Rickenbacker twelve-strings. Tom Petty and Mike Campbell both played Rickenbackers, along with Fenders, Gibsons, and Gretsches, and Mike Campbell played a Rickenbacker six string on "American Girl" at the Hollywood Bowl, but Rickenbacker twelve-strings are somewhat fragile and temperamental for touring, as they are notorious for having tuning problems and being susceptible to temperature changes. The Fender XII is more of a workhorse. But the Fender XII is also a California guitar, an archetypally American icon, streamlined, sting ray sleek, with the swooping lines of a modernist hot rod fever dream, and for this song, in this place, it was an inspired choice, a mid-twentieth century Beach Boys looking slice of the California subconscious, reminiscent of the guitars a teenage boy would have seen on TV in Florida in 1965, on Shindig, a Los Angeles rock and roll show that featured James Burton on lead guitar in the Shindogs, the house band.

Tom Petty begins "American Girl" with a ringing, jangly, Fender XII string chord, and then the band kicks in. Oh my. Here we go. The finely tuned machine is there once more in front of us, with three members that go all the way back to Gainesville in the early seventies, Mike Campbell on guitar, Benmont Tench on keyboards, and Ron Blair on bass, along with the new guys, Scott Thurston on second guitar, only around 26 years, and Steve Ferrone on drums, only twenty two years, and then we are off, into the land of myth and dreams, roaring down the open road searching for the heart's true home. "American Girl" is a vision in miniature, a microcosm of sound and image that can only be approximated in words in a kind of remote way, which is the hopefully understood curse of anyone trying to write about music, especially rock and roll, when you only have black marks on the page at your disposal, but I'll swing for the fences here and maybe a tiny bit will connect.

In *Moby Dick* there are many levels of interpretation, as there always are with any serious and even great works of literature, and one of these interpretations takes the Pequod, the whaling ship that Ishmael ships out on from Nantucket, as arguably a symbol of America in mid-nineteenth century, when the country was becoming industrialized but had not yet reached anything close to its incredible potential in manufacturing. At that time whaling was the country's biggest industry, and although it would only last until the discovery of oil in western Pennsylvania, at the time, in the 1850's, whaling was huge, and Melville goes to great lengths to describe the dark, savage, and even satanic forces at work in the harvesting of the whale oil the country needed. It was a hunting vessel, yes, but it was also a factory ship, and the stripping of the whales of their blubber and the rendering of the flesh into oil in the middle of night on the open sea is an indelible scene, dark, with flashing lights, and huge clouds of stinking black smoke.

Twists and Turns of Life's Fortunes

But the Pequod is also radically multicultural, with white New Englander, native American, African American, south sea islander, African, and South American all represented, a kind of emblematic sampling of the country as a whole, with all of it being led by a megalomaniacal, mystical madman, Captain Ahab, the man with the absent leg that had been bitten off by Moby Dick and then replaced with a wooden peg, holding the flaming harpoon that he juts aloft as the Pequod sails silently on in the emptiness of the open sea. This was a symbol of mid-nineteenth century America if there ever was one, a still young and explosive country in the years before the approaching cataclysm of the Civil War, a different kind of white whale that split the timbers of the republic and drowned nearly 800,000 young Americans, more than all of our other wars combined, including the charismatic if darkly possessed leader, who Whitman wrote about in "O Captain, My Captain."

Tom Petty is part of a long line of not only American writers but American characters, like Huck Finn, who lights out for the territories, while Mr. Petty went to Los Angeles from Florida, but Tom Petty was also in a sense our Ishmael, the sole survivor who remains to tell us the stories and legends of the road. And in so many ways, but perhaps especially in "American Girl" Tom Petty channeled American identity in ways so many of his fans could identify with, and one of these ways was by embracing the idea of just getting up and leaving, going to some place that might be better than that which fate and circumstance, money and class, family dynamics and the twists and turns of life's fortunes and misfortunes, has placed you in, and even if things do not work out as well as you had planned or hoped, well, at least it is something different, and at least if nothing else you tried, and you kept a promise that you had to yourself, and even if it was not a complete escape, it was a way to step out and feel something that was not programmed already for you to do, a preordained life for you to live that you had not even chosen for yourself. It might sound very adolescent when put like that, and perhaps it is, but one could also say that about Whitman and the open road, or Kerouac, or even Melville, with his all male band of ne'er-do-wells sailing on the open sea, running away from whatever complications they had found themselves wrapped up with on shore, but when Tom Petty sings "American Girl" he is making a statement that, although it does not at first sound like it, must be at least a little bit steeped in ambiguity.

What does it even mean to be an American girl? It sounds like something we all should understand intuitively, without even a little bit of explanation, but if we do, it seems to me that it rather quickly becomes at least somewhat meaningless. It is a supremely general idea that sounds great, at first, but if you give it even a little bit of examination it falls apart, at least when taken literally. All of the girls in America are American girls, on some level, but then it becomes clear that Tom Petty is talking in some kind of archetypal sense, with the girl in the song somehow representing something that is quintessentially American. Dean Young asserts that "The heterogeneity of "Song of Myself," of its formal experimentation and tonal swerves, is explicitly seen as an aspect of self-making American, a citizen of expanding frontiers, varied populations, scientific advances, and cultural gusto. "The United States themselves essentially is the great poem," he wrote in his 1955 preface to *Leaves of Grass*. The very nature of the poem and the social vitality it represents, its self-making, are explosive" (Young 140). Furthermore, in an article entitled "Seeking a Second Chance at Landmark Status, Aluminum Siding and All," by James Barron, Matt Miller, an associate professor at Yeshiva University, is quoted as saying, "If you talk to Americanists, experts in American literature, they'd agree that 'Song of Myself' is to the U.S. what Dante's 'Inferno' is to Italy. It's America's epic."

If, I want to argue, we can then place "American Girl" within these contexts, and look at it as part of a continuous stream that flows from Whitman's American epic to Tom Petty's final song in the last concert on his last epic tour, and, in addition, we can then think of the open road, the road that Whitman and Kerouac wrote about, as being a quintessentially American image and experience, we can then combine this image or trope with leaving home and hearth and all of the comforting familiarities of the world you had known. If we can furthermore accept that the road is perhaps a part of what defines us as being American, and then couple that with the intrinsic, inevitable loss that must come with leaving home, a presence of ineluctable sadness and melancholy which intrudes unbidden, like the crash of surf in the distance, then all of a sudden we find ourselves in a place where being an American Girl starts to make some kind of expanded yet still at least somewhat amorphous sense, although thinking too much about the meaning of a rock and roll song that is blaring out of your car radio speakers might kind of defeat the purpose, at least a little bit.

But then again, maybe not entirely, and, in fact, it is this kind of complex haiku-like mirror power that gives American Girl some of its clout, in the same way that Bruce Springsteen's "Born in the USA" undercuts its own seemingly jingoistic chorus when one listens to the verses and finds that the song is both praising the life of the character that the singer is inhabiting in his performance of the song, while at the same time condemning the circumstances that seemed to have conspired together and led to him to make the choices that he did. Tom Petty is not doing precisely that same kind of role-playing as a singer in "American Girl," he is more of an offstage narrator in this case, but he is still calling up some of the same archetypal echoes from the complex American past, combinations of dark chthonic forces that bubble up from the unconscious of our nation, tensions and reverberations folding and vibrating together to create some kind of loosely defined yet somehow clearly expressed national identity, one that will always be filled with paradox and contradiction, tension and release, electric and acoustic, soft and loud, fast and slow.

The Pequod, the open road, and a girl standing on her balcony are all different expressions, perhaps, of the same waking dream, and as long as we have the music of Tom Petty, we can listen. We can escape all of the limitations that bind us for a moment, not permanently and probably for only a few minutes, but that is enough sometimes, as we roll down the windows and listen to Tom sing about an American Girl while the Heartbreakers rock the house, and maybe we can feel some of what Jack Kerouac and Walt Whitman felt when they looked over the horizon at the unfolding American stars spinning in the firmament, and maybe every now and then, it will be Tom Petty who brings the past into the present and the present into the past, as the cars go by on the highway and the surf crashes day and night, rolling in and out on the coast of Florida with the changing phases of the moon.

WORKS CITED

Bangs, Lester. *Psychotic Reactions and Carburetor Dung*. Edited by Greil Marcus. 3rd ed. New York: Random House, 2003.

Barron, James. "Seeking a Second Chance at Landmark Status, Aluminum Siding and All." *New York Times*, 17 July 2018.

Clover, Joshua. "Bob Dylan Writes 'Song to Woody.'" *A New Literary History of America*. Edited by Greil Marcus and Werner Sollors. Cambridge: Harvard University Press, 2009. 904–908.

Dylan, Bob. "Bob Dylan 2016 Nobel Lecture in Literature." Online posting, 4 June 2017. https://www.nobelprize.org/nobel_prizes/literature/laureates/2016/dylan-lecture.html.

Dylan, Bob. *Chronicles: Volume One*. New York: Simon & Schuster, 2004.

Epstein, Daniel Mark. *The Ballad of Bob Dylan*. New York: HarperCollins, 2011.

Melville, Herman. *Moby Dick*. 1851. Second Norton Critical Edition, Herschel Parker and Harrison Hayford, eds. New York: W.W. Norton & Company, 1988.

Olson, Charles. *Call Me Ishmael*. Eastford, CT: Martino Publishing, 2015.

Wild, David. "Ten Things That Piss Off Tom Petty," *Rolling Stone*, November 14, 2002. https://www.rollingstone.com/music/features/the-ten-things-that-piss-off-tom-petty-20021114.

Young, Dean. *The Art of Recklessness: Poetry as Assertive Force and Contradiction*. Minneapolis: Graywolf, 2010.

Place, Race and Mutability

Everyman's Hillbilly Rhetoric

MARA LEE GRAYSON

Almost immediately following Tom Petty's death in October of 2017, music critics, entertainment writers, and fans memorialized the late musician as rock's "everyman." In tributes published in the days after his death, *Variety's* Chris Willman called Petty the "least polarizing figure in rock history" and *NPR's* Stephen Thompson called Petty "unassuming," identifying him as "an everyman for everyone."

Simultaneously the cause and effect of this "everyman" label is Petty's apparent impermeability to musical categorization: Thompson, Willman, and countless others who honored the artist in the weeks after his death spoke of Petty's multiplicity and the difficulty of situating him or his song catalogue in any single genre. To some, Petty's position as a "musical institution" is the direct result of his "relatability" and "unpretentiousness," characteristics that more closely connect him with the youthful free-spiritedness of early rock and roll (Williams). At the same time, however, the "everyman" label itself serves to place Petty into a particular musical genre—though perhaps not the one these writers and critics intend. Intentionally or not, those who have assigned Petty the "everyman" identity have also connected the rocker with one of the classic tropes of country music and the White Southern culture it is traditionally believed to reflect.

How closely the instrumental elements and overall sound of Petty's music adhere to the country genre is debatable; however, like those obituaries and the critical reception to much of his work during his forty-year career, both Petty's lyrics and his artistic persona recall many of the tropes that have long defined country music. At certain points in his career, such as the recording and release of his 1985 album with the Heartbreakers, *Southern Accents*, these connections were intentional and artistically motivated. At other times, Petty's connections to the genre appeared tenuous or even contentious. Often, in fact, the elements of Petty's work that bear the greatest similarity to country music appear to be the result not of his artistic intentions but of his deep roots in the American South, roots he at times actively resisted yet to which he could not help but remain tethered.

Here I seek to analyze and contextualize Petty's original work as well as critical and cultural responses to his work within American cultural and racial discourse and rhetorics of White southernness and rurality. Through this intersectional framework, I rhetorically analyze both the narratives of his songs and his actions and statements as a public figure. Ultimately, I address the implications of studying Petty's life and work for music fans as well as scholars of race rhetoric, focusing in particular on the following questions: (1) What are the features and limitations of this rhetoric in Petty's body of work? (2) Does this rhetoric offer any insight into Petty's wide-ranging audience appeal? and (3) In what ways does Tom Petty offer a counter narrative to the stereotypical story of the southern hillbilly?

"Hillbilly" Rhetoric and American Racial Discourse

Place and race are two of the defining characteristics of hillbilly rhetoric. Usage of the term *hillbilly* dates back at least to the year 1900, when it was defined by the *New York Evening Journal* as a descriptor of a White Alabama who "lives in the hills, has no means to speak of, talks as he pleases, drinks whiskey when he gets it, and fires off his revolver as the fancy takes him" (qtd. in Beech). The term "Hillbilly music" emerged in the 1920s to describe a commercial genre of Appalachian folksong that would evolve into what we now know as country music. Music scholars argue that the rise of hillbilly music was a pivotal part of southern cultural development. Ryan Carlson Bernard writes:

> Mass-produced, commercialized hillbilly music was a vital and pivotal feature of southern acclimation to modern industrialized society and northern urban centers. Examining the rise and fall of the hillbilly genre provides insight into socioeconomic variables that ultimately affected the identities of southern Appalachians and the commercial music industry and its role in shaping rustic, rural values and mores through modern modes of media [8].

The term "hillbilly music" has since been described as "derogatory" (Country) and some artists associated with the genre are said to have resented the descriptor; Hank Williams, for example, called his genre "folk music" (Ribowsky). The concept of the hillbilly, after all, is fraught with racial, socioeconomic, and geographic stereotypes. Scholars who have studied the discursive framing of White southern poverty have pointed out that the hillbilly is identified externally as such and that the label is one of ascription rather than self-identification (Beech; Newitz). This term and similar others like *redneck* have been increasingly appropriated by those who might once have had that label forced upon them. Since the 1990s, comedian Jeff Foxworthy's *You Might Be a Redneck if …* series of books, comedy specials, and merchandise has both made fun of and celebrated the features of hillbilly discourse. Country musicians Blake Shelton and Trace Atkins's 2005 song "Hillbilly Bone" celebrates the food and live music of the rural American south, suggesting that everyone has a little hillbilly in them.

While such commodification and dissemination has helped to normalize hillbilly discourse in popular culture, the discourse remains exceedingly problematic in the context of a broader American discourse on race. Terms like *redneck* and *White trash* allow middle-class and wealthy White people to assert their racial and socioeconomic agency by pointing out how poor Whites behave "in ways supposedly unbecoming to or unexpected of Whites" (Beech 175). In doing so, Whites with social and cultural capital are able to displace racism onto poor, southern, and less educated Whites while simultaneously reifying racist ideologies of essential distinctions between Whites and Blacks. In other words, when "class status is understood and defined as lifestyle" (Jarosz and Lawson 10), the severity of poverty and the systemic political and societal structures that contribute thereto are obscured.

In what Critical Race Theory calls *interest convergence*, both White elites and poor White benefit from systemic racism: White elites benefit materially whereas poor Whites benefit psychically. However, when racism is assigned to the poor White redneck, those who have both racial and socioeconomic privilege are not forced to examine or even admit the ways in which they benefit from structural inequity. For example, the successful cable television show *Duck Dynasty*, which presented its star, Phil Robertson, as a prototype of "the rural, poor, white redneck from the south that is racist, sexist, and homophobic," drew much critique after Robertson gave interviews spouting remarks that were, unsurprisingly, racist, sexist, and homophobic (Schippers). While Robertson, the so-called "reality" star, received considerable backlash for his comments (which were neither the first nor last such statements he would make over the course of the show's eleven-season run), the television network A&E and other corporate forces behind the show's framing largely evaded critique.

The lens of critical media literacy (Kellner and Share) demands that we, as consumers of visual and material culture, consider the ideological and structural forces that influence their construction and dissemination. While rhetoricians and critical race scholars have examined the ideologies behind terms like *hillbilly* and *redneck*, these terms' prevalence in contemporary popular culture enables the discourse to thrive without the close critical address medial literacy demands. From here on, I refer to this hillbilly discourse as rhetoric because, given its commodification and prevalence in American culture, the discourse has long been employed deliberately, strategically, and broadly in music, television, and other media. It is not merely a way of speaking or thinking about place and identity; it is also a marketing plan foisted upon those who are consumers of that culture as well as those who are not. Therefore, I argue that this rhetoric is intentional and systematic—whether the artists who employ it are consciously aware of that or not. As such, my usage here of the label *hillbilly rhetoric* emphasizes the persuasive nature of musical storytelling.

Place: Small Town, Big City

While Tom Petty is most often thought of as an L.A. musician (arguably due as much to the name dropping of Los Angeles streets and neighborhoods in "Free Fallin'," his first solo single and arguably one of his biggest hits, as to the many decades he spent living and recording there), his southern hometown was perhaps an even greater influence upon the music and persona that made him famous. "However long it had been since he'd run away from Gainesville, Florida, from the rednecks and the college boys ... he knew it was the place that made him," writes Petty biographer Warren Zanes. "He didn't find rock and roll in Malibu. He'd brought it with him" (5).

Petty and his early band Mudcrutch arrived in California in 1974 but had spent years performing in Gainesville's then-thriving music scene. By all accounts, however, the primary reason artists like Petty strove for success *in* Gainesville was to achieve enough success to get *out* of Gainesville. As a college town, Gainesville in the 1960s was, in Zanes's description, "the Deep South with a door punched in its side for strangers to walk through" (Zanes 33). Zanes's framing here is telling but complex. The violence of the punch in the door's creation contrasts with the covertness of its location. The easiest interpretation of the metaphor employed here is that the strangers themselves—the academicians and college kids—punched that door through in an act of colonization. The Floridians in this interpretation have no control over the strangers' access. On the other hand, the door might have been punched out from the inside: the college, after all, did bring people and money to a place that might otherwise have remained another working-class southern town.

This duality, of course, is the same tension ever present in Petty's music—and in other music that has come out of the south. Mainstreaming threatens authenticity—but it also provides a platform for stories to be voiced and a venue for dissemination. In this sense, many musicians struggle to balance artistic truth, both in the stories they tell and their artistic expression, with the genre conventions to which they are expected to adhere. We must remember that the messages conveyed by a song are not solely artist-driven but also are developed to appeal to distributors and audiences and to appease investors. For example, many musicologists have argued that sex and violence are prevalent in rap songs (as they are in other genres of music) primarily because sex and violence sell (Rebollo-Gil and Moras 120).

Seen through this lens, artists who are marketed as country musicians or southern rockers *perform* southernness as much as they embody it. Petty himself was never marketed as a country artist. He did, however, routinely cover songs by classic country musicians Carl Perkins and Conway Twitty at live shows; in the eighties, he topped the charts covering Hank Williams's "Mind Your Own Business" with country stars Willie Nelson and Hank Williams, Jr.; and, in 1996, Tom Petty and the Heartbreakers played backup on country legend Johnny Cash's album *Unchained* (Leahey). Petty was able to slip in and out of country music by performing southernness when he was in that world—and rejecting it when he wasn't.

Of his Gainesville hometown, Petty claimed that just outside of town, one was "back in redneck land" (qtd. in Zanes 33). This distancing language implies Petty's belief that he was separate from the people and culture he describes as "redneck." This language, then, is one of othering, not of identification. Petty separates himself from the place where he was raised and the people who populated it. This urge to escape the small town is one of the defining features of Petty's song catalogue: "Mary Jane's Last Dance," "Learning to Fly," "Into the Great Wide Open," "You Don't Know How It Feels," "Time to Move On," "Runnin' Down a Dream," "American Girl," and many others feature variations of the escape or journey narratives. This escapist narrative is in fact a common trope in the country music songbook and in the country music genre, journey narratives often conclude with the protagonist returning home to the rural spaces s/he initially fled (Neal).

Petty's 1986 release *Southern Accents* features what is perhaps Petty's most direct lyrical address of his southern environs from which he hailed. Petty claimed that his goal with *Southern Accents* was to create a concept album about the south but that the concept eventually "slipped away" (Greene). The speaker of the title song claims to have his own way of talking, working, and praying, each of which is filtered through his southern accent, a term that is figurative as much as it is literal. On this track, Petty assumes an ownership of the south that he had not previously attested. Petty performs southernness most directly, however, on "Rebels," another song from the album, a narrative approach that indirectly led to one of the biggest controversies of his career. During performances of the song on his Southern Accents tour, Petty included a Confederate flag as part of the stage dressing. It quickly became a prominent part of the marketing campaign for the tour and merchandise featuring the flag was soon available for purchase at concerts. Of his decision to introduce the Confederate flag onstage, Petty told *Rolling Stone*:

> "It's spoken from the point of a view of the character, who talks about the traditions that have been handed down from family to family for so long that he almost feels guilty about the war. He still blames the North for the discomfort of his life, so my thought was the best way to illustrate this character was to use the Confederate flag" [qtd. in Greene].

Petty's audience, however, latched onto the song's narrative and its characterization rather than the critical lens through which Petty depicted the song's narrator, and, years after the Southern Accents tour, once it was no longer part of the stage dressing, fans still brought Confederate flags and memorabilia to his concerts. In 1990, a fan threw a Confederate flag onto the stage. Fred Blurt, a music writer in attendance at the concert, describes feeling a "collective thought ripple through the air" seemingly asking for Petty to "wave it proudly at all your fellow Southerners" (qtd. in Williams). Despite the chorus of boos that followed, Petty stopped performing, explained that the decision to ever use the symbol had been a mistake, then wadded up the flag and tossed it aside, proclaiming "So we don't do *this* anymore" (qtd. in Williams, emphasis original).

While Petty claimed *Southern Accents* was a concept album and the flag a prop that illustrated the world it depicted, public reception to the work raises crucial questions about the audience's role in meaning-making and the limitations of authorial intent. Given his audience's literal rather than critical interpretation of "Rebels," does it matter that Petty's intentions were to depict a character and evoke a sensibility rather than to celebrate that character's ideology? Especially troubling is that the southern man Petty impersonates is an essentialized one whose story is fraught with the many thematic tropes and stereotypes of hillbilly rhetoric. Ultimately, the characters and narratives that populate the album are stock ones: working class drunks; southerners long bitter about the Civil War; the domineering wife in "Rebels"; the doting religious mother in "Southern Accents." Are these characters true to life? Perhaps. They are not, however, dimensional enough to counternarrate the stereotypes and essentialist narratives of hillbilly. As such, the concept that undergirds Petty's "concept album" is a normative one that does little justice to the dimensions of Petty's music, craft, or persona.

Petty's use of stereotypes may stem from his frustration with his early life in the south: Petty described himself as a "geeky, artistic kid" with no interest in hunting and fishing, common hobbies in Gainesville, and said that throughout his early life he felt like "a duck out of water" (qtd. in Tannenbaum 40). As much as the American South remained a part of Petty and his work, he struggled just as hard to separate himself from the Florida town where he got his start. "Something connects a man to the hometown he pushes against to get going in the first place," writes Zanes (33). It is not atypical, of course, for a person to struggle to extract himself from the roots to which he has been long tethered but it is an important element of Petty's work.

The 1975 single "American Girl" projects this struggle onto the song's female protagonist, who, in one verse, listens to the sound of the cars on Florida's Route 441 and, in another, imagines a bigger life somewhere else. Following his journey back to the south with *Southern Accents*, with 1989's *Full Moon Fever* and 1991's *Into the Great Wide Open*, Petty returns to the Los Angeles landscape. Songs like "Free Fallin'" and "Into the Great Wide Open" pay homage to the West Coast home Petty adopted. While "Free Fallin'" seems a celebratory tour through LA, the landscape of "Into the Great Wide Open" is an ephemeral one, as is the stardom his protagonist achieves. The narrator describing Eddie's attempts to make it in LA is older and wiser than Eddie and presents the story sardonically, emphasizing the impermanence of success and his protagonist's naïveté.

"Last Dance with Mary Jane," released in 1993, depicts another young woman from a small town. In this song, the title protagonist hails from small town Indiana but moves to another unnamed town where she meets—then leaves—the song's narrator. Given that "Mary Jane" is a common reference to marijuana, many have interpreted this song as an homage to drug use. Whether or not the protagonist's identity is symbolic, in a 2010 interview with *MOJO* magazine, Petty described Mary Jane as the same character as the woman from "American Girl" but "with a few hard knocks" (Snow). Nearly twenty years separate the songs but both are defined by tensions of place: in "American Girl," the character longs to leave the small town; Mary Jane has already left the small town but has not found the better life she imagined. Ultimately, she leaves again. "Last Dance with Mary Jane" also includes numerous references to the narrator's frustration with that unnamed town where she has left him, but at this point, it is unclear if that town is one he has run to or one he longs to flee. By the 1990s, then, it appears that Petty's perspective on place has become more nuanced: his aim to escape is less assured, the ties that ground him less certain.

Similar themes abound in 2006's "Saving Grace" and Petty appears to take yet another perspective on the relationship between person and place. The narrator here claims to be flying over cities and country landscapes. Playing the role of observer rather than participant, Petty's maturation is evident and he the song evokes a sense of reflection: the narrator here is not mired in the struggle to escape one place and find another but instead is critical of that struggle. He speaks to an unnamed second person, questioning the need to escape and identifying it as the struggle for salvation. At times it appears

"I" and "you" are one, the addressed a mere projection of the speaker. At other times, it appears that Petty is calling out to a second person, employing the technique of "implied conversation," which Jocelyn R. Neal suggests is a narrative paradigm of the country music genre. This technique is particularly compelling, Neal explains, because "the listener becomes an active participant in the song through the inference of the omitted dialogue" (46). However, with this song, Petty illuminates both the inevitability and the pointlessness of the search for salvation that defines so much of his music.

In doing so, "Saving Grace" draws upon Protestant conceptions of identity, self-searching, and salvation, adding another dimension to the everyman label so easily ascribed to Petty's music and persona. The everyman archetype has conceptual and cultural origins in Christianity, dating back to the 15th century morality play known by the same title; *Everyman* and other early morality plays existed to promulgate Christian ideals of good morals and behavior. Country music, too, has long been rooted in Christian ideology. Communications scholar Jimmie N. Rodgers claims that country music "holds no attraction for those who do not want to be reminded of where they come from, where they are, or where they are likely to be going," arguing that the genre's configurations of life and place are rooted in Christian ideas of an afterlife (163, qtd. in Neal, 42).

In Protestant Christianity, the relationship between man and God is individual; one is achieves God's grace not as a reward for external works but as a result of his or her individual faith. Tom Petty was an outspoken critic of organized religion, particularly Christianity (despite having been raised in a Baptist community). Following the release in 2014 of "Playing Dumb," a song that criticizes the Catholic Church's handling of molestation accusations, Petty told Billboard: "Religion seems to me to be at the base of all wars.... It seems to me that no one's got Christ more wrong than the Christians" (qtd. in Schruers 2014).

Despite his views on organized religion, the lyrics of "Saving Grace" imply that the journey to find oneself by seeking it externally—in other physical spaces—is futile and unending. In "Saving Grace," it seems that at last we hear the artist looking back. He is older and wiser, and his new perspective invites us, his audience, to question our own escapist tendencies. That this perspective on salvation is rooted in Protestantism provides another link between Petty's songbook and the everyman trope that prevails in country music.

Race: White Masculinity and Americana

It is important to note that the concept of the "everyman" is not gender-neutral. An archetypal protagonist with whom audiences are intended to identify and empathize, the everyman is ordinary rather than heroic and, while he often must overcome extraordinary odds, his feats are not heroic but a result of human strength and ability. Given the allegorical nature of morality plays and their socio-religious function, everyman figures were intended to stand in for all mankind—an outdated universality that discursively marginalizes the female experience. Medieval scholar Douglas Bruster argues that women may in fact play a larger role in Everyman and other morality plans than their titles suggest, but that their "male protagonists and their sermonic motives ... can strike readers as virtually defining a male-centered aesthetic and worldview" (57).

Andrew Leahey writes that Petty's music seemed to be "universal" and "belonged everywhere, to everyone" (Leahey). In this way, Tom Petty has functioned as that everyman: magnanimous enough to command attention and adulation yet ordinary enough to be a stand-in for whatever the audience wanted him to be. Nicholas Dawidoff points out that Petty's songs are "unspecific enough that they become vulnerable to many kinds of interpretation." Many listeners "located something hopeful and persevering" in Petty's music; "they listened and thought, That's me" (Dawidoff).

Psychologist Michael Addis has suggested that songs like "I Won't Back Down" serve to cement Petty's image as a "rebel" and a "man's man" (Perry), a persona that recalls the men with whom Petty spent his early life. Petty's father was a "charming, carousing good ol' boy" (Tannenbaum 40) who "drank too much too often. He beat his son. He fought with his wife" (Zanes 21). In an interview with journalist and musician Paul Zollo, Petty recalled an incident during his childhood in which his father attacked an alligator that had swum up to their fishing boat: "I actually saw my dad take his forefinger and thumb ... and punch the eyes in on the alligator. To show me that he could knock the alligator out" (qtd. in Zollo). Petty claimed that his father wasn't afraid of anything but that he was, as a result, afraid of his father. While Earl Petty wanted his sons to do the things "American boys that age were supposed to be doing" (Zanes 26), young Tom Petty had little interest in school, sports, fishing, or hunting. Petty later confessed:

> "I'm not the best authority on the relationships fathers have with their sons. I didn't understand that there could *be* a relationship. I thought a father just put shit on the table, made a living, and we owed him respect because he put a roof over our head, because for some reason our mother married him.... I didn't realize there were kids who had really genuine relationships with their fathers" [qtd. in Zanes 18, emphasis original].

According to Zollo, Petty's "father's attitude towards him mirrored how he was treated by most of the town" as a child and young adult. As a "longhair" in the south, Petty had difficulty getting a job to finance his musical ambitions, eventually working as a gravedigger.

Even in music, Petty did not entirely fit in: the music scene in Gainesville during the sixties and seventies was dominated by the "long jams" of the era's southern rock (Tannenbaum). Petty's first musical love was rockabilly (Zollo). At twelve, he met Elvis on the set of a movie, who "quickly became a symbol of a place Tom Petty wanted to go" (Zanes 27). By the time Petty became a performer in Gainesville, he was writing short songs that more closely resembled early rock and roll and the songs of the British Invasion.

Petty's music throughout his career reflects his early experiences as a misfit. Michael Addis suggests that music (particularly rock and blues) provides one of the only venues "where men's true emotional selves are expressed" but that the expression is far more indirect than it is overt. "It's often done in this 'sleight of hand' way," Addis explains, "where the persona of the musician is masculine, rebellious and very cool. And the emotionalism is often snuck in through either the lyrics or the way the instrument is played" (qtd. in Perry). For Petty, that emotionalism is balanced out with a strong dose of self-righteous indignation.

Billboard's Rob Tannenbaum describes Petty's "most frequent lyrical tone" as "a wounded perseverance," citing as examples the popular refrains from "I Won't Back Down," "Refugee," and "You Don't Know How It Feels" (40). Nicholas Dawidoff writes that Petty's song catalogue is filled with "so many songs of grievance, so many songs casting unhappily inward, so many songs expressing the perpetually injured and afflicted American male." The narrative voice that prevails in Petty's work, from early songs with the Heartbreakers like "Don't Do Me Like That" to later solo hits like "You Don't Know How It Feels," is stubborn, often self-pitying, and "suggests that a man can subsist a long time on nothing more than his favorite grudge" (Dawidoff).

Tannenbaum writes that "if denim could start a rock band, it would sound like Tom Petty" (40) equating the musician with one of the most American of fabrics—and symbols. The fabric grew out of the American cotton industry, a market sustained by slave labor, and was initially popularized when prospectors during the gold rush needed fabric that would withstand mining conditions. Denim was later associated with soldiers, cowboys, and rebellious teenagers, cementing its status as the uniform of blue-collar workers and nonconformists.

Perhaps most problematic is that, despite Petty's progressive political views, the power and anger of Petty's narrative voice have long resonated with the very same white, conservative population from which he struggled for so long to dissociate. In 2000, Petty sent a cease and desist letter to then-presidential candidate George W. Bush to prevent the Republican from playing "I Won't Back Down" at campaign rallies (Chao). Today, amidst a sociopolitical climate in which white blue-collar Americans lament the decline of the coal mining industry, blame the leftist elite for ignoring and wear hats proclaiming "Make America Great Again," Petty seems to have become "an accidental bard of white resentment" (Dawidoff). Ultimately, the man's man persona that narrates so much of Petty's music communicates—and is heard—in a way that is uniquely white.

Trent Watts has pointed out that in recent decades, "the 'blue collar' man" stereotype of the white southern male has come to be seen as "the most solid and patriotic of Americans" (6) and that contemporary conceptions of masculinity in the United States are heavily drawn from southern stereotypes. "Many white American males now embrace an inner white southerner," Watts writes, "and apparently believe that we are, to one degree or another, rednecks now" (6). This stock character, however, particularly in pop culture iterations by Jeff Foxworthy, Larry the Cable Guy, and others, has been wiped clean of both his overt racism and his working class solidarity (4–5). The result of this benign iteration is that none of the systemic issues that lead to the development of such identities (specifically structural racism and inequitable socioeconomic class structures) are subjected to exploration, let alone criticism.

Just as Petty's narrative persona gives voice to white male emotion, the genre of country music appears to provide the soundtrack to white American culture. Given its nostalgic adherence to tropes that have largely long disappeared from American life, country music is typically seen as socially and politically conservative—and raced as White. Its association with political and cultural conservatism and its bent toward what Jocelyn R. Neal calls "nostalgia" stem as much from the narrative tropes promulgated in popular song narratives as the cultural ideologies that influence the genre's musical production. In other words, beliefs and values common to rural Whites may have influenced the thematic development of country music narratives but as time passes, those songs and stories serve to maintain those traditions. The ongoing association of the music with the subject matter may also lead artists to continue to incorporate themes common to the genre.

Historically, however, country music has not been the "overwhelmingly, perplexingly white" genre it is thought to be (Petrusich 4). Country music has come to be seen as a White genre much in the way hip-hop is seen as a Black one—but as Amanda Petrusich reminds us, while hip-hop "was born specifically from an experience of blackness" and "emerged, in part, to give voice to that experience—country music was not born from an experience of whiteness" (5).

Erich Nunn points out that early hillbilly music, like that by Jimmie Rodgers, known as the "Father of Country Music," existed in the "crosscurrents of folk traditions and commercial forms, black- and white-identified styles, reactionary plantation nostalgia, and forward-looking jazz-inflected pop" (624–25).

Rock and roll too is a genre of hybridity and one that historically has drawn a great deal from African-American music. It must be acknowledged that, to some extent, Tom Petty's ability to move between genres—or to be beyond easy classification—is a raced characteristic and a marker of White privilege.

Tom Petty's music has been described as "apolitical" (Dawidoff) but Petty was not hesitant when it came to sharing his opinions, whether that meant airing grievances with the recording industry or voicing his beliefs about oft-controversial social and political issues like organized religion or the industrial prison complex. Despite his seeming directness, Petty's statements on matters of racism have ranged the gamut from evasive and problematic to overt and complex. For example, decades after he stopped featuring it on tour, Petty described his use of the Confederate flag as "stupid" (Greene). While it is tempting to forgive his behavior in light of his remorse, it should be noted that even Petty's apologies are fraught with remnants of the hillbilly rhetoric he appears to disown. In a *Rolling Stone* interview he gave following the removal of the Confederate flag from the South Carolina statehouse in 2013, Petty said:

> "I have good feelings for the South in many ways. There's some wonderful people down there. There are people still affected by what their relatives taught them. It isn't necessarily racism. They just don't like the Yankees. They don't like the North. But when they wave that flag, they aren't stopping to think how it looks to a black person. I blame myself for not doing that" [Greene].

On the surface, Petty seems to be providing historical context for the attitudes he has witnessed in the south, both as a born southerner and as a performer with a complex relationship to so-called southern pride. The generalizations he employs, however, weaken the conclusions he draws. Petty again here uses distancing language to describe southerners as other. While Petty assumes some blame for his own past ignorance about the Confederate flag, his pronoun usage (*they*) separates those who "don't like the Yankees" from those like himself—southerners who have left the South. Through his broad use of the third-person plural, Petty effectively claims that all southerners influenced by their families' teachings harbor resentment toward the North. As Trent Watts reminds us, "it is often analytically useful to consider white southern men as a group, but they are no more homogeneous than any other group" (Watts 7). Petty's grouping flattens the differences among individuals and demonstrates his essentialist perspective on the south; that Petty, himself born in the south, seems to neither fit this stereotype nor associate himself with it makes the conflation even more perplexing.

At the same time as he attempts to distance himself rhetorically from the Confederate flag-wavers, Petty appears to apologize for them, attributing their (and his own) affinity for the discriminatory symbol to historicism, regional pride, and ignorance. Petty noted of the flag: "I'm sure that a lot of people that applaud it don't mean it in a racial way" (Greene). This statement, though couched in apologies and caveats reiterates common conservative rhetoric of southern pride. Despite this similarity, Petty's seeming apologia may in fact be less about defending the individual actions of those who bear the Confederate flag than it is about redirecting responsibility toward the broader racist ideologies and institutions of American society. In that same interview, Petty claimed that

> "Beyond the flag issue, we're living in a time that I never thought we'd see.... As a country, we should be more concerned with why the police are getting away with targeting black men and killing them for no reason. That's a bigger issue than the flag. Years from now, people will look back on today and say, 'You mean we privatized the prisons so there's no profit unless the prison is full?'" [Greene].

Here Petty demonstrates a broader understanding of the systemic nature of racism in the United States and a more pointed critique of structural racism. He identifies popular discussion of the Confederate flag as a distraction from more pressing concerns of racially motivated police brutality and the industrial prison complex.

Again, however, Petty's statements are filled with discursive contradictions. He acknowledges the prevalence of institutional racism but then describes a time he "never thought we'd see." In the latter statement, racism is dehistoricized, which downplays its systemic insidiousness. That Petty would express a decontextualized view of racism is perplexing, given his own background. While Petty expressed distaste for the racism he witnessed in Florida, racism had in fact played a large part in bringing Petty's family to Florida in the first place. Petty's paternal grandmother was a Cherokee Indian; she and his paternal grandfather had fled Georgia after a "fracas over interracial marriage" resulted in Petty's grandfather killing another man (Schruers 1995).

Given Petty's difficulties shaking the tropes of hillbilly rhetoric, it would be a stretch to say that his persona and song catalogue offer complete counternarratives to stereotypes of the White southern man. Even when attempting to convey his own observations in lyrical narratives on albums like *Southern Accents*, his distancing from southernness is too absolute and his embrace of West Coast enlightenment too uncritical. Petty's music, then, can be defined by its simultaneous resistance to and reinforcement of hillbilly discourse. Petty's version of the white Southern male is one simultaneously rooted in Americana and critical thereof, patriotic and dissentious, macho and sensitive, boastful and self-critical. The push and pull between Petty and his southern roots is a defining component of Petty's legacy—and it offers, if not a counter narrative, at least a more dimensional depiction than those that prevail in American racial and regional discourses.

Country's Rock 'n' Roll "Everyman": Mutability and Mass Appeal

Despite his attempts to dissociate himself from the "rednecks" and "good ol' boys," Tom Petty's adherence to the tropes of hillbilly rhetoric, intentional or otherwise, helps to explain why the "everyman" of rock and roll is so often associated with country music—and perhaps why he was able to fill arenas with liberals, conservatives, young fans, and older classic rock enthusiasts. Songwriter and critic Dave Hickey writes that, historically, the authenticity of country music "was presumed to reside in the authenticity of the culture— the virtues of country life and country people—and not in the performers themselves, so it was possible for a performer to betray his or her purportedly authentic country roots" (843). As long as he told stories that resonated with a country audience, Petty seemed to be accepted as a country artist.

Tom Petty was not a fan of modern country music. During a 2013 performance, Petty derided modern country music as "bad rock with a fiddle," and, in an interview shortly thereafter, added that popular country reminded him of "rock in the middle eighties, where it became incredibly generic and relied on videos" (Leahey). Ironically, Petty made numerous award-winning music videos during the nineteen-eighties and nineties, including "Don't Come Around Here No More," famous for its Alice in Wonderland imagery; "Last Dance with Mary Jane," which features an intricate narrative and Kim Basinger playing a corpse; and "You Don't Know How It Feels," a continuous shot in which all sorts of strange events occur as backdrop while Petty calmly sings and strums a guitar in the foreground. In fact, Petty was in some ways a music video pioneer—his video for "You Got Lucky" was the first to establish a narrative that would be threaded throughout the length of the video through the use of a non-musical introduction (Schiff).

Petty, of course, was critical of the music video genre even when he and his band were making music videos. The 1981 video for "Letting You Go" is tongue-in-cheek and self-referential and appears as much a send-up of the genre as it is a legitimate music video. The video depicts a band making a music video and highlights the musicians' discomfort at being filmed: in a particularly telling scene, a cameraman on a lift approaches Petty, who glares at the cameraman and backs up. The camera is depicted as invasive and inorganic. Despite his discomfort, however, Petty embraced the music video format rather than rejecting it and his videos have been widely celebrated as some of the greatest and most influential of all time.

Given the context, then, Petty's comments about country music and music videos, critical though they may be, appear to be more the inward explorations of his own career than the outward assessments they are at surface. Petty was resentful of being associated with the south, particularly when his origins put his image at odds with the Los Angeles persona he had so passionately cultivated. This misdirection seems the struggle of a man who, after all these years, is still trying to figure out where he belongs.

In a brief article exploring Petty's influence on country music, *Rolling Stone* writer Andrew Leahey eulogized Petty as "part of America's daily soundtrack" and categorized his music as "universal, forged from street-smart Southern sneer, garage-rock grit and the stoned shimmer of California folk-rock" (Leahey). In fact, it seems that every Petty critic and fan has a different perspective on the genre with which Petty ought to be associated. Attempts to categorize Petty have been debatable, at best, and divisive at worst. When Alex Young's obituary of Petty for the web magazine Consequence of Sound identified Petty as a "southern rock legend" (Young), an angry commenter noted that "just because a guy grew up in Gainesville doesn't mean he played southern rock" (KellyCNY).

The difficulty in categorizing Petty's music may stem from the fact that Petty was himself resistant to such categorizations: he disliked the word "demographics" and the marketing schemes record companies employed. "That kind of thinking—how best to divide an audience for maximum marketing potential—was antithetical to the spirit of rock and roll. His goal was never to direct material to any one segment of the populace" (Zollo). GQ's Steve Kandell claims that Tom Petty and the Heartbreakers "made conventional music conventionally" and that it was this conventionality that enabled the band to pack arenas "with multiple generations of fans over the span of four decades." Rock and roll is, like country, a genre of hybridity, and Kandell's description of Petty's music as "conventional" does not seem a full enough explanation for Petty's long-term success.

In light of the complexities of Petty's relationship with rhetorics of race and rurality, I argue that Petty's appeal among diverse audience was due in large part in his ability to position himself as a dynamic character in the music world whose discursive and rhetorical evolution reflected the changes occurring more broadly in American society over the past forty years. This ability to evolve and respond—to admit mistakes and to speak out against matters on which he was once silent or complicit—helped to position Petty not only as a celebrated musician but also as a significant figure in American popular culture.

While Petty's complexity, viewed with a more critical eye, might be described as vagueness or indecision, his ability to see multiple perspectives of contentious sociopolitical issues (such as organized religion and the use of the Confederate flag) and his willingness to change his behavior as a performer are two of the defining characteristics of his artistic and public persona. Whether genuine or by rhetorical design, Petty's ability to change his music and behavior over time is arguably the reason for the difficulty in placing him neatly in one genre—and at least partly the reason behind the "everyman" label so easily ascribed to him.

To his audiences, Tom Petty was an everyman, a drifter between genres. He was a shapeshifter whose stubbornness and admonitions of standing his ground seem more about self-soothing than outward assertion. More than anything, however, it seems that Tom Petty always wanted to be somewhere else—and someone other than who he was. Music, it seems, was the only thing that felt like home. In his last interview with *Rolling Stone*, Petty claimed that Tom Petty and the Heartbreakers' fortieth anniversary tour would be their last major tour but that they would not stop performing: "to stop playing is unimaginable to me" (qtd. in Rodrick). Petty confessed that outside of touring and recording, there was "no other life situation" in which he felt truly comfortable. Speaking of his time on the road and in the studio, Petty claimed: "I am completely O.K."

WORKS CITED

Beech, Jennifer. "Redneck and Hillbilly Discourse in the Writing Classroom: Classifying Critical Pedagogies of Whiteness." *College English*, Vol. 67, No. 2, 2004.

Bernard, Ryan Carlson. *The Rise and Fall of the Hillbilly Music Genre: A History, 1922–1939*. Unpublished thesis. East Tennessee State University, 2007.

Bruster, Douglas. "Women and the English Morality Play." *Medieval Feminist Forum*, Vol. 45, No. 1, 2009, 57–67.

Chao, Eveline. "Stop Using My Song: 35 Artists Who Fought Politicians Over Their Music." *Rolling Stone*, 8 July 2015.

"Country Music." *Encyclopedia Britannica*. September 29, 2014.

Hickey, Dave. "The Song in Country Music." *A New Literary History of America*. Edited by Greil Marcus and Werner Sollors. Cambridge, MA: Belknap Press of Harvard University Press, 2009, pp. 843–846.

Hilburn, Robert. "Tom Petty Tries His Hand at Southern Rock." *Los Angeles Times*. March 31, 1985.

Jarosz, Lucy and Victoria Lawson. "'Sophisticated People Versus Rednecks': Economic Restructuring and Class Difference in America's West." *Antipode*, 2002, 8–27.

Kandell, Steve. "Tom Petty Never Overstayed His Welcome." GQ.com. October 3, 2017.

KellyCNY. Comment on "RIP Tom Petty: Southern Rock Legend Has Died at 66." Consequence of Sound, October 3, 2017, https://consequenceofsound.net/2017/10/r-i-p-tom-petty-rock-legend-has-died-at-66/.

Leahey, Andrew. "Why Tom Petty Is Contemporary Country Music's Biggest Rock Influence." *Rolling Stone*, October 3, 2017.

Mann, Geoff. "Why Does Country Music Sound White?: Race and the Voice of Nostalgia." *Ethnic and Racial Studies*, Vol. 31, No. 1, 2008.

Marr, Madeleine. "Tom Petty Had His Roots in Florida and He Never Let Go." *Miami Herald*. October 4, 2017.

Massey, Carissa. "The Rhetoric of the Real: Stereotypes of Rural Youth in American Reality Television and Stock Photography." *Discourse: Studies in the Cultural Politics of Education*, Vol. 38, No. 3, 2017, 365–376.

Neal, Jocelyn R. "Narrative Paradigms, Musical Signifiers, and Form as Function in Country Music." *Music Theory Spectrum*, Vol. 29, No. 1, 2007.

Nunn, Erich. "Country Music and the Souls of White Folk." *Criticism*, Vol. 51, No. 4, 2009, 623–649.

Perry, Jim. "Clark Forum Tackles Music with Professor, Biographer." Worcestormag.com. October 13, 2016.

Petrusich, Amanda. "Darius Rucker and the Perplexing Whiteness of Country Music." *The New Yorker*, 25 October 2017.

Rebollo-Gil, Guillermo and Amanda Moras. "Black Women and Black Men in Hip Hop Music: Misogyny, Violence and the Negotiation of (White-Owned) Space." *The Journal of Popular Culture*, Vol. 45, No. 1, 2012, 118–32.

Ribowsky, Mark. *Hank: The Short Life and Long Country Road of Hank Williams*. New York: Liveright, 2017.

Rodrick, Stephen. "Tom Petty's Last Rolling Stone Interview." *Rolling Stone*, 5 October 2017.

Rogers, Ashley. "The Ten Biggest Tropes in Country Music." Westword.com. 5 September 2013.

Schiff, Mark. "7 Overlooked Music Videos That Prove the Genius of Tom Petty and the Heartbreakers." AXS.com, 29 July 2014.

Schippers, Mimi. "We're Right to Criticize Phil Robertson, but Why Are We So Quick to Let A&E Off the Hook?" Thehuffingtonpost.com. 21 February 2014.

Schruers, Fred. "Tom Petty Isn't 'Playing Dumb' About Church Sex Abuse Scandal on New Song." Billboard.com. 21 July 2014.

_____. "Tom Petty on the Road: This Is How It Feels." *Rolling Stone*, 4 May 1995.

Snow, Mat. "Tom Petty: The Darkness That Drives Him." *MOJO Music Magazine*, Issue 94, 1 January 2010.

Thompson, Stephen. "Tom Petty's Was Rock's Everyman." Npr.com, 3 October 2017.

Vinson, Christina. "Eric Church Addresses Tom Petty's Criticism of Country Music." Tasteofcountry.com, 26 August 2013.

Watts, Trent. "Telling White Men's Stories." *White Masculinity in the Recent South*, edited by Trent Watts. Baton Rouge: Louisiana State University Press, 2008.

Williams, Stereo. "Tom Petty's Remarkable Stand Against the Confederate Flag." Thedailybeast.com, 7 October 2017.

Willman, Chris. "An Appreciation of Tom Petty: Rock's Superstar Everyman." *Variety.com*, 3 October 2017.

Young, Alex. "RIP Tom Petty: Southern Rock Legend Has Died at 66." *Consequence of Sound*, 3 October 2017, https://consequenceofsound.net/2017/10/R-I-P-Tom-Petty-Rock-Legend-Has-Died-At-66/

Zanes, Warren. *Petty: The Biography*. New York: Henry Holt and Company, 2015.

Zollo, Paul. "On the Life and Times of Tom Petty." Americansongwriter.com, 6 October 2017.

Tom Petty's "Magic" of Success and the Craft of a Writer

CRYSTAL D. SANDS

> "It's [writing] always been my sanctuary. I could always withdraw into that music. I think that goes back to my childhood. I withdrew into music. I went into that world. And it was this nice, safe, wonderful world. And so, I think it shaped my personality for life, that I can always go into that. It's like slipping on a suit of clothes. You can go into that world of writing, and it's soothing and rewarding at the same time."
>
> —Tom Petty, *Conversations with Tom Petty*

I have been teaching people how to improve their writing for over twenty years. During that time, I have taught and studied over 15,000 students. Some may not believe that I have actually *studied* my students, but I have—at least to the best of my ability given the teaching situations I was in. I do not know any other way to do it. I teach writing process as a way to improve, and, because everyone works differently, I have to study my students to figure out what is going to work best for each and every one of them. It is no easy task, and I am not always as successful as I would like to be. But I learn from my students, and this learning helps me be better at helping them.

I have been able to study some writers more than others. Ten years ago, I married a writer, a poet to be exact, and studying his process so up-close and personally has taught me even more about writing process than my graduate studies or research in composition theory could have. By studying my husband's writing process, I began to understand that strong, effective writers would *naturally* develop strong, effective writing processes—processes that seemed to align closely with that we teach in writing courses across the country. I grew more interested in writing process and began reading as much as

I could about the writing processes of writers—when they would talk about it. I have found that not everyone is willing to talk about their writing processes; I have also found that not everyone is *able* to speak to their processes with the kind of depth someone who studies writing hopes to see. Doing so requires a high amount of metacognition. Thankfully, Tom Petty did both.

I was the Tom Petty fan who took Tom Petty for granted. As so many others have written, I was certain Tom Petty had written the soundtrack to my life. I grew up with him. He was there for me during my divorce. He was there for me when I was falling in love again—with the poet—of course. I always had this sense that Tom Petty's songs were speaking directly to me. He "got it," I thought. He knew what life was about. He "got me," I thought. So, when I learned of his death on October 2, 2017, I took it hard. Over the next months, my husband and I embarked on a kind of journey with Tom Petty. For nearly four months, we listened exclusively to Tom Petty music, and many days, we listened to Tom Petty's work for eight to ten hours a day. I found myself changed by his music, and I found myself fascinated by the diversity of his writing in those deep tracks and by the profound way in which I felt like he was speaking directly to me because, while I was going through this, I was also reading online about others who were going through similar experiences—others who also felt that Tom Petty was speaking directly to them.

I began to wonder how a writer could become *that* effective. How could Petty's lyrics be general enough to apply to so many people and yet specific enough to feel deeply personal to each and every one of us? How could someone write so consistently and effectively for so many decades? His work, undoubtedly, sets a standard in Rock and Roll music and is a major part of the Canon of American songwriting. Since I am a writing teacher and study writing processes extensively, I began to wonder about Tom Petty's writing process.

In this essay, I embark on a journey into Petty's writing process and explore, mainly through his own words, what Tom Petty's writing process was like and how it was so effective. Through my study of his process, I argue that anyone who wants to write or teach writing can learn a great deal from studying the processes of highly effective writers like Tom Petty. In my over twenty years of teaching, I have found that the vast majority of my students want to be effective writers and want to do well. I contend that studying the writing process of a highly successful writer like Tom Petty can not only teach us how to improve our processes and become effective writers but can also teach us a little something about what it takes to become one of the *greats*— one of those writers who touches people's lives with their messages and whose words will live long after they are gone. Ultimately, an examination of Petty's writing process reveals that process is important and that the way to "catch" a creative thread within the universe is to be diligent in our habits. It is through the rigor of writing process that connections to the universe can be formed.

What Is a Writing Process?

All writers, even beginning writers, have some kind of process. It is the process we go through when we set out to write something, anything, and most beginning writers need help developing a stronger writing process. For example, many of the students I work with will draft one time and consider their process complete. This stunted process leads to writers who are not writing their best work. By contrast, people who are strong, experienced writers have writing processes which are strong, include many stages that work well for them, and have become almost a kind of ritual for them. Those of us who teach and coach writing often teach to basic writing processes that can help beginning writers, processes that involve better invention stages, drafting, revision, and, usually, collaboration.

At times, however, writing teachers and coaches will view the writing process as a rigid one, one with steps that must be followed by everyone in order to be effective. Unfortunately, rigidity in the writing process has led to some critique of writing process instruction. But when writing process is taught as important but organic and unique to the individual, research shows that writing process instruction can be highly effective. According to a 2007 meta-analysis of writing instruction techniques conducted by Graham and Perin, writing process instruction, when provided by writing instructors who have been trained in the process, is an effective strategy to help improve writing. Of course, critical to the study is that teachers were trained in writing process instruction, which, I would argue, increases the chances of a more organic and authentic approach to the process. When I have seen teachers approach the writing process with rigidity, it has been teachers who have not been well trained yet.

Tom Petty's Writing Process

Of course, Tom Petty was never trained by a writing instructor in writing process, yet, as an highly successful writer, it is interesting and important to note that his effective process involved many of the key strategies we teach in writing courses. His process involved collaboration, persistence, and stages of the process from invention to, of course, publication for a very wide audience. Thankfully, Tom Petty left a highly detailed record of his writing process though interviews, documentaries, and programs like VH1's *Storytellers*. What we glean from these materials is a man who worked hard at his process and also possessed a kind of genius way of viewing the world and the people in it, which led to one of the longest and most successful careers in songwriting America has known.

Learning the Genre

Petty was learning the genre of the rock and roll song since childhood. His encounter with Elvis Presley when he was very young is the stuff of legend, and Petty was so inspired by meeting Elvis that he spent all of his money growing up on music, buying albums when he could. Petty was also greatly influenced by the Beatles and the Byrds, and he recounts his childhood as one of turmoil and trauma but one in which he used music as an escape. In writing instruction, we teach the importance of learning the genre, and new research points to genre instruction as a highly-effective instructional method. It makes sense, of course. If one is going to write well within a genre, one must possess a keen understanding of said genre. Essentially, Tom Petty spent his entire life studying his genre.

But Tom Petty also had a remarkable work ethic, and when he made the move from Gainesville to Los Angeles, he worked diligently on his craft. In *Petty: The Biography*, Warren Zanes wrote of the way record producer Denny Cordell got Petty to work. "Cordell was sitting with Petty, playing records for him, making him think about where Mudcrutch fit in the world, making him write" (89). Zanes went on to describe the way Cordell would get Petty to listen to record after record. Tom Petty said, "[H]e was also teaching me something about taste. 'Cause if you have good taste, then you at least know what you're chasing, right" (90)? During this early stage of his career, Petty was deeply learning his genre, and this, coupled with his perceptive mind, which would naturally be observant of key aspects of the genre anyway, certainly must have been a part of what helped Petty develop into such an effective writer.

Working with Others

There is a myth that writing is a solitary endeavor, and certain parts of a writing process can be; at some point, however, writing becomes social, and surrounding ourselves with other strong writers and creative minds makes our writing better. In their 1990 work, *Singular Texts, Plural Authors:*

Perspectives on Collaborative Work, Composition instructors and theorists
Lisa Ede and Andrea Lunsford were among the first in the field of writing
instruction to challenge the assumption that writing is a solitary act. Using
formal research coupled with their own experiences, Ede and Lunsford assert
the truly collaborative nature of the writing process. Tom Petty intuitively
knew this and enjoyed working with the best, learning from them, and building a creative process that worked well for him. One key in the social aspect
of writing is that it seems for the process to work best, strong relationships
of trust and respect must be built.

In a presentation I attended in 2005 with Lisa Ede at the University of
Oregon, she offered follow-up advice on her groundbreaking work with
Andrea Lunsford. In her talk, Ede emphasized again the social nature of writing but also emphasized that writing with others cannot be forced and that
there must be a relationship of trust between the authors for co-writing to
work well. She used her experiences writing with Andrea Lunsford as an
example. Again, this is something that Tom Petty seemed to know intuitively.

Tom Petty's process of working with some of the great minds in the
music industry exemplifies important lessons about writing process, and,
when Petty discusses his writing relationships with others, there is a clear
emphasis on mutual respect and trust. One of Tom Petty's most long-lived
creative relationships was with his guitarist, bandmate, and friend, Mike
Campbell. Mike Campbell was with Tom Petty from the beginning of Tom
Petty and the Heartbreakers, and over the years, he would be an important
part of Petty's writing process. While Campbell also helped write songs for
other artists, such as Don Henley's hit, "Boys of Summer," Campbell would
play an important role in Petty's creative processes and co-authored many of
the greatest hits from Tom Petty and the Heartbreakers.

In his book, *Conversations with Tom Petty,* Paul Zollo shared a conversation he and Petty had about how Petty and Campbell worked together to
write songs:

So you write the melodies and words to his [Mike's] tracks.
Yeah, sometimes I even write a bridge, or change a chord here or there.
Do you work to the tape?
He'll give me a tape, but what I like to do is learn it on piano or guitar. Then I
work on it that way. Because that gives me the luxury of going somewhere else. If you
work just with the tape, it can get a little monotonous...
*Do you have lyrics in mind when you're writing to one of Mike's tracks, or do you
allow the music itself to dictate what the words should be?*
I start cold. I just start cold. If something's there that I get a feel for, it starts to
happen. And if I don't, I just don't pursue it.... I remember writing ["Refugee"] really
quick to his tape. The words came really quick. I just had to come up with a melody,
really...
That's how we write together. We never sit down face-to-face [Zollo].

While Petty's self-professed introverted nature comes through in this strategy for working with Campbell, it is clear Petty was great at surrounding himself with talented people, and these talented people created a creative atmosphere where greatness could be born. Petty knew this of course, and throughout his career, he would write with creative minds, such as Bob Dylan, George Harrison, Jeff Lynne, Benmont Tench, and David Stewart.

Writing Consistently

One thing that all writers must understand is the importance of consistency with writing, the making of writing habits. Petty's dedication to his writing and his music exemplified the kind of discipline a writer needs in order to succeed, in whatever way that is measured for the writer. For Tom Petty, success as a songwriter meant producing songs that were powerful and meaningful, and, of course, in his case, commercial success often came along as well. But consistency and persistence are key. Not all of his songs came to him easily, but some of them did. It is the nature of the process—sometimes, it feels like the writing gods smile upon us, and, other times, writing is so difficult that we feel cursed. But persistence always pays off.

Petty spoke about the differences he would experience in his song writing, about how some songs would come quickly and easily while others were struggles, in a 2002 interview. In speaking about his experience writing "Southern Accents," Petty said, "that may be my favorite among my songs—just in terms of a piece of pure writing. I remember writing it very vividly. It was in the middle of the night and I was playing it on the piano at home in Encino. I was just singing into my cassette recorder and suddenly these words came out" (Hilburn). One can almost hear the joy in Petty's voice as he spoke about this piece. He mentioned the words coming to him quickly, but this was not always the case for him as a writer. In other songs, he struggled to find the right words and the right music.

In the same interview, Petty spoke of his experience writing "The Waiting." He said, "That was a song that took a long time to write. Roger McGuinn swears he told me the line—about the waiting being the hardest part—but I think I got the idea from something Janis Joplin said on television. I had the chorus very quickly, but I had a very difficult time piecing together the rest of the song" (Hilburn). Petty spoke of his writing process at various points in his career, and it is important to take his comments about his writing process as a collective.

At times, he spoke of the almost high one feels when the writing just comes, when it feels like magic. Still, other times, he spoke of the work, the drudgery. For example, in the 2007 documentary, *Tom Petty and the Heart-*

breakers: Runnin' Down a Dream, Petty mentions the work of writing while others in his band were out having fun. He also specifically described an example of struggling with the title of the song, "You Wreck Me." For a period of time, he could only come up with "You Rock Me," but everyone in the band agreed it was not right and sounded cliché. In his description of the process of trying to find the right word, one can sense the struggle and impatience of searching so hard for the right word for the title of the song. One can sense the work and dedication to his craft and to making a song "right." However, in a 2014 interview with Jian Ghomeshi, Petty describes the other side of the process, the side when the songs come quickly. Petty said, "Sometimes, a song can some so fast that you're suspicious of where it came from" ("Tom Petty On Making Great Songs"). Moreover, in Petty's narrative for VH1's Storytellers, he spoke of the "magic" of song writing and compares the process of success in writing a good song to an orgasm.

If someone heard just one side of his writing process, they would most certainly have an incomplete picture of Petty's process. Writing is very much about the hard work and being persistent, and when good writers practice these good habits, sometimes, they "catch a thread."

Catching the Thread

In her book, *Big Magic*, author Elizabeth Gilbert spoke to the concept of "catching a thread." In the book, she described the importance of persistence in writing and dedication to the craft. It is only with this persistence and dedication that a writer can hope to experience a phenomenon that Gilbert described as "supernatural" and "magical." Of course scientists and many professors would disagree that there is anything magical to anyone's writing process. In the past, I would have thought the same thing. I would ascribe moments like the ones that Tom Petty described where the song came so quickly to him that he questioned where it came from as a kind of luck which was a result of good writing process habits. But, as I have now spent over 20 years studying writers and their processes quite deeply and work as a writer myself, my mind has been opened to a potentially broader understanding of the writing process.

I mentioned in the beginning of my essay that my husband is a writer as well, a poet. It is difficult to make a living as a poet, of course, but I would most certainly describe my husband as a skilled poet, and when he works consistently and persistently, he produces good material. I have read hundreds of his poems. Most of them are quite good to me, though I can recognize when a few need some work. Even though I am married to this poet, I have my years of experience and training to keep me grounded in my opinions of his writing. In the ten years we have been married, I have seen magic happen with him a few times, and I cannot fully explain it within anything in my training. I have seen him become obsessed with a poem. I have seen difficult poems and structures come to him very quickly, almost magically. And I have had him hand me a poem to read that he wrote in one evening that shook me to my core and made my soul yearn. Because I also see his normal process and how long most poems take him to write, when something comes quickly and beautifully, like Tom Petty, I have to wonder where that comes from.

I have experienced this myself as a writer once or twice; interestingly, one of my best writing ideas came to me while I was in the middle of my mourning Tom Petty's death and was listening to his music all day every day. I could not believe I had the idea. I wrote the piece quickly, over the period of a day, almost in hiding, because I was confused about how I had the idea. I keep researching on the web to see if, indeed, my idea was original. It seemed too good and came to me too quickly. I did not know where it came from. But I could not find that it existed anywhere else, so I published it; later that afternoon, it was on the front page of a major national newspaper.

When I first began to study Petty's writing process, I suspected that he was one of those gifted writers who had the ability to take an idea from the universe and put it into words and forms for the rest of us to experience. One needs only to see the way people react to his music to think this. Petty's songs had and continue to have a broad appeal, across social class, the political spectrum, gender, and more. As I looked more deeply into his process, I had no doubt. While, he did not seem to use the same vocabulary as Gilbert did in her work on writing process, his processes and experiences that he described in interviews very much align with Gilbert's assertions about the writing process.

In summary of her argument about writing process, Gilbert wrote:

> Most of my writing life, to be perfectly honest, is not…. Big Magic. Most of my writing life consists of nothing more than unglamorous labor, disciplined labor. I sit at my desk and I work like a farmer, and that's how it gets done. Most of it is not fairy dust in the least.
>
> But sometimes it is fairy dust. Sometimes, when I'm in the midst of writing, I feel like I am suddenly walking on one of those moving sidewalks that you find in a big airport terminal; I still have a long slog to my gate, and my baggage is still heavy, but I can feel myself being gently propelled by some exterior force. Something is carrying me along—something powerful and generous—and that something is decidedly not *me* … I only rarely experience this feeling, but it's the most magnificent sensation imaginable when it arrives. I don't think there is a more perfect happiness to be found in life than this state, except perhaps falling in love [66–67].

In his 2014 interview with Ghomeshi, Petty addressed writing process and magic in his words:

PETTY: It's kind of a dangerous business, looking really deeply into the germ that creates songs. I don't like to stare at that light very long. I get a little superstitious about it, but...

GHOMESHI: Like you'll lose your mojo or something?

PETTY: Well, there is some kind of actual magic going on there. I feel that, for some reason, I was born with some kind of conduit to this energy force or whatever it is, and I can have that happen through me if I really try to do it or sometimes when I'm not. ("Tom Petty On Making Great Songs").

Ownership

In addition to just being a kind, understanding human being, perhaps it was Petty's understanding of this "magical" aspect to writing that led him to be as lenient as he was in terms of copyright and ownership of his songs. Petty was famously kind and forgiving with other artists who accidentally copied parts of his work. The Red Hot Chili Peppers' hit "Dani California" from 2006 shared too much music and theme with Tom Petty's 1993 hit "Mary Jane's Last Dance." Tom Petty's publishing team wanted to sue the Red Hot Chili Peppers, but Petty said no, citing being a fan of the band and asserting that there was no negative intent (Rice). Even when the Grammy winning song from Sam Smith's 2014 "Stay With Me" borrowed too heavily from Petty's "I Won't Back Down," to the point where Smith ended up listing Petty and Jeff Lynne in the credits for his song, Petty reportedly handled the situation with extensive kindness. In an official statement on his website, Tom Petty said that "these things can happen" and went on to emphasize an amicable agreement (Rice). In *Conversations with Tom Petty*, Zollo asked Petty how he felt about the Grateful Dead making a song entitled "Built to Last," which was the same title Petty had used in an earlier song. Petty explained that these kinds of things happen to him as a writer as well. He said:

"That happens sometimes. You look up, and you think you've come up with something, and you realize somebody else has done it first. You try not to let it bug you. What bugs you the most is when you write something and then realize it's somebody else's song. That'll happen to me two times a month. I'll be working with something and then realize I'm channeling this melody from somewhere else, and then I have to abandon the idea. But there's only so many words and so many notes, so sometimes you do cross somebody else's territory."

Petty would go on to say that he throws his work out when this happens, but an understanding of the limits in ideas and musical variations as well as the connectedness of ideas likely aided in Petty's patience and understanding with artists who would borrow far too heavily from his work.

Understanding That Writing Is Hard Work

Writing is hard work in terms of the cognitive load it requires. While Petty sometimes mentioned the "magic" associated with writing, as noted earlier, he also mentioned that it is hard work. In a study published in 2014, researchers from the University of Greifwald in Germany studied the brains of writers and found that beginning writers activate a high number of regions in their brain, and while more experienced writers activated different regions of their brains in many cases, there was a great deal of activity going on during the creative process. "The inner workings of the professionally trained writers in the bunch, the scientists argue, showed some similarities to people who are skilled at other complex actions, like music or sports" (Zimmer). Petty mentioned having struggles writing when he was feeling low or depressed, and this would make sense given the complexity of brain activity that is required to write.

In his 2014 interview with Ghomeshi, Petty said, "'I'm not one to write when I'm bummed out'" ("Tom Petty On Making Great Songs"). This example is further illustrated in Zanes' biography of Petty. Zanes described Petty's struggle with some serious depression before and during the making of Petty's album *Echo*. Zanes described the situation as Petty worked with producer Rick Rubin on the album. Rubin had produced *Wildflowers* (1994) with Petty and had been so inspired by Petty's writing. In an 2014 interview with *Rolling Stone*, Rubin had this to say about Petty's writing, "'He wrote constantly and called me to come and hear new songs often. There is a poetry about them that spoke to me'" (Grow). Rubin continued and spoke of both Petty's dedication and genius that he witnessed during the creation of *Wildflowers*.

> "I remember when Tom lived in Encino and I would go to his house to listen to demos he was working on…. One day, between cassette recordings of songs he was working on, he began strumming the guitar. After a couple of minutes of strumming chords, he played me an intricate new song complete with lyrics and story. I asked him what it was about. He said he didn't know it just came out. He had written it or more like channeled it in that very moment. He didn't know what it was about or what the inspiration was. It arrived fully formed. It was breathtaking" [Grow].

But as Rubin worked with Petty on *Echo* (1999), Petty was not the same writer due to his struggles with depression. Zanes wrote:

Echo didn't stimulate Rubin in the same way. He liked working closely with artists, and

> this artist was under a few layers that couldn't be unwrapped…. There were efforts to change the mood. Rubin went to Barns and Noble and purchased several magnetic poetry sets, the boxes of words intended for building phrases on refrigerators. "I went through them all," explains Rubin, "and took out all the little words…. Then, when Tom had songs without words, just chord changes and melodies, he'd randomly

look at words and make up sentences. I could show you specific lines he wrote that were words from the poetry set. It was remarkable and beautiful. He could draw on this pool of information to create the stories. His mind works *very* fast" [261].

Although Petty's genius could shine through even difficult writing situations, such as this case of a kind of writer's block due to his depression, we see that the writing was work. In this case, we see Rubin using a classic strategy of invention to get Petty's process going, and it worked. Of course, this example teaches the importance of persistence even through difficult times, but Petty's experiences with the difficulties of writing also teach us that writing is not an easy thing to do. There are some who think it is, and I have seen writers get quite down on themselves when they struggle. However, writing requires work, sometimes intense work, and the cognitive load is real.

Writing Under the Influence

Although more difficult to talk about, no discussion of a legendary Rock and Roll writer's writing process would be complete without discussing the impact of drugs or alcohol on the writing process. It is important to note that there is a long history of writing under the influence from many of the great writers throughout history. It is well known that Edgar Allan Poe struggled with alcohol, as did Stephen King. King writes about his experiences having to learn to write "clean" in his work *On Writing*. Mary Shelley may have been on laudanum when she wrote her famous novel *Frankenstein*, and there are rumors that even Shakespeare smoked marijuana in order to stimulate his writing. It is also well known that marijuana had a profound influence on the Beatles' music, and Alanis Morisette has spoken about the clarity marijuana brought to her writing process.

The topic is not one academics discuss when exploring writing process, but Tom Petty did speak of marijuana and other drugs and their impact on his writing process. In *Conversations with Tom Petty*, Petty had nothing good to say about the impact of cocaine on his writing, but he did mention some helpfulness in relation to marijuana use, though he contended that pot did not have a strong influence on him as a writer. Zollo shared the following exchange on the topic:

> *Smoking pot had a big influence on The Beatles; it changed their songwriting and their recording. Did it have an influence on you and the Heartbreakers?*
> [Laughs] Probably not. There was certainly plenty of pot around. I don't think all The Heartbreakers were pot smokers. I've never been a drinker; it just never worked for me. So pot kind of appealed to me, because I could get into another space, and it was kind of groovy [Zollo].

Petty continued, "I don't think drugs really make anything better. They're probably more detrimental than helpful. But I'm sure there were times when it helped me focus, or get in the mood to write something" (Zollo).

Although Petty dismissed drugs having much of an influence on writing process, he did note that marijuana helped him get into the mood to write or helped him focus. Later, in a piece for *Men's Journal*, Petty spoke about marijuana again. When speaking about drugs and alcohol, Petty said he was never a drinker and that he was "more a reefer guy." He went on to call marijuana "a musical drug" (Eells). These insights align with some of the latest scientific research about the benefits of marijuana to the creative processes in the brain. Although there is still debate about whether or not people who use marijuana are just more open and creative people to begin with, a research study published in 2017 in the journal *Consciousness and Cognition* found that in a test of 979 participants, people who used marijuana out performed people who did not on tests that measured a type of creative thinking called convergent thinking, or a "thought process that involves judging a finite number of solutions to arrive at one 'correct' answer" (Johnson). While Petty made it clear that he was not greatly impacted as a writer by being under the influence, his experiences and processes align with many great writers and other creative thinkers who report being able to write better when they can use a substance like marijuana or alcohol to turn off the "noise" or distractions in their heads. Dr. Alice Weaver Flaherty a neurologist and professor at Harvard Medical School points out that marijuana's effectiveness on the creative processes varies from person to person. She said, "A very anxious person may get some benefit from cannabis. In calming them down, it could help their creativity" (Johnson). What we can learn from this is that, again, the writing process is a complex one and varies for different people. Some people do seem to be helped creatively by being under the influence of something like marijuana. Therefore, while no one could *encourage* drug use as a part of writing process, more openness to varied effective writing processes can help both writers and those who instruct others in writing.

Conclusion

In my years of teaching writing, I have often been asked if writing is a gift or if it is a skill that can be taught. To a certain extent, it is a skill that can be taught, of course, and we do that in my field, in part, by helping people become better writers by developing a better process. I see people improve as writers every day. It takes work, but they can grow. Still, in the thousands of students I have taught, I have seen some who seem to have a gift—a gift that is difficult to define, a kind of genius. Stephen King describes the genius in this way: "These are the really good writers … the Shakespeares, the

Faulkners, the Yeatses, Shaws, and Eudora Weltys. They are geniuses, divine accidents, gifted in a way which is beyond our ability to understand, let alone attain. Shit, most geniuses aren't able to understand themselves…" (King 142). I contend that Tom Petty is one of those divine accidents and that his work will prove to be a lasting part of the canon of American songwriting and, to some extent, American writing in general.

It is as if some of us have a different, deeper way of seeing the world, and some of those seem to be able to articulate that for the rest of us. In Zollo's book, Petty had this to say about Bob Dylan as a writer: "He can enunciate his view of the world really well. And he can enunciate it in a way that is poetic. That's a gift. That's not something you learn, or get out of a manual. It's just a gift" (Zollo). Of course, these same words are also true for Tom Petty.

But even for those with the gift, having the gift is not enough. There is work and rigor through a strong writing process that allows those with the gift to write in powerful ways, to tap into the thread of the universe, and, especially, to be prolific with their gift. We are fortunate in that Tom Petty was not only a gifted writer and musician but also dedicated to his process; his process teaches us not only that process is important but also that it must be flexible and authentic to the writer in order to work best. And, maybe, when our process is rigorous and the conditions are right, we can all catch the thread every now and again.

WORKS CITED

Ede, Lisa, and Andrea Lunsford. *Singular Texts/Plural Authors*. Carbondale: Southern Illinois University Press, 1992.

Eells, Josh. "Tom Petty Still Won't Back Down." *Men's Journal*, 20 October 2015, https://www.mensjournal.com/features/tom-petty-still-wont-back-down-20151020/.

Gilbert, Elizabeth. *Big Magic: Creative Living Beyond Fear*. New York: Riverhead Books, 2015.

Graham, Steve and Delores Perin. "A Meta-Analysis of Writing Instruction for Adolescent Students." *Journal of Educational Psychology*. Vol. 99, issue 3, 2007, pp. 445–476.

Grow, Kory. "Rick Rubin Talks 'Breathtaking' Poetry of Tom Petty." *Rolling Stone*, 5 October 2017, https://www.rollingstone.com/music/music-features/rick-rubin-talks-breathtaking-poetry-of-tom-petty-120292/.

Hilburn, Robert. "Tome Petty Breaks Down 10 of His Songs, Including Big Hits and Obscure Gems." *Los Angeles Times*, 2 March 2002. http://www.latimes.com/entertainment/music/la-et-ms-tom-petty-songs-archive-20020315-story.html.

Johnson, Stephen. "Does Smoking Weed Make People Creative, or Do Creative People Smoke Weed?" *Big Think*, 2 December 2017. https://bigthink.com/stephen-johnson/does-smoking-weed-make-people-creative-or-do-creative-people-smoke-weed.

King, Stephen. *On Writing*. New York: Scribner's, 2000.

Rice, Alex. "Five Musicians Who Ripped Off Tom Petty." *City Pages*, 3 Feb. 2015, http://www.citypages.com/music/five-musicians-who-ripped-off-tom-petty-6634114.

Tom Petty and the Heartbreakers: Runnin' Down a Dream. Directed by Peter Bogdanovich, Warner Brothers, 2007.

"Tom Petty on Making Great Songs." CBC News: The National. 25 July 2014, https://www.youtube.com/watch?v=J7oN4mkbz-I&feature=share.

Zimmer, Carl. "This Is Your Brain on Writing." *The New York Times*, 20 June 2014, https://www.nytimes.com/2014/06/19/science/researching-the-brain-of-writers.html.

Zollo, Paul. *Conversations With Tom Petty*. London: Omnibus Press, 2015, Kindle Edition.

A Career in Review

Spencer Rowland

Tom Petty's career spanned over four decades. In that time, he released twenty albums and performed as a solo musician, as a front man with The Heartbreakers, as a friend in Mudcrutch, and as Charlie T. Wilbury, Jr., in the Travelling Wilburys. With his passing in 2017, the music industry and the world lost one of its most recognizable faces. While Tom Petty is undoubtedly a household name, little research has been done on how his music influenced Rock and Roll and popular culture. Is he a Rock God, a legend, an innovator, or something else entirely?

To answer these questions, I scoured Petty album reviews of all kinds. How was he received with The Heartbreakers, as a solo artist, with The Traveling Wilburys, and with Mudcrutch? While reading these reviews I wondered what praise Petty received, how he changed rock and roll, how he innovated his genre, and whom he influenced.

I analyze Petty's body of work, dividing it into four sections: his time with The Heartbreakers, his time as a solo artist, his time with The Traveling Wilburys and his time with Mudcrutch. To be fair, there is a large amount of overlap between these groups. Many of The Heartbreakers performed on Petty's solo albums, one of his many producers, Jeff Lynne, was a member of The Traveling Wilburys, and Mudcrutch shared half its lineup with Tom Petty and the Heartbreakers. What is more is that these are not four distinct time periods over Petty's career either. He would release solo albums between albums with The Heartbreakers—the same is true for The Traveling Wilburys and Mudcrutch.

The paper is organized this way, then, to show the nuances (or possibly lack thereof) between these bands. I analyze what is different between them (if anything) and how reviewers accepted or rejected each band on its own merits and in relation to other bands in the Petty Canon. Based on these reviews, I also analyze the legacy of Tom Petty's influence on his fellow musicians and on pop culture.

Tom Petty and the Heartbreakers

Tom Petty and the Heartbreakers' high water mark is undoubtedly *Damn The Torpedoes*. Not only was it their best-reviewed album at the time of its release, but it was also the standard that all following Petty and Heartbreaker albums were held up to. Somewhat surprisingly, then, is the fact that Ariel Swartley's 1979 *Rolling Stone's* review gave it only 3.5 out of 5 stars and says, "*Damn the torpedoes* is the Tom Petty and the Heartbreakers album we've all been waiting for—that is, if we were all Tom Petty fans, which we would be if there were any justice in the world" (Swartley). While this is pleasant and pro–Petty, it is not exactly what one would consider a rave review—from the star rating down to the analysis.

Rolling Stone goes on to give Petty and the Heartbreakers further middling responses saying, "Petty takes a middle position between rock's romantic visionaries and urban nihilists—his observations are as flat and down-to-earth as his heartland twang," and, "...for Petty, rock is neither a cash crop nor a code of honor, not salvation or a cultural neutron bomb" (Swartley). In short, Petty plays very matter-of-factly. He is making no grand statement, nor is he innovating music. Rather, he is just playing pure rock and roll like his heroes did.

Interestingly enough, a 2004 review by Warren Zanes of *Rolling Stone* gave the same album 5 stars (Zanes). This review originally ran in *Rolling Stone* as part of a series that looked back at classic albums. This is a pattern that many reviews would follow—at the time of an album's release it would receive middle of the road reviews, but reflecting on the albums after several years had passed, they would receive substantially higher and upper percentile reviews. Similarly, later albums in the Petty and Heartbreakers canon seemed to rate, on average, higher than his previous albums. While this could be due to the band improving, I began to wonder if there was a correlation between the two. It seems that, as Petty continually established himself, his albums began to rate higher simply by virtue of being Petty albums. Furthermore, reviews of past albums closer to the time of Petty's death rated these albums higher than they were rated on their initial release. This *could* speak to the fact that Petty continually improved his reputation or came to be seen as a bonafide songwriter in his own right.

Petty's next album, *Hard Promises,* cemented the fact that Petty and the Heartbreakers were a force to be reckoned with. In 1981, at the time of its release, *Hard Promises* received 3 stars from *Rolling Stone* and a B (on a plus or minus alphabetic scale) from Robert Christgau (Cohen; Christgau "Robert Christgau Dean of American Rock Critics"). Stephen Erlewine's *All Music* review that came several years after the album's release grants *Hard Promises* a 4.5/5 and posits that it, "offered reaffirmation that *Damn the Torpedoes* wasn't a fluke" (Erlewine "Tom Petty and the Heartbreakers/Tom Petty Hard Promises"). In accordance with this, *Rolling Stone* wrote, "It's as if the Heart-breakers have to be restrained so as not to show more confidence than Tom Petty's willing to admit" (Cohen). Given these reviews, *Damn the Torpedoes* and *Hard Promises* are what initially established Petty and the Heartbreakers as a group for listeners to keep their ears on.

That said, even supposed flubs like Petty and the Heartbreakers' *The Last DJ* do not receive many negative reviews. Greg Kot of *Rolling Stone* gave the album 3/5 stars, even while asserting, "Tom Petty sounds like the crankiest middle-aged punk this side of Neil Young" (Kot "Tom Petty: The Last DJ"). Similarly, Robert Christgau gave the album a C+ questioning, "does [Petty] whine … in that weird, self-pitying child drawl? Sure, he regresses every time out" (Christgau "Robert Christgau Dean of American Rock Critics"). Despite critics' qualms regarding the content of the album, *The Last DJ* does not fare much worse than his best-reviewed album, *Damn the Torpedoes*. In fact, *Entertainment Weekly* rated *The Last DJ* as an A- despite calling it, "an album-length rant about greed and corruption in the music biz" (Weingarten). In spite of being arguably Petty and the Heartbreakers' worst reviewed effort, *The Last DJ* still manages to maintain average reviews. The above average ratings of Petty's negatively reviewed albums (relative to his other work) go to show how consistently good his work is. This is a pattern that Petty and the Heartbreakers' weakest albums maintain.

Critics treated Petty and the Heartbreaker's *Let Me Up (I've Had Enough)* similarly. This poorly received album was granted 3/5 stars by *Rolling Stone* and *Blender* and a B+ from Robert Christgau (DeCurtis; Tom Petty: Let; and Christgau "Robert Christgau Dean of American Rock Critics"). In fact, *All Music's* Erlewine writes that *Let Me Up (I've Had Enough) is*, "Filled with loose ends, song fragments, and unvarnished productions, it's a defiantly messy album, and it's all the better for it," and while, "there aren't any stand-outs on the record … there's no filler either—it's just simply a good collection of ballads" (Erlewine "Tom Petty and the Heartbreakers/Tom Petty Let Me Up (I've Had Enough)"). Two of Petty and the Heartbreakers' most divisive albums were still *above average*—which sums up their career nicely.

Petty and the Heartbreakers never had a five-star record. At the release of each of their albums, they were never rated as five-stars. The closest Petty and the Heartbreakers ever came to a five-star rating (at the release of an album) was Kenneth Partridge's 4.5 star *Billboard* review of Petty and the Heartbreakers' 2014 release, *Hypnotic Eye* (Partridge). Indeed, both *The Guardian* and *Rolling Stone* granted the same album 4 stars (Woodcraft; Dolan). While this comes close to the elusive 5 stars that albums such as The Beatles' *Sgt. Peppers Lonely Hearts Club Band* or Bob Dylan's *The Freewheelin Bob Dylan* obtained, it does not reach it. In fact, *Spin* and *Exclaim* felt the album deserved a 7/10 (Soto; Côté). Despite *Hypnotic Eye* receiving Petty and the Heartbreakers' highest review at the time of its release, it was not universally acclaimed.

In their 38-year run, Petty and the Heartbreakers received a 4/5 star rating at the release of their albums from *Rolling Stone* for *Southern Accents,* *Rolling Stone* for *Into the Great Wide Open, The Music Box* and *Rolling Stone* for *Songs and Music from "She's the One," The Music Box* for *Echo, Rolling Stone* for *Mojo,* 4.5 stars from *Billboard* and 4 stars from *The Guardian* and *Rolling Stone* for *Hypnotic Eye* (Millman "Tom Petty: Southern Accents"; Puterbaugh "Tom Petty: Into the Great Wide Open"; Metzger "Tom Petty Songs and Music from the motion picture *She's the One*; Puterbaugh "Tom Petty: Songs and Music from *She's the One*"; Metzger "Tom Petty & the Heartbreakers Echo"; Fricke; Partridge; Woodcraft; and Dolan). Thus, Petty and the Heartbreakers received a grand total of *nine* 4 star reviews for the thirteen studio albums they released. On the other hand, Petty and the Heartbreakers were reviewed for less than 3/5 stars on only a few occasions including 2.5 stars from *Rolling Stone* for *You're Gonna Get* It, from *Slant* for *MOJO,* and 2 stars from *The Guardian* and *NOW* for *MOJO.* Given this, Petty and the Heartbreakers only received four reviews below 3 stars for their thirteen studio albums (Carson; Hann; Gillis; Cole). While Petty and the Heartbreakers never received 5 stars, they rarely received negative reviews and were often received positively. To put it simply, they were good more than they were bad. In 38 years, Petty and the Heartbreakers maintained average reviews— average reviews that leaned further towards praise than they did criticism.

Tom Petty Solo Albums

Petty released three solo albums—*Full Moon Fever* in 1989, *Wildflowers* in 1994, and *Highway Companion* in 2006. While they were billed as solo albums, they were frequented by The Heartbreakers and most notably by Mike Campbell—lead guitarists of Tom Petty and the Heartbreakers. Critics often have difficulty finding a sonic difference between Petty's solo albums and his albums billed as Petty and the Heartbreakers.

Full Moon Fever received a 3.5 star review from *Rolling Stone's* Jimmy Guterman who writes, "The opening song, the delicate "Free Fallin'," is not only the standout on *Full Moon Fever* but also one of the most concise, well-rounded performances of Petty's career" and ""Free Fallin' " isn't the only high point on this sprawling album" (Guterman). It seems that Petty may have saved his best for himself; *Fool Moon Fever* produced an astonishing five singles—"I Won't Back Down," "Runnin' Down a Dream," "Free Fallin'," "A Face in the Crowd," and "Yer So Bad." Stephen Erlewine of *All Music* review gave the album 4.5 stars and said it, "didn't have a weak track; even if a few weren't quite as strong as others, the album was filled with highlights" (Erlewine "Tom Petty Full Moon Fever"). With *Fool Moon Fever,* Petty continued his record of highly accessible albums.

While *Fool Moon Fever* does not innovate, it does entertain. Christ Williams of the *Los Angeles Times* writes that "Petty didn't make this album to break ground. He just wants to kick up a little dirt" (Willman). Petty is a preserver of sounds of the past more than he is a trailblazer. Just like the Petty and Heartbreaker albums, *Fool Moon Fever* was reviewed as above average but not outstanding. *Blender* gave the album 4 stars; *The Chicago Tribune* gave it 3.5 stars; *Pitchfork* gave it an 8.1 out of 10, and Robert Christgau even rated it as a B+ saying, "if guys made roots-rock albums anymore, anything here would spruce one up" (Tom Petty—Full; Silverman; Johnston; and Christgau "Robert Christgau Dean of American Rock Critics"). Petty used *Full Moon Fever* to display a nuance to his sound that, while similar to his other work, added more layers than what had been heard on Petty and the Heartbreakers' albums. In essence, *Full Moon Fever* sounds at home with Petty's prior work but has more going on beneath the surface than his previous efforts.

Petty's second solo album, *Wildflowers,* is arguably his best album. Sam Sodomsky of *Pitchfork* gave *Wildflowers* an 8.8 out of 10 and said, "When he was 44 years old, Petty released his second and greatest solo album" (Sodomsky). As he did with *Full Moon Fever,* it seems that Petty may have left the best for himself. Working with Rick Rubin, Petty composed a stripped down album that was more vulnerable than his previous work. *All Music* gave the album 4.5 stars saying, "the finest songs here … match the quality of his best material, making *Wildflowers* one of Petty's most distinctive and best albums" (Erlewine "Tom Petty *Wildflowers*"). Between Petty's solo career and his career with The Heartbreakers, his solo albums consistently rise to the top of all around best Tom Petty albums.

As usual, Petty's work was not without detractors. Robert Browne of *Entertainment Weekly* claims, "[Petty] and the Heartbreakers have come up with some good singles … and kept alive the traditional rock-band ensemble when everyone considered it dead, yet Petty hasn't had an original guitar lick in his head his whole career" and gave *Wildflowers* a B- (Browne). Working as Petty and the Heartbreakers or by himself, Petty could not escape critiques of being unoriginal, uninspired, or just grumpy. Robert Christgau also gave *Wildflowers* a B- and notes, "if [Petty] were a flower, he'd be wilted, but since he's more of a dick, call him torpid" (Christgau "Robert Christgau Dean of American Rock Critics").

In the face of all these criticisms, though, *Wildflowers,* and by extension Petty, remain not only relatively unblemished but come out triumphant in the end. Sam Sodomsky of *Pitchfork* writes that "[Petty] never floundered like Dylan in the '80s or Springsteen in the '90s. Instead, he attacked and retreated more consistently" (Sodomsky). From the critics' perspective, Petty never strayed from his vision—regardless of how single-minded they perceived that vision to be. Again, this vision proved fruitful for Petty. *Entertainment Weekly* continues, "Of course, Petty has become a classic-rock god himself, and what better proof than an actual Petty tribute album, *You Got Lucky*" (Browne). Whether or not he should be considered a "classic-rock god," Petty has left a lasting impression on his genre. Elysa Gardner of *Rolling Stone* writes, "*Wildflowers* is worthy of that longstanding impact and evidence that this American boy is moving through middle age with all the gusto and poise that his admirers have come to expect" (Gardner). Whether Petty was innovating Rock N Roll or not, he left his thumbprint on the industry, especially with *Wildflowers*.

Petty's last solo effort is *Highway Companion,* which was released in 2006 and proved to be a combination of elements that worked well from both *Full Moon Fever* and *Wildflowers. All Music* wrote that it, "is precise and polished, yet it's on a small scale, lacking the layers of overdubs that distinguish Lynne's production, and the end result is quite appealing, since it's at once modest but not insular" (Erlewine "Tom Petty *Highway Companion*"). Petty maintained his streak of above average, but not exceptional album ratings. True to form, this solo effort rose to the top of Petty's discography as well. Even if *Highway Companion* is not his best outing, it still garnered high praise. Noel Murray of *A.V. Club* praised *Highway Companion* saying, "something about stepping outside the rock-band format frees Petty up, letting him write batches of songs that are stylistically eclectic, yet unified by mood" (Murray). It is a trend that Petty's solo albums are often better received than his work with the Heartbreakers. Yet, even his well-received solo albums were not rated as five stars at the time of their release.

By 2006, critics began to reflect on the fact that Petty had not released a 5-star album. Even so, *Highway Companion* entertained and glowed. Instead of going big—in terms of both his music and his success—Petty preferred to narrow his focus. Randy Lewis of the *Los Angeles Times* gave the album 3 stars and commented, "*Highway Companion* ... musically represents time spent cogitating next to a gurgling brook in a hidden meadow rather than standing in awe in front of Niagara Falls" (Lewis). Interestingly enough, the same is true of Petty's career as a whole. Multiple critics commented on Petty's staying power, despite the fact that he never released a five-star record. Similar to the *Los Angeles Times*, the *A.V. Club* continued, "Tom Petty's recording career has been a persistent curiosity, because while he's imminently capable of putting together a classic album, he's rarely actually done it" (Murray). To that point, though, Petty never released a low-quality album either.

As Alan Light from *Rolling Stone* put it in 2006, "In a career that has now reached its thirtieth year, Tom Petty has never made a bad album … the man's consistency is pretty astounding" (Light). Just like with Petty and the Heartbreakers, Petty's solo career did not have highs and lows. While Petty may not have managed any grand victories, he won the war—and every battle of the war too. His genius comes from tried and true practices instead of innovation and novelty. From the onset, Petty knew what made a great song; instead of building on what that could be, he distilled it. As Jeff Vrable from *Pop Matters* puts it, "Petty's not out to reinvent the wheel; he never has been. He's just happy to be behind it, and happy that you are, too" (Vrabel).

The Traveling Wilburys

The Traveling Wilburys is a high point in Petty's long career. The Traveling Wilburys is one of Rock and Roll's most successful supergroups. In this case, a supergroup is a band formed by members of other hit bands that successfully produces a sound that is more than the sum of its parts. In The Traveling Wilburys, Tom Petty played alongside George Harrison from The Beatles, Bob Dylan, Roy Orbison, and Jeff Lynne from ELO. Among these four, Harrison, Dylan, and Orbison are undisputed legends in their own right. Each member of the band took a pseudonym. Petty was the only member who didn't have the last name "Wilbury"; instead, Petty went by Charlie T. Jr.

The Traveling Wilburys first release, *The Traveling Wilburys Vol. 1*, which was released in 1998, was one of the best-reviewed albums that Petty played on. If anything, this band pushed Petty to a level of success that he had not yet achieved with Petty and the Heartbreakers. *All Music* notes that The Traveling Wilburys, "[set] the stage for…. Petty's first solo album, *Full Moon Fever*, produced by Lynne (sounding and feeling strikingly similar to this lark)" (Erlewine "The Traveling Wilburys *The Traveling Wilburys Vol. 1*"). At the formation of The Traveling Wilburys, Petty might not have been as famous as his fellow band members. Yet, by sharing an album and a stage with them, Petty's fame elevated.

As aforementioned, *The Traveling Wilburys Vol. 1* was one of the best-reviewed albums that Petty ever played on. *Rolling Stone* gave the album 4 stars and Robert Christgau gave the album an A- (Wild; Christgau "Traveling Wilburys"). While Petty does share the writing credits and success with his four other bandmates, he received some notable mentions in the album reviews. In particular, David Wild of *Rolling Stone* wrote that "Petty acquits himself well on "End of the Line" and "Last Night"; he and Orbison share lead on the latter song, a shuffling tale of good love gone bad" (Wild). With this album, Petty proved that he could stand among the legends of Rock and

Roll and hold his own. In addition, Bud Scoppa of *Uncut* wrote that "Petty's "Last Night," suffused with bonhomie, and the synth-meets-horns production number "Margarita" exemplify the extremes of his longstanding partnership with Lynne" (Scoppa). One way or the other, it is notable that Petty (and Lynne) can stand out at all when playing with such musical giants.

The Traveling Wilburys' second album, *The Traveling Wilburys Vol. 3*, which was released in 1990, while still praised, was not as well received as their first outing. This could have been for a number of reasons, including the passing of bandmate Roy Orbison. However, like many other albums Petty released, it was far from negative. In fact, it was rated above average at the time of its release receiving 3/4 stars from *The Chicago Tribune* and a B+ from *Entertainment Weekly* and Robert Christgau (Kot "Traveling Wilburys Traveling Wilburys Vol. 3"; Tucker; Christgau "Traveling Wilburys"). Similarly, *All Music* rated *The Traveling Wilburys Vol. 3* a 3/5, several years after its release (Erlewine "The Traveling Wilburys *The Traveling Wilburys Vol. 3*"). Perhaps because Orbison was not on the album and, therefore, Petty ostensibly had more songs that he wrote on, Petty received further acclaim for his contributions on the second album. *All Music* wrote that "Lynne and Petty dominate this record ... but it's striking that this sounds more like their work, even when Dylan takes the lead on "Inside Out" or the doo wop-styled '7 Deadly Sins'" (Erlewine "The Traveling Wilburys *The Traveling Wilburys Vol. 3*"). It's impressive that Petty and Lynne's sound shines through the musical giants that are George Harrison and Bob Dylan. True, Harrison and Dylan were older than both Petty and Lynne, but they both had more experience and larger followings. While The Traveling Wilburys might not have had a five-star album, they are widely considered one of the best, if not the best, supergroups of all time. The Traveling Wilburys provided Petty and company a chance to explore more whimsical and laid back ideas. While they might have ultimately proven to be more "fun" than Petty's solo work, they also allowed Petty to explore yet another creative avenue. Like Petty's other bands, The Traveling Wilburys did not top the charts, but they did leave their mark.

Mudcrutch

Mudcrutch was Petty's pre–Heartbreakers band in the '70s and consisted of multiple musicians including Tom Petty, Mike Campbell, Benmont Tench, Tom Leadon, Randall Marsh, Jim Lenahan, Danny Roberts, and Charlie Souza. Shortly after moving to California, Mudcrutch split up and reformed as Tom Petty and The Heartbreakers while keeping Mike Campbell on guitar and Benmont Tench on piano. In 2008, Mudcrutch reformed with much of the '70s lineup including Tom Petty, Mike Campbell, Benmont Tench, Tom

Leadon, and Randall Marsh. Mudcrutch's eponymous debut album was released in 2008 and, like all Petty albums, was met with varying degrees of favorable reviews. The lowest of these reviews being Alex Young of *Consequence of Sound* who writes that "Mudcrutch's debut album begins with a clear message: this is not Tom Petty and the Heartbreakers,"; yet, "one can feel Petty's signature smile beaming through the lyrics" (Young). At this point, Petty had made enough of a name for himself that he could successfully carry two unknown musicians under his wings—with the aid of longtime partners Campbell and Tench. However, in doing so, Petty leaves a distinct, if light, thumbprint on the material. Even though Young writes positively about *Mudcrutch*, *Consequence of Sound* gave it a C+, citing that "it lacks the power of other Petty material" (Young). That said, Petty does his job to shape the band without crushing it.

It would not be one of Petty's albums, though, if it did not receive above average reviews. Clark Collis of *Entertainment Weekly* counters by saying that "it sounds like a pretty good Tom Petty record" and grants the album a B+ (Collis). *Now* and *Rolling Stone* both rated the album with 4 stars with *Now* positing that "the sound isn't all that different than what Petty does with The Heartbreakers" ("Mudcrutch"; Hermes). Even with the changed name and altered line-up, it seems that Tom Petty cannot help but sound like Tom Petty. While Petty plays in multiple bands and under multiple names, he has a distinct sound that, apart from a few albums, did not change much over the years. *Mudcrutch*, like nearly all Petty albums, was not a means to innovate, but a way to look back and pay homage to the music of yesterday. Far from an innovator, Petty performs much more as a curator by bringing old material to light again.

While *Mudcrutch* received a fair amount of press, the band's second album, *2*, did not. For this paper, I found no reviews that could be used in a worthwhile analysis of the second album. This is perplexing given Petty's stellar track record. For this paper, then, I will omit any reviews of *2* affecting the conclusion. Released in 2016, Mudcrutch's *2* was the final full-length recording released by Tom Petty.

Conclusion

Tom Petty's professional career ran for forty-one years and began in 1976 and lasted until 2017 with his passing. At the conclusion of his career, Petty had released twenty studio albums—thirteen with Tom Petty and the Heartbreakers, three solo albums, two albums with The Traveling Wilburys, and two albums with Mudcrutch. While Petty never received a five-star review of an album (at the time of its release), of his twenty albums, Petty received few—if any—negative reviews. As Alfred Soto of *Spin* put it, Petty is "kind of not bad and often very good" (Soto). In over forty years, Petty never released a total flub.

While Petty consistently released commercially viable, enjoyable, and, for the most part, good albums, his playing missed the mark of being categorized as masterful or innovative. Petty's lead guitarist, Mike Campbell, was frequently cited for his guitar prowess, but Petty was rarely cited for his skill. In fact, Browne of *Entertainment Weekly* claims that "Petty hasn't had an original guitar lick in his head his whole career" (Browne). In addition to this, Petty's voice is often criticized for its less-than aesthetically pleasing quality. As Dave Dimartino of *Entertainment Weekly* puts it, Petty, "at his worst has tended to bray rather than to sing" (Dimartino). Simply put, Petty wasn't at the top of his music class.

Given that Petty was not generally considered a guitar virtuoso and was often critiqued for his singing, it is hard to argue Petty innovated rock and roll, but that is not to say he did not influence it. Rather than being a trailblazer, Petty played the role of curator. His music was inspired by the sounds of his past, and he kept playing it until he could not anymore. Petty was routinely cited as, "embracing the Byrds as much as the stones," remaining "unflinchingly loyal to the sound of Sixties-era Stones and Byrds," or continuing "to reflect and abiding appreciation for the three B's: Byrds, Beatles, and Bob Dylan" (Erlewine "Tom Petty & the Heartbreakers *Tom Petty & the Heartbreakers*"; Kot "Tom Petty: Echo"; and Kot "Tom Petty: The Last DJ"). While he was not as innovative as trailblazers such as The Beatles, Jimi Hendrix, or Led Zeppelin, Petty had other skills that were just as valuable—he was a curator and editor. Petty continually returned to the sounds of his past to find old gems, put a new polish on them, and make them new again. In doing so, Petty made songs that never seemed to grow old and were accessible to people of all generations and all walks of life. In addition to this, Petty's career has influenced contemporary rock bands such as the Foo Fighters, Cage the Elephant, and Kings of Leon, to name a few.

Throughout Petty's career, he was content to be himself. He did not want to be a Rock God. He was too real to be that. Petty was human and his music explored the human condition. His music was accessible because he was not afraid to look at all of his perfections and imperfections, to acknowledge that he could be wrong, and to always try to be better. Petty's music spoke to so many people because he was authentic. He was not to be put on a pedestal above listeners; instead, he was the voice of the unsung heroes. In short, Petty was an everyman. By the end of his career, Petty perfected his sound and established himself as one of the most accessible faces of rock and roll.

In his enduring career, Petty never received the elusive five-star rating at the release of any of his albums, yet he managed to release consistently good albums, which featured timeless music that was always human and always accessible. Petty might not have had the same chops as The Beatles, Hendrix, or Zeppelin, but he had heart and soul. During his time in the spotlight, Petty expressed the feelings that many had, but they did not know how to communicate. In that sense, listeners not only connected with Petty, but with one another. Petty wove himself into popular culture and in doing so, made the world smaller and made the unfamiliar recognizable. Like Petty, his music was not meant to stand above its listeners; rather, it was meant to inspire them to appreciate where they had been and to always try to be better. Petty's legacy is this—whenever listeners are feeling alone, misunderstood, or out of place, Petty will be waiting on them to be their voice, to be their comfort, and, most of all, to be their highway companion.

WORKS CITED

Browne, David. "Music Reviews: 'Wildflowers' and 'You Got Lucky.'" *Entertainment Weekly*, 4 November 1994, https://ew.com/article/1994/11/04/music-reviews-wildflowers-and-you-got-lucky/.

Carson, Tom. "Tom Petty: You're Gonna Get It!" *Rolling Stone*, 7 September 1978, https://www.rollingstone.com/music/music-album-reviews/youre-gonna-get-it-196711/.

Christgau, Robert. "Robert Christgau Dean of American Rock Critics." http://www.robert christgau.com/get_artist2.php?id=2365.

_____. "Traveling Wilburys." *Robert Christgau Dean of American Rock Critics.* https://www.robertchristgau.com/get_artist.php?name=Traveling+Wilburys.

Cohen, Debra Rae. "Tom Petty: Hard Promises." *Rolling Stone*, 23 July 1981, http://archive.li/nlk1Q.

Cole, Matthew. "Tom Petty and the Heartbreakers Mojo." *Slant*, 14 June 2010, https://www.slantmagazine.com/music/review/tom-petty-and-the-heartbreakers-mojo.

Collis, Clark. "Mudcrutch." *Entertainment Weekly*, 2 May 2008, https://www.thepettyarchives.com/archives/magazines/2000s/2008-05-02-entertainmentweekly.

Côté, Thierry. "Tom Petty & the Heartbreakers Hypnotic Eye." *Exclaim! Music*, 25 July 2014, https://exclaim.ca/music/article/tom_petty_heartbreakers-hypnotic_eye.

DeCurtis, Anthony. "Tom Petty: Let Me Up (I've Had Enough)." *Rolling Stone*, 4 June 1987, https://www.rollingstone.com/music/music-album-reviews/let-me-up-ive-had-enough-252035/.

Dimartino, Dave. "Into the Great Wide Open." *Entertainment Weekly*, 19 July 1991, ew.com/article/1991/07/19/great-wide-open-2/.

Dolan, Jon. "Tom Petty and the Heartbreakers: Hypnotic Eye." *Rolling Stone*, 29 July 2014, https://www.rollingstone.com/music/music-album-reviews/hypnotic-eye-102047/.

Erlewine, Stephen Thomas. "Tom Petty & the Heartbreakers *Tom Petty & the Heartbreakers.*" *All Music*, https://www.allmusic.com/album/tom-petty-the-heartbreakers-mw0000191386.

_____. "Tom Petty and the Heartbreakers/Tom Petty Hard Promises." *AllMusic*, www.allmusic.com/album/hard-promises-mw0000650625.

_____. "Tom Petty and the Heartbreakers/ Tom Petty Let Me Up (I've Had Enough)." *AllMusic*, www.allmusic.com/album/let-me-up-ive-had-enough-mw0000191385.

_____. "Tom Petty Full Moon Fever." *All Music*, https://www.allmusic.com/album/full-moon-fever-mw0000197322.

_____. "Tom Petty *Highway Companion*." *All Music*, https://www.allmusic.com/album/highway-companion-mw0000573384.

_____. "Tom Petty *Wildflowers*." *All Music*, https://www.allmusic.com/album/wildflowers-mw0000119270.

_____. "The Traveling Wilburys, the *Traveling Wilburys Vol. 1.*" *All Music*, https://www. allmusic.com/album/the-traveling-wilburys-vol-1-mw0000787431.

_____. "The Traveling Wilburys, the *Traveling Wilburys Vol. 3.*" *All Music*, https://www. allmusic.com/album/the-traveling-wilburys-vol-3-mw0000787432.

Fricke, David. "Tom Petty and the Heartbreakers: Mojo." *Rolling Stone*, 15 June 2010, https:// www.rollingstone.com/music/music-album-reviews/mojo-203303/.

Gardner, Elysa. "Tom Petty: Wildflowers." *Rolling Stone*. 3 November 1994, https://www. rollingstone.com/music/music-album-reviews/wildflowers-184067/.

Gillis, Carla. "Tom Petty and the Heartbreakers Mojo." *Now*. 10 June 2010, https://nowtoronto. com/music/album-reviews/tom-petty-and-the-heartbreakers-2010-06-10/.

Guterman, Jimmy. "Tom Petty: Full Moon Fever." *Rolling Stone*, 4 May 1989, https://www. rollingstone.com/music/music-album-reviews/full-moon-fever-248625/

Hann, Michael. "Tom Petty and the Heartbreakers: Mojo." *The Guardian*, 17 June 2010, https:// www.theguardian.com/music/2010/jun/18/tom-petty-and-the-heartbreakers-mojo-cd-review.

Harvey, Eric. "Tom Petty/The Heartbreakers *Damn the Torpedoes.*" *Pitchfork*, 10 October 2017, https://pitchfork.com/reviews/albums/tom-petty-and-the-heartbreakers-damn-the-torpedoes/.

Hermes, Will. "Mudcrutch." *Rolling Stone*, 1 May 2008, http://archive.li/elppf.

Johnston, Maura. "Tom Petty *Full Moon Fever*" Pitchfork, 10 October 2017, https://pitchfork. com/reviews/albums/tom-petty-full-moon-fever/.

Kot, Greg. "Tom Petty: Echo." *Rolling Stone*, 29 April 1999, https://www.rollingstone.com/ music/music-album-reviews/echo-124259/.

_____. "Tom Petty: The Last DJ." *Rolling Stone*, 17 October 2002, https://www.rollingstone. com/music/music-album-reviews/the-last-dj-99574/.

_____. "Traveling Wilburys, Traveling Wilburys Vol. 3." *The Chicago Tribune*, 15 November 1990, http://articles.chicagotribune.com/1990-11-15/features/9004040589_1_wilburys-star-tom-petty.

Lewis, Randy. "Petty's Route Gets Complex." *The Los Angeles Times*, 23 July 2006, http:// articles.latimes.com/2006/jul/23/entertainment/ca-rack23.

Light, Alan. "Tom Petty: Highway Companion." *Rolling Stone*, 20 July 2006, https://www. rollingstone.com/music/music-album-reviews/highway-companion-190025/.

Metzger, John. "Tom Petty & the Heartbreakers Echo." *The Music Box*, October 1999, http:// www.musicbox-online.com/tp-echo.html#axzz2Gqpq2Bwd.

_____. "Tom Petty Songs and Music from the Motion Picture *She's The One.*" *The Music Box*, February 1997, http://www.musicbox-online.com/tp-one.html#axzz4xXmNuoSM.

Millman, Joyce. "Tom Petty: Southern Accents." *Rolling Stone*, 23 May 1985, https://www. rollingstone.com/music/music-album-reviews/southern-accents-92415/

"Mudcrutch." *Now*, 8 May 2008,https://nowtoronto.com/music/album-reviews/mudcrutch/.

Murray, Noel. "Tom Petty: *Highway Companion.*" *A.V. Music*. A.V. Club, 26 July 2006, https:// music.avclub.com/tom-petty-highway-companion-1798201855.

Partridge, Kenneth. "Tom Petty and the Heartbreakers Return to Form with 'Hypnotic Eye': Track-By-Track Review." *Billboard*, 29 July 2014, https://www.billboard.com/articles/review/ 6192892/tom-petty-and-the-heartbreakers-return-to-form-with-hypnotic-eye-track-by.

Puterbaugh, Parke. "Tom Petty: Into the Great Wide Open." *Rolling Stone*, 11 July 1991, https:// www.rollingstone.com/music/music-album-reviews/into-the-great-wide-open-251781/.

_____. "Tom Petty: Songs and Music from the Motion Picture *She's the One.*" *Rolling Stone*, 5 September 1996, https://www.rollingstone.com/music/music-album-reviews/songs-and-music-from-the-motion-picture-shes-the-one-203940/.

Scoppa, Bud. "The Traveling Wilburys Volumes 1 and 3." *Uncut*, 6 June 2018, https://www. uncut.co.uk/reviews/album/the-traveling-wilburys-volumes-1-and-3.

Silverman, David. "Tom Petty Full Moon Fever." *The Chicago Tribune*, 11 May 1989, http:// articles.chicagotribune.com/1989-05-11/features/8904110871_1_star-full-moon-fever-tom-petty.

Sodomsky, Sam. "Tom Petty *Wildflowers.*" *Pitchfork*, 10 October 2017, https://pitchfork.com/ reviews/albums/tom-petty-wildflowers/.

Soto, Alfred. "Tom Petty and the Heartbreakers Preserve Their Legacy on 'Hypnotic Eye.'" *Spin*, 29 July 2014, https://www.spin.com/2014/07/tom-petty-and-the-heartbreakers-hypnotic-eye/.

Swartley, Ariel. "Tom Petty: Damn the Torpedoes." *Rolling Stone*, 13 December 1979, https://www.rollingstone.com/music/music-album-reviews/damn-the-torpedoes-191894/.

"Tom Petty Album Guide." *Rolling Stone*, web.archive.org/web/20110714025349/http://www.rollingstone.com/music/artists/tom-petty/albumguide.

"Tom Petty—Full Moon Fever." *Blender*, 11 June 2010, web.archive.org/web/20100611073757/http://www.blender.com/guide/back-catalogue/55145/full-moon-fever.html.

"Tom Petty: Let Me Up (I've Had Enough) Review on Blender: The Ultimate Guide to Music and More." *Blender*, 15 June 2008, web.archive.org/web/20080615225026/http://www.blender.com/guide/reviews.aspx?ID=5171.

Tucker, Ken. "Traveling Wilburys Vol. 3." *Entertainment Weekly*, 2 November 1990, https://ew.com/article/1990/11/02/traveling-wilburys-vol-3/.

Vrabel, Jeff. "Tom Petty: Highway Companion." *Pop Matters*, 23 July 2006, https://www.popmatters.com/tom-petty-highway-companion-2495685458.html.

Weingarten, Marc. "The Last DJ." *Entertainment Weekly*. 11 October 2002. *Entertainment Weekly*, https://ew.com/article/2002/10/11/last-dj/.

Wild, David. "The Traveling Wilburys: Traveling Wilburys Vol. 1." *Rolling Stone*, 18 October 1988, https://www.rollingstone.com/music/music-album-reviews/traveling-wilburys-vol-1-103329/.

Willman, Chris. "Petty Laughs Last on 'Full Moon Fever': On His Own, the Wilbury Delivers Sad Stories, Ridiculous Details : Tom Petty 'Full Moon Fever.'" *The Los Angeles Times*, 23 April 1989, http://articles.latimes.com/1989–04‑23/entertainment/ca-1720_1_free-fallin-full-moon-fever-wilburys.

Woodcraft, Molloy. "Hypnotic Eye Review—Tom Petty and Company Are Impossible to Dislike." *The Guardian*, 26 July 2014, https://www.theguardian.com/music/2014/jul/27/hypnotic-eye-tom-petty-and-the-heartbreakers-review.

Young, Alex. "Mudcrutch—Mudcrutch." *Consequence of Sound*, 22 May 2018, https://consequenceofsound.net/2008/05/album-review-mudcrutch/.

Zanes, Warren. "Tom Petty: Damn the Torpedoes." *Rolling Stone*, 16 September 2004, https://www.rollingstone.com/music/music-album-reviews/damn-the-torpedoes-2-255319/.

Psychedelic Strangeness

"Don't Come Around Here No More" and Other Magical Music Videos

TOM ZLABINGER

On the day of his death, Tom Petty's youngest daughter, AnnaKim Violette Petty, remembered her father as a "magical human" on Instagram (Delbyck). This may seem odd to those who know Petty better as a staple of classic rock radio and an MTV icon, but if we begin to view Petty through the lens of his daughter's words, a more profound image of the rock legend begins to snap into focus. After he and his band, the Heartbreakers, had established themselves in the late 1970s, Petty went on to pioneer the new visual medium of music videos and skillfully used the creative outlet to enhance his music. In his remembrance of Petty in *The Washington Post,* Chris Richards attempted to explain the root of Petty's magic by discussing a conversation he had had with the rock legend regarding Petty's approach to making music:

> "My musical quest [is] to get more and more purity into the music." That's something Tom Petty told me over the telephone once. Years later, I wonder if he died … pushing that boulder uphill. Because it was always the impurity of Petty's music that made it feel so sublime. Even back in the '70s, when he was just a blond smirk in a black leather jacket, Petty's brand of Americana was already exuding its own mood, its own smell. As handsome as they were, his rock-and-roll songs came coated in a thin residue of psychedelic strangeness. And they still glisten in the light.
>
> Some of it had to do with Petty's thing for electric guitars that jangled and wheezed, and the rest of it had to do with his voice—an unmistakable mewl that could sound vaguely sinister, gently pleading or stylishly aloof. All the while, his songbook seemed to move across the map like a vagrant weather system, fluctuating from heartland warmth to California cool to whatever dank vibes must have been hanging over Florida when Petty first marched his Heartbreakers out of Gainesville in 1976 [Richards].

The images and storytelling in Petty's music videos helped illuminate this "psychedelic strangeness" that sprang from his creative mixture.

Petty's psychedelic nature comes as no surprise, as he credits "the radio and the 60s" as some of his major influences. Petty specifically drew from the psychedelic sounds of the Byrds. He highlighted the creative debt he and the Heartbreakers owed the Byrds, stating, "Some of our earliest songs were influenced by the Byrds. They brought a kind of folk influence to rock." (Bogdanovich) When listening to the Byrds, we can hear similar vocal inflections between lead singer Roger McGuinn and Petty. Petty also incorporated the Byrds' characteristic 12-string electric guitar-based sound when he recorded "American Girl" (1977) and also posed with a 12-string on the cover of *Damn the Torpedoes* (1979). Petty would continue to include the 12-string electric guitar, most notably on "Free Fallin'" (1989). The Byrds are inarguably a large part of Petty's musical identity. By covering the Byrds' "So You Want to Be a Rock and Roll Star" (1967) on his first official live album *Pack up the Plantation* (1985), Petty cemented his connection to the Byrds and by extension psychedelic music. Petty was later able to deepen his relationship with the music of the Byrds when he sang and co-wrote "King of the Hill" on McGuinn's *Back from Rio* (1991).

The purpose of this essay is to celebrate Petty's link to psychedelic music and magic by focusing on sonic and visual aspects heard and seen in several of his music videos, with special emphasis on arguably one of his most famous psychedelic moments, "Don't Come Around Here No More" (1985). His early traditional music videos will first be examined, and the fantastic images found in several other of Petty's major videos are then connected together to weave a larger psychedelic tapestry.

Early Traditional Petty Music Videos

Before the dawn of MTV in 1981, Petty and his band made some very simple music videos. For example, the music video for "Here Comes My Girl" from *Damn the Torpedoes* (1979) depicts Petty and the Heartbreakers performing on a well-lit soundstage. The band performs without microphones, as not to obstruct the view of the members of the band. On one hand, the music video captures an up-close and realistic image of the band. But the music video is also a little unreal, as the band's vocals and overall sound would not be accurate without microphones. This discrepancy may be lost on most viewers, but is worth noting, as this is the beginning of the music video aesthetic, a mixture of intimacy and inauthenticity. The music video for "Refugee," from the same album, is similar to "Here Comes My Girl" but includes an additional opening scene where Petty is seen in the alleyway walking past members of the Heartbreakers before he enters a building and descends the stairs to what is probably a rehearsal space for the band. The addition of an opening scene is an example of exploring the storytelling possibilities of the medium of the music video beyond a simple performance by the band.

Petty begins to explore the visual potential of the music video medium in "The Waiting" from *Hard Promises* (1981). The video begins with a black and white still of Petty that morphs in slow motion into a color performance. The band performs on a white soundstage with white steps (again with no microphones). Large blue, yellow, and red triangles hang in the background and accompanying colored paint spills are on the steps and floor. Blue, yellow, and red ropes are also seen in the video, creating an almost artsy atmosphere. At one moment, Petty stops playing and smashes his 12-string guitar against a grey paper wall that slices open to reveal lead guitarist Mike Campbell performing a solo. The band performs the rest of the song relatively normally on the soundstage. The video ends with keyboardist Benmont Tench and drummer Stan Lynch goofing off and switching instruments while the playback of the song is still going on. This moment heightens the unreal nature of the video. The fourth wall between the band and audience is then broken as members of the film crew enter the shot, place a clapperboard over Petty's face, and halt the performance with the shutter of the clapstick. But Petty gets the last laugh as he smiles before the video ends. Though not radically unreal, "The Waiting" foreshadows Petty's use of the medium as an extension of his music, and we see the seeds of what later evolves into Petty as narrator or guide through his videos.

Two other music videos from *Hard Promises* are much more typical of MTV at the time. In "A Woman in Love (It's Not Me)," Petty and his band are shot in black and white in what appears to be an abandoned factory. The urban landscape is made unreal by the use of spotlights, shadows, and slow motion. This is another example of an exploration of the storytelling and other creative possibilities afforded by the medium of the music video. In the video for "Insider," Petty and his band perform with Fleetwood Mac's Stevie Nicks in a realistic recording studio, in color and with microphones. There are several dissolves between camera angles. In addition to close shots of each musician, there are sweeps across the entire band. Several times the camera zooms in and out of shot. Though this video is the most realistic so far, the editing of shots creates a filmic atmosphere and thus the video feels more like a short film that helps tell the story of the Petty and Nicks' duet.

The four videos mentioned are the foundation for what would later evolve into Petty's masterful use of the music video as a storytelling medium. Though none of these videos are psychedelic or related to psychedelic culture, we can observe that Petty and his creative team are experimenting with the new creative outlet.

Petty's First Otherwordly Music Video

The video for "You Got Lucky" from *Long After Dark* (1982) can be seen as a bridge from his early performance-oriented videos to his later fantasy-oriented videos. Echoing the a dystopian future similar to the sci-fi film *Mad Max* (1979), "You Got Lucky" opens with an otherworldly intro not featured in the original recording of the song. Accompanied by synthesizers, percussion, and guitar effects orchestrated by Petty, the video depicts Petty and Campbell arriving in a dusty, space-age car that stops on the side of the highway in front of an abandoned building covered in black tarps. After the gulf-wing doors of the car open, Petty and Campbell step out of the car dressed as futuristic cowboys. This is the first time we see Petty in a top hat, which would become an integral part his persona in future videos. On the side of the road, Petty and Campbell find an old boombox wrapped in a plastic bag. After tearing open the bag, Petty presses play on the cassette deck and the song begins. Shortly, the rest of the band arrives on a motorcycle with a side-car and tailfin. Petty and the band enter the building which contains television sets, recording equipment, video games, computers, jukeboxes, slot machines, and other technology from a previous era, covered in clear plastic to protect the objects from years of dust.

After entering the building, Lynch switches on the power, and all of the technology comes to life. The many televisions show images of sci-fi movies, the Marx Brothers, Chuck Berry, and live footage of Petty and the Heartbreakers, among other things. At the perfect moment in the song, Campbell discovers an electric guitar and performs the guitar solo. Afterwards, Petty discovers a video game that he pushes over and acts as if it were an opponent he had killed in a shootout, twirling has revolver and shoving it back into its holster. The band leaves the building, but Campbell takes the guitar with him. The boombox is left on the side of the road as we see the car and motorcycle drive off in the distance.

The video for "You Got Lucky" begins Petty's legacy of mythical story-telling in his videos. Except for the futuristic intro, "You Got Lucky" features typical sounds heard in most of guitar-driven classic rock at the time. But the futuristic nature of the video adds new meaning to the song, as it now is heard through a boombox from a previous era. Petty has placed himself and the Heartbreakers in a future far from himself. Similar to breaking the fourth wall in "The Waiting," Petty has now taken himself, his band, and us out of the picture. Via the video, everyone is now at a temporal (and most likely physical) distance from the original song and its recording. Here we see Petty bend time and space, which is part of his "psychedelic strangeness." His next video would take temporal and physical transportation to an extreme.

Petty in Wonderland

Much has already been written about the incongruent nature of Petty's *Southern Accents* (1985). Originally intended to be a concept album focusing on the South and its relationship to the history of rock and roll, *Southern Accents* evolved into an eclectic mix of styles, including dance-oriented tracks, symphonic moments, free jazz, Motown sounds, *musique concrète*, and classic Petty. At the time, Petty was impressed by the musical freedom he heard and saw on MTV, most notably Prince's *Purple Rain* (1984). Petty explained, "I saw Prince doing what looked like an attempt at psychedelia.... And I loved it. It inspired me" (Zanes). Though Petty's new album included long-time producer Jimmy Iovine, it was the introduction of the Eurythmics' guitarist Dave Stewart that had greatest impact on the album and led to the creation of Petty's most psychedelic video from the album, "Don't Come Around Here No More."

Petty had heard and admired Stewart after hearing the Eurythmics' hit "Sweet Dreams (Are Made of This)" (1983). When Iovine asked Petty for new material for the upcoming Stevie Nicks album he was producing, Petty suggested that Iovine contact Stewart. While Iovine and Stewart were working together on the Nicks material, Petty visited them in the studio. During this time, the basic tracks for "Don't Come Around Here No More" were created. Petty took the material from the Nicks session and used it for his own album. The song was nothing like anything Petty had recorded before, with synthetic drums, keyboard bass, synthesizers, electric sitar, and other sounds not heard previously on Petty's albums. These sonic elements laid the foundation for what would be Petty's most fantastical video (Zanes).

Lewis Carrol's *Alice's Adventures in Wonderland* (1865) has been a cultural touchstone of psychedelic rock since Jefferson Airplane released "White Rabbit" on *Surrealistic Pillow* (1967). The mere mention of the phrase "rabbit hole" evokes images of lost time and space. Petty took rock's relationship with the Carroll classic even further in his video for "Don't Come Around Here No More." The video not only includes Alice, but also the Caterpillar, the Mad Hatter, flamingos, musical chairs, a pig baby, and (most memorably) cake.

Alice (played by Louise "Wish" Foley) is first seen in Wonderland among large mushrooms. Looking up, she sees Stewart as the hookah-smoking Caterpillar atop a mushroom playing the famous sitar intro. Alice climbs up to meet Stewart, who hands her a piece of mushroom that sends her falling backwards into a black and white checkered room with Petty as the Mad Hatter sitting at the head of a long table, clad in a top hat and rectangular, McGuinn–like sunglasses, and drinking a large cup of tea. Throughout the video, both Alice and Petty change in size. And the members of the Heartbreakers eat chaotically around the table, periodically playing musical chairs. All the while, Petty is the narrator throughout Alice's adventures.

During the video, Alice has many hallucinatory visions. She gazes into a bassinet and sees a baby version of herself that morphs into a piglet and back again. She shrinks and finds herself in Petty's teacup, bombarded by sugar cubes and a doughnut dropped by Petty. Finally, she awakes as an Alice-shaped cake that is then devoured by Petty, his band, and the three women adorned in black and white checkers that have appeared throughout the video. Alice screams, and we see her face swallowed by Petty, who then burps and pats his mouth with a black and white checkered napkin.

The video was in high rotation on MTV and later nominated for and won several awards. At the time, however, the images in the video were quite shocking (though they seem quite tame today). In addition to drug references, the eating of Alice as a cake stirred up some controversy. In a 2013 interview, Foley commented about the reaction to the video at the time:

> After the *Alice in Wonderland* video, I was invited to do another video for the [sequel video "Make It Better (Forget About Me)"]. While I was in the makeup chair, [I was] asked if I would respond to some questions. One of the questions was "How do you feel about the women's group rallying against the video due to its violence against women?" Another was "Do you think that the fact that Dave Stewart gives you a mushroom in the beginning to start the hallucination was promoting drug use?"
>
> I was too young to articulate what I was thinking at the time, but my thought on violence against women was "It's just a video!" It doesn't have any deeper meaning. It is a fantastical, funny, imaginative concept, committed to film. It is not a statement video with a hidden message.
>
> When they asked about the drug use, my first thought was "Drugs? Huh? What are they talking about?" I guess I was naïve to drugs at the time, though I had dabbled quite a bit, but I never made the connection at the time.
>
> …I was surprised that anyone would have been offended by it in any way because it was rock and roll. What're you, new? If the music industry didn't have sex and drugs, they quite possibly wouldn't have true rock and roll [Foley-Cohen].

In the video for "Make It Better (Forget About Me)," Foley appears as herself while Petty and the Heartbreakers perform inside her brain in miniature. The sequel is not nearly as memorable as the original, but it is another instance where Petty bends time and space. Foley does have the upper-hand at the end of the video, as she cleans Petty out of her ear with a cotton swab. Though this may be a humorous reply to the original cannibalistic scene in "Don't Come Around Here No More," the producers at MTV had suspected that the video for "Don't Come Around Here No More" could be controversial. Petty recounted that MTV asked to delete a scene in "Don't Come Around Here No More" that went too far: "[MTV] actually made me edit out a scene of my face when we were cutting [Alice] up. They said it was too lascivious. It was just a shot of me grinning, and they were like, 'Well, you can do it, but you can't enjoy it that much'" (Petty).

Despite the controversy, "Don't Come Around Here No More" remains

Petty's most remembered video and further strengthens his connection to psychedelic rock, simply by incorporating the legacy of *Alice's Adventures in Wonderland*. In addition, "Don't Come Around Here No More" was called a "psychedelic curveball triumph" by *The Atlantic*, due to its genesis, sonic content, and cinematography (Kornhaber). But most importantly, the song was a creative risk for Petty at the time that displayed his willingness to create new and adventurous music and storytelling.

Postmodern Petty

After the success of "Don't Come Around Here No More," Petty's next video "Jammin' Me" from *Let Me Up (I've Had Enough)* (1987) was an exercise in postmodernism that bent time and space by diving deep into the creative possibilities of the medium of the music video. The video starts with static that then converges into a dot that flies away, revealing Petty and the Heartbreakers performing on a synthetic landscape of a green-and-grey-striped floor with a static backdrop. Immediately, the band's performance is edited with television commercials, newsreels, and other television footage, as either a backdrop or somehow inserted into a scene. The video is composed of numerous "green screen" (also known as "blue screen" or "chroma key") sequences. Though a version of the technology had been used in movies since the 1930s and became prevalent in the 1970s, Petty's video is shocking as he squeezed as many synthesized scenes together as possible, making one's optic nerve feel strained.

In addition to the fabricated footage, Petty creatively uses the static as some kind of video goop that he could move or hold. Petty first squeezes a bunch of static goop in his hand as it leaks out from between his fingers. At another point, the static goop is seen leaking out of someone's television set. Later, Petty is seen pulling pieces of static goop piece-by-piece out of one television set that he then uses to smear across our television screen, again breaking the fourth wall.

This video can be thought of as an abstract psychedelic trip. The faces of each band member quickly flicker in sequence. Non-related images are juxtaposed together. Members of the Heartbreakers are seen driving a car embedded in a video game, that then drives out of Petty's mouth. An atomic bomb explodes superimposed with Petty's face, which then becomes a photo negative. Finally, the video ends with the melting of the film in an unseen projector, again breaking the fourth wall.

The message of the video is that we are being overloaded by the media and the visuals in the video masterfully create the feeling of overload. The lyrics ask us to take back several cultural and historical icons, like famous actors (like Eddie Murphy, Joe Piscopo, and Vanessa Redgrave), famous people (like Ayatollah Khomeini and Steve Jobs), and famous places (like Pasadena and El Salvador). Watching it decades later, the feeling of overload created by the video is still relevant, if not more so.

Petty with Beatles

Over the course of his life, Petty performed or recorded with several of rock's greatest musicians, including Johnny Cash and Del Shannon. But most notably, Petty was among rock royalty in the supergroup the Travelling Wilburys, with Bob Dylan, George Harrison of the Beatles, Jeff Lynne of the Electric Light Orchestra (ELO), and rock 'n' roll pioneer Roy Orbison. Despite their huge success, the Traveling Wilburys never performed live and recorded only two studio albums: *Traveling Wilburys Vol. 1* (1988) and *Traveling Wilburys Vol. 3* (1990). (The missing second volume was never released.) Petty had previously toured with Dylan in 1986. But more notably, in addition to writing and recording with Lynne and Orbison, the Travelling Wilburys was the beginning of Petty's relationship with Harrison, a member of the world's most famous psychedelic band.

Petty was a huge fan of the Beatles as a teenager. And one could argue that Petty probably had heard his beloved 12-string guitar in the first chord Harrison played in "A Hard Day's Night" (1963) before he heard the Byrds. The music the Traveling Wilburys created contains references to psychedelic rock, including the Beatles cover of "Twist and Shout" (1963) and Jimi Hendrix's "Purple Haze" (1967). And one could also argue that the mere existence of the band bends time and space, as it seems that such a supergroup could only happen in a dream!

In addition to the Traveling Wilburys, Harrison performed with Petty in the video for "I Won't Back Down" from *Full Moon Fever* (1989), along with fellow Beatle, Ringo Starr. The video opens with Petty wearing his iconic top hat as he opens a box with him and other musicians performing inside. In addition to Harrison and Starr, we see Lynne and Campbell. One could argue that the video is surreal as many of Petty's previous videos are referenced: "Don't Come Around Here No More" with Petty's top hat and the change in scale, "Jammin' Me" with superimposed video, and the Traveling Willburys (with the presence of Harrison and Lynne). Time and space is bent with all these worlds colliding together, plus the video backdrop of a rotating mirrored ball and flying over oceans. Additionally, Starr is seen drilling a hole in a model of the Earth and peering inside, which could be a "rabbit hole" reference. Petty also holds a book that includes footage of the himself and the band performing, another postmodern (or meta) moment.

Petty rightly belongs alongside these members of rock's royalty. And the videos created for the mentioned songs continue to add to Petty's trippy catalog that bends both time and space in their own ways.

Animated Petty

The video "Runnin' Down a Dream" from *Full Moon Fever* is quite possibly the most chaotic of all the videos discussed. Petty is seen in the beginning similar to "I Won't Back Down" in his iconic top hat, but instead of a box, this time, Petty opens a book titled *Runnin' Down a Dream*. The black and white cartoon that emerges features an animated Petty awakened in bed by a cigar-chomping little person with a crown and in coveralls. Could this be a dream of Petty's? While Petty and the little person climb a ladder, Alice and the Mad Hatter fly by in a balloon. The Wonderland reference confirms that Petty is in a dream or at least an alternate reality.

Petty and the little person traverse a world filled with killer clowns, gigantic insects, gigantic rabbits, and Native Americans. At one point, Petty grows in size and climbs the Chrysler Building in a reference to *King Kong* (1933). At the end of the video, Petty continues to grow in size and falls off the edge of the Earth, but is caught by his bed and flies away, possibly returning home.

This fully-animated video allows Petty to take almost any creative leap imaginable. He is no longer limited to the confines of real video or enhanced video. This is a completely unreal landscape with fantastic adventures. One could argue that we are now beyond time and space and that this could be the logical conclusion of Petty's video creations, a true trip down the rabbit hole to Wonderland.

Petty Comes Down

Full Moon Fever would spawn three more videos: "Free Fallin'," "A Face in the Crowd," and "Yer So Bad." Interestingly, all three videos can be seen as Petty's snap back to reality. Though "Free Fallin'" creates a spacy atmosphere sonically, the stories in the song and video are about actual people who exist in our world over the years. As earlier, Petty remains the narrator throughout, but with no top hat, possibly signaling that he is rooted in our reality as opposed to an alternate world like Wonderland. Rather than someone from or travelling to a bent time and space, he is now firmly rooted in our world. Yes, he is seen riding escalators, above people atop buildings, and driving in cars. But there is no fantastic nature to the video. In "A Face in the

Crowd," Petty is a storyteller relating stories from another time and place. He is seen singing into a classic 1930s microphone and strumming his beloved 12-string guitar. There are mythic images of mermaids, love lost, and wars gone by. But we do not go with him to those worlds, and he does not truly visit those worlds. Finally, "Yer So Bad" is a similar series of stories, with Petty as a detached narrator telling the stories of bad people in a mad world. Similar to "Free Fallin'," Petty is above or outside all the stories he is telling, but the stories are only slight exaggerations of realistic tales of infidelity and other human tragedies.

Petty's video for "Learning to Fly" from *Into the Great Wide Open* (1991) continues the trend of Petty as detached observer. The band is seen performing on abandoned planes in the desert. There are some surreal moments (like when the chorus line dancers appear as the boy sees an atom bomb explode). But again, Petty neither bends time and space nor visits those worlds. These are simply stories about people who really exist and what happens to them. There is a psychedelic moment when a kid in McGuinn–like glasses takes acid during a rock show, but this could have really happened. Finally, a kid driving a car thinks he sees spaceships flying overhead and crashes the car in his confusion. But this too could have happened. Time and space are not bent.

One could argue that the above four videos are slightly psychedelic or trippy. But they are not nearly as intense or complex as the previously-discussed videos. We see a stylized and safer version of Petty's adventures in song, and Petty is no longer a participant, but rather an omnipresent observer. The videos are still strange, just not transformative as the others.

Petty in Fairytale Land

"Into the Great Wide Open" from *Into the Great Wide Open* (1991) is a return to form for Petty. This mini-film tells the story of the fictitious musician Eddie and his adventures. The video starts as a book titled *Into the Great Wide Open* opens. Eddie (played by Johnny Depp) moves from an unnamed rural state to make it big as a musician in Hollywood. Petty returns as the top hat wearing narrator persona with storybook in hand. We see the rest of the Heartbreakers in miniature performing on a desk beneath Petty: Campbell stands in a coffee cup; Tench plays a keyboard made out of office supplies; Howie Epstein plays bass sitting on an ashtray; and Lynch plays drums made of upside-down paper cups with matchsticks.

In addition to the narrator, Petty plays Eddie's roadie named Bart and a journalist. Members of the Heartbreakers also play small parts throughout the video. Faye Dunaway appears as Eddie's manager and fairy godmother. Her presence eventually gives the tale a magical quality that we have not seen since "Runnin' Down a Dream." Dunaway's character first makes Eddie's career by getting him gigs and record deals that lead to his success. She then ends his career after she was slighted by Eddie. We see her cast an evil spell with lightning above her after he refuses to allow her to accompany him into a club. Eddie's wife leaves him; he becomes an embarrassment, and he loses his record deal. The tale comes full circle as Eddie sees the latest version of himself (played by Matt LeBlanc) arrive to Hollywood.

Though "Into the Great Wide Open" does not bend time and space like earlier videos, Petty does take us on a journey to another world and shows us elements from his previous videos. Magic plays a central role to the video and the story told in the song, which is not far from the psychedelic nature of the previous videos.

Petty Resurrects Alice

In "Mary Jane's Last Dance" from *Greatest Hits* (1993), we again see magic. The video begins with Petty opening his eyes while lying on a gurney in a morgue. Has he awakened from a dream? Has he entered a dream? Has he died? We do not know. But the location of the morgue sets an eerie tone nonetheless. Petty discovers the body of Mary Jane (played by Kim Bassinger) and steals the cadaver from the morgue, complete with toe tag.

Petty drives Mary Jane to his gothic home, dresses her in a wedding gown, and sits her at his table to dine. Petty dons his top hat and dances with her. The parallels to the images of *Alice's Adventures in Wonderland* in "Don't Come Around Here No More" begin to surface. In addition to Mary Jane sitting at a table at a party, she has been transported from one world (the dead) to another (the living). After Petty is frustrated with her, he takes her to the sea and submerges her. This rejection of Mary Jane's body is also a parallel to the consumption of Alice's body. Then magic transpires as Mary Jane's eyes open.

Petty has come full circle from "Don't Come Around Here No More" to "Last Dance with Mary Jane." Though he may not be the source of the magic, he has gone from deconstructing a female form to resurrecting a female form. Time and space have now been bent a different way. Instead of Petty's character narrating a fantastic story, Petty's character has fallen through a rabbit hole and is part of the story.

Petty Down the Rabbit Hole

Finally, Petty may now have consciously become the traveler. In the video for "Walls (Circus)" from the film *She's the One* (1996), Petty is seen arriving at a circus in a yellow taxi cab with guitar in hand. The video is a mixture of black and white plus color. Though the cab is yellow, the rest of the world is black and white. Petty leaves the cab and enters the circus grounds and sets up with the rest of his band on a stage. A little girl (quite possibly an angel) approaches him, and as she touches his head, the world becomes colorized. As Petty begins to sing, a book opens up behind him with a lotus. Then the lotus opens, and Petty emerges a second time inside the lotus. The circus features many images from Indian culture: the Indian gods Gnesh and Krishna, meditation, elephants, Indian clothing/jewelry/makeup, and more. Petty is no longer in New York. He may not even be in reality.

Later, in a hall of mirrors, Petty performs among a sea of flowers and trees. When the camera pulls back, Petty and his reflections are seen either in the frame of a picture or another mirror. The space Petty is in quickly becomes confusing. Petty is seen struggling and even wrestling with his guitar and reflections. The colors within the hall of mirrors also change. There are cutaways to images of the circus and Petty performing. At one point, Petty wipes his eyes and then falls down. The little girl reappears and Petty's head is in her lap, as Petty lies on the floor in front of the stage. The camera pulls away above the little girl, Petty, and the circus. Petty is seen leaving the circus and returning to the yellow taxi cab and black and white world. But this time we see colorized Indian images in front of him as he returns to a colorized New York seen in the distance.

It is unclear if Petty has been transformed after his trip down the rabbit hole in "Walls (Circus)." But the world around him has possibly been transformed. And if the world has been transformed, maybe we can deduce that time and space have been bent for Petty and his character thus may see the world differently. Some sort of magic or dream state has happened. Whether Petty's character realizes it or not, we as observers have been transformed as we accompanied him on his adventures.

Conclusion

The "psychedelic strangeness" and magic found in the discussed videos by Petty are undeniable. Over the course of seventeen years, Petty developed a mode of storytelling with the medium of music videos that masterfully augmented and illuminated his music. Contained within many of the videos are images and sounds that transport the listener to other worlds. And within the context of his videos and sounds, Petty tells stories of characters who are transformed as time and space bend. Hopefully, time and space may bend for us as we revisit these videos and we too can be transformed as we learn something about Petty, the world, others, and ourselves.

WORKS CITED

Bogdanovich, Peter, dir. *Runnin' Down a Dream.* Warner Bros., 2007.

Delbyck, Cole. "Tom Petty's Daughter Remembers 'Magical Human' in Heartbreaking Tribute." *The Huffington Post,* 3 Oct. 2017, huffingtonpost.com/entry/tom-pettys-daughter-remembers-magical-human-in-heartbreaking-tribute_us_59d3849fe4b0655781556690.

Foley-Cohen, Louise "Wish." "The Girl in the Video: 'Don't Come Around Here No More.'" *Noblemania,* 22 July 2013, http://www.noblemania.com/2013/07/the-girl-in-video-dont-come-around-here_22.html.

Kornhaber, Spencer. "Tom Petty's Psychedelic Curveball Triumph." *The Atlantic,* 2 October 2017.

Petty, Tom. "Tom Petty: A Portrait—*Billboard's* 2005 Century Award Honoree." *Billboard,* 3 December 2005.

Richards, Chris. "Tom Petty's Americana Felt Stranger than the Rest." *The Washington Post,* 3 October 2017.

Zanes, Warren. *Petty: The Biography.* New York: Henry Holt and Company, 2015.

Running Down an American Dream

Tom Petty and the Tour T-Shirt

LAUREN ALEX O'HAGAN

Whether it is used as an identity marker, a cultural signifier or a symbol of prestige, the tour t-shirt is a wardrobe staple for any die-hard fan of a particular artist. Unlike its band t-shirt counterpart, which has saturated the high street in recent years and become more about fashion than fandom, the tour t-shirt remains a firmly entrenched part of the practices of avid concertgoers and music lovers. While the band t-shirt creates a dichotomy between the owner's desire to be seen differently and their need to fit in, through its rituals of consumption and possession, the tour t-shirt conveys a "secret identity" that is bound up with the notions of musical tribalism, collective experience and shared meanings, offering tangible proof of attendance at a particular concert. Tour t-shirts read like a biography of their owner, each becoming an entry on a timeline that marks age, place and state of mind at the moment of purchase. Their "time-travelling" ability often means that tour t-shirts become the most cherished items of band merchandise, providing a direct link between the owner, the musician(s) in question, and the army of fans who shared the event together. Fonarow notes that tour t-shirts even have an unspoken etiquette; she cites immediately putting on a new tour t-shirt upon purchase as a rookie mistake because it communicates the status of a novice and inexperienced fan, while donning a t-shirt from a past tour is believed to give the wearer a certain prestige amongst other fans, as it is indicative of the longevity of their support for the band.

Despite their widespread popularity and well-established position in popular culture today, tour t-shirts are still generally considered to be little more than *curios* and, consequently, are yet to be addressed from an academic perspective. In this paper, I will use three Tom Petty tour t-shirts to demonstrate how a sociolinguistic approach can shed new light on their functions. While the creative mastery of Petty's videos, lyrics, and album covers is widely acknowledged, the tour t-shirt is a neglected part of originality in the Petty story. This paper offers a first effort to readdress this imbalance by conducting a multimodal analysis of three t-shirts from the 1991–92 *Touring the Great Wide Open* tour, the 1995 *Dogs with Wings* tour and the 2002–03 *The Last DJ* tour. It will reveal how choices of imagery, color, typography and materiality are used as symbolic, visual representations of a theme that runs throughout all of Petty's work: the American Dream.

The Evolution of the T-Shirt: From Practical Undergarment to Vehicle of Expression

The t-shirt is generally believed to have started its life in 1898 when it was issued by the U.S. Navy as an undergarment (Easby and Oliver 1). Its adoption by the U.S. and UK armies in the early 20th century firmly established the t-shirt as a symbol of masculinity, and by 1920, it had earnt its first entry in the Merriam-Webster Dictionary, described as "a collarless short-sleeved or sleeveless usually cotton undershirt." In the 1930s, the t-shirt became adopted as outerwear by dockworkers, farmers, miners, and construction workers who recognized the practicality of its lightweight and easy-to-clean fabric. Soon, manufacturers began to mass-produce t-shirts, selling them in mail order catalogues and department stores across the world.

Up until this point, t-shirts had been plain and unembellished garments. However, this trend soon changed following the outbreak of World War II. Realizing that their white t-shirts made them easily visible targets, soldiers began to dye them with coffee grinds. They also started to print their own t-shirts using stenciling to mark their station post, corps, and place of origin (Anticonformity USA 1).

Outside of the military, the plain t-shirt skyrocketed to its position as a fashionable outer garment following its use by Marlon Brando in *A Streetcar Named Desire* (1951), *The Wild One* (1953), and James Dean in *A Rebel Without a Cause* (1955). The t-shirt epitomized a new American youth that was emerging (Easby and Oliver 2) and of which Petty was part. Struggling to find their place in post-war suburban society, the t-shirt enabled these adolescents to create their own sub-culture. As the 1960s arrived, the potential of the t-shirt as a vehicle of self-expression became recognized. Taking advantage of its blank and mobile canvas, young adults used the t-shirt to write slogans, protests, and advertisements. Music festivals played an important role in this countercultural shift that swept America, leading manufacturers to think about using the t-shirt as a promotional device for bands. And so, the rock t-shirt was born.

The earliest example of a music t-shirt dates from 1956 when Elvis Presley's record company produced a promotional t-shirt alongside the release of one of his singles. However, the first known t-shirt to be sold at a concert was by The Beatles in 1964 followed by the Monkees in 1967. At this time, the t-shirt was one of many items of merchandise for sale and was considered to be just another fad (Easby and Oliver 4). Its permanent fixture at concerts is widely attributed to Bill Graham who established Winterland Productions in 1971, producing the first concert t-shirts for the Allman Brothers and the Grateful Dead. The year of 1973 marked a new landmark in the history of the tour t-shirt, as the first festival t-shirt was made promoting three bands at once (the Allman Brothers, Grateful Dead and The Band). This established the classic characteristic of the tour t-shirt, which distinguishes it from the simple band t-shirt: the dates on its back.

Come the 1970s and the iron-on transfer increased the availability of mass-produced t-shirts. Since then, the t-shirt has firmly established its place as a defining feature of rock concerts no matter the size, venue, or location. Fans on the Tom Petty Nation (the largest Facebook group for Tom Petty fans) recall the existence of rock t-shirts at Petty concerts as early as 1977, the first design being the now-iconic Tom Petty and the Heartbreakers logo of a heart with a Gibson Flying V running through it.

The 1981 *Hard Promises* tour was the first to have a name—a sure sign of the band's growing popularity. Their increasing recognition is reflected in the change in t-shirt designs that occurred at this time, moving from simple album covers and images of Petty to clever puns, symbolism,

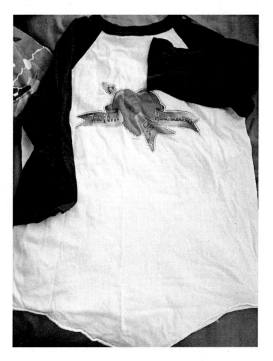

Classic Tom Petty and the Heartbreakers t-shirt design (photograph by Paul Kelly).

and humor. The importance of the t-shirt to the Tom Petty story is even apparent in the fact that guests to his funeral were given their own personalized t-shirts in recognition of Petty's final swansong. The t-shirt shows an image of a young Petty foregrounded by the Latin "nil desperandum" (no need to despair) from Horace's *Odes*.

Over the years, Petty's tour t-shirts continued to push boundaries, sitting on the cutting edge of design. They helped to expand the visual identity of the Heartbreakers beyond record sleeves and concert posters and enabled fans to integrate the band's aesthetic into their own. The result is a treasure trove of multimodality in which color, typography, image and texture all work together to represent the American Dream.

American Dream, Political Scheme?

Although the set of ideals that it evinces is rooted in the Declaration of Independence, the term "American Dream" was first coined in 1931 by James Truslow Adams in *The Epic of America*, described as "that dream of a land in which life should be better and richer and fuller for everyone, with opportunity for each according to ability or achievement" (214–215). It was not a material dream of motor cars or high wages, but a dream of social order in which everybody was able to accomplish what they were innately capable of and recognized for what they were, regardless of social class or circumstances of birth. Indeed, Martin Luther King rooted the civil rights movements in the African-American quest for the American Dream.

Historically, the Dream originated in the mystique of frontier life. Writing in 1772, a British official declared that Americans "forever imagine the Lands further off are still better than those upon which they are already settled" (qtd. in Cavallo 83). By the 19th century, the frontier had become popularly romanticized as a barren landscape that provided an idealistic way of living, which was in strong contrast to the harsh realities faced by those who inhabited the area. This concept of the American Dream ran deep in Petty's blood, his paternal grandmother having been a Cherokee who married a white man from Georgia and consequently, found themselves drifting from town to town in pursuit of happiness until they finally settled in Reddick, Florida (Zanes 10–12). It was a topic that Petty would revisit time and time again in his songs from *Two Gunslingers* and *Rebels* to *Time to Move On* and *Into the Great Wide Open*.

Over the past eighty years, the meaning of the American Dream has changed considerably. While Rank *et al.* argue that its fundamental aspect remains the expectation that the next generation should do better than the previous generation (98), Dixon equates the new American Dream with the possession of material items, as mythologized in Fitzgerald's *The Great Gatsby*. Since the 1980s, Hanson and Zogby have carried out a series of public opinion polls to examine trends in attitudes about the American Dream. They note that most Americans believe that the American Dream is becoming increasingly unattainable. Despite this skepticism, Blanden *et al.* affirm that "the idea of the U.S. as 'the land of opportunity' persists" (33), albeit misplaced.

While the idea of the American Dream is complex and multifaceted, Petty created stories that struck at the soul of all of its aspects: frontier life, personal dreams, material aspirations, and even its rough and distorted reality. We see it in Eddie Rebel whose future was wide open, the American girl who thought there was a little more to life somewhere else, the loser who got lucky sometimes. Petty's music makes it clear that, although no single individual or group has an exclusive claim to the American Dream, everybody has a vision of what it is as a way of life.

In a 2014 interview with *The Sun* newspaper, Petty stated that the American Dream "is a very upfront issue for this generation." However, he also acknowledged the importance of balancing hope and belief with this new perverted view of America: "Young people have been taught cynicism. They've been bred cynicism. So, I think it's important to give them hope and realism in the same package. You can be realistic but there should be hope in it. Because hope's what we're about. If we don't have hope, then we don't go on." With this in mind, Petty sets the scene nicely for a new type of American Dream. An American Dream that offers hope in the face of despair. An American Dream that recognizes the struggles of life, yet uses music to make sense of these pains, desires, pleasures, and fears. An American Dream Plan B.

Multimodality and Visual Grammar

Multimodality is a theory of communication that describes communicative practices in terms of the different semiotic modes (i.e. image, writing, layout, music, gesture etc.) used to compose messages. Jewitt and Oyama see multimodality as a form of visual grammar which involves "the description of semiotic resources, what can be said and done with images and how the things people say and do with images can be interpreted" (136). Multimodalists argue that modes have equal significance as ways of conveying meaning, and each shapes and carries the ontological, historical and social orientations of a society and its cultures with it into every sign (Kress, 79). Although texts have always been multimodal in nature, certain modes have not always been recognized as legitimate or culturally accepted forms of expression. However, in order to completely understand a text, the many modes used to communicate and their affordances, defined by van Leeuwen (4) as "the potential uses of a given object," must be observed and recognized.

Multimodality is a relatively new theory, having developed over the past twenty-five years within the field of "social semiotics" to address many of the changes in society in relation to new media and technologies. The most important and influential work on multimodality was carried out in 1996 by Kress and van Leeuwen. They established the first social semiotic framework for analyzing images in their seminal work, *Reading Images: The Grammar of Visual Design*. Within this framework, Kress and van Leeuwen recognize that an image simultaneously performs three metafunctions: the representational, the interpersonal and the compositional.

The representational metafunction is concerned with the people, places, and objects within an image and the actions or narratives in which they are involved, while the interpersonal metafunction deals with the relationships between the visual, the producer, and the viewer. Among the visual techniques that contribute to interpersonal meaning are the absence or presence of gaze towards the viewer, gestures which make offers or demands, degrees of social distance, and intimacy and perspective. The compositional metafunction, on the other hand, relates to the layout of a text (i.e. positioning, framing, salience) in order to determine the coherence between visual and verbal elements to the meaning-making of the entire unit.

Since Kress and van Leeuwen's framework for analyzing images was established, much work has been carried out on creating similar frameworks of analysis for other semiotic modes (i.e. van Leeuwen on music, Kress and van Leeuwen on color, Stenglin on space, Stöckl on typography, Djonov and van Leeuwen on texture and van Leeuwen and Djonov on kinetic typography). In my PhD thesis, I develop a model that draws together the most important elements of these frameworks when exploring visual artefacts and demonstrate how incorporating ethnographic methodologies into multimodal analysis can provide material evidence that strengthens the potential subjectivity of the arguments put forward. This model will be used to explore Petty's tour t-shirts.

Most work on multimodality has been principally concerned with the exploration of digital media, particularly the moving image (Burn and Parker; Rowsell), interactive CD-ROMS (Adam and Wild; Jewitt) and advertising (Gregorio-Godeo; Sørensen). Recently, there has also been an increase in research on the impact of multimodality on language pedagogy (Walsh; Kitson). Despite being a vast source of multimodality, musical artefacts, such as album covers, promotional videos and tour t-shirts, have been widely overlooked by scholars. As a result, there is currently a lack of knowledge of the ways in which choices of imagery, color, typography, and materiality are used to transmit important messages about musicians and their ideas. Thus, it is apparent that there is an urgent need to explore the tour t-shirt within an academic context in order to change its perception from a walking billboard for a band to a significant medium of multimodal communication. Given the ingenuity of their designs, there is no better place to start exploring tour t-shirts than with those of Petty.

Methodology

Three Petty tour t-shirts have been chosen for multimodal analysis with the aim of establishing how words and images are used to convey the American Dream. The three tour t-shirts come from the 1991–92 *Touring the Great Wide Open* tour, the 1995 *Dogs with Wings* tour and the 2002–03 *The Last DJ* tour. They have been chosen for the fact that each offer a different interpretation of the American Dream (the allure of the frontier, personal aspirations and material prosperity) and the ways in which it has changed over time. Despite their varied perspectives of the American Dream, these t-shirts share some common factors that make them suitable comparable sources of analysis. Perhaps most obviously, the site of purchase was the same for all three t-shirts: the merchandise stand at a Tom Petty concert. Additionally, each t-shirt is made of the same cotton fabric and features a screen-printed image on its front and writing on its back.

The model for analysis can be seen in Figure 1. It compiles aspects from previous multimodal frameworks that are most important when exploring the tour t-shirt, as well as ethnographic information that helps to situate the tour t-shirts within their social context and to reconstruct the social practices involved in their creation. These two approaches offer a complementary way in which to think about tour t-shirts, as multimodality provides ethnography with an analytical tool to understand artefacts, while ethnography gives an ideological quality to multimodality (Rowsell and Chen 176).

Under "Image," Kress and van Leeuwen's three metafunctions are summarized in terms of what the image is about, how it engages the viewer, and how it is arranged to make sense to the viewer. "Typography" encompasses two chief aspects: cultural connotation and style. Cultural connotation refers to the specific intentions, inherent associations and cultural references associated with the physical qualities of a typeface, while style is characterized by a type's weight, width, slope and orientation, which have vast meaning potential in terms of personalization. "Color" comprises two features: value and modulation. Value is linked to the physical and emotional effect that a color's symbolism has on viewers, while modulation considers the importance of tints and shades in terms of cultural ideologies and positive/negative valuations. "Materiality" is divided into three components: fabric, printing technique, and expression. While fabric and printing technique refer to the physical production of the tour t-shirt, expression relates to the metaphorical meaning of texture within images in terms of relief, density, regularity, and consistency.

"Context" draws upon the work of linguistic anthropologists Hymes and Saville-Troike to consider the production process and the key participants involved, the topic and purpose of the tour t-shirt, as well as its norms of interpretation. "Ethnographic Resources" lists the most useful documents to consult for supporting information. Of these resources, the Petty Archives (http://thepettyarchives.com), a non-profit website dedicated to preserving Tom Petty and the Heartbreakers' related history, has been invaluable for its collection of original newspaper and magazine articles, interviews, tour information and setlists. The fans on the Facebook group, Tom Petty Nation, have also been an endless source of knowledge on all things Petty related. Warren Zanes' *Petty: The Biography*, Andrea Rotondo's *Tom Petty: Rock 'N' Roll Guardian* and Peter Bogdanovich's *Running Down a Dream* documentary film have also provided extremely useful supporting information.

Figure 1.
The Tour T-Shirt

Image	Typography	Color Value	Materiality
Representational What is this image about?	**Cultural Connotations** What specific intentions, inherent associations and cultural references are associated with the physical qualities of the typeface?	What physical and emotional effect does the color's symbolism have on viewers?	**Fabric** What material was used to create the t-shirt?
Interpersonal How does the image engage the viewer?		**Modulation** How do the use of tints and shades transmit particular cultural ideologies and positive/negative valuations?	**Printing Technique** How was the image on the t-shirt printed?
Compositional How is the image arranged to make sense to the viewer?	**Style** How does the weight, width, slope and orientation of the type contribute to the text's meaning potential?		**Expression** How is texture used in the t-shirt to convey metaphorical meaning?

Context	*Ethnographic Resources*
Production Process How was the t-shirt produced?	**Petty Archives** —Newspaper and magazine articles, interviews, tour information and set lists from 1971 to 2017.
Participants Who was involved in the t-shirt's production?	**Tom Petty Nation** —Interviews with fans
Topic What is the referential focus of the t-shirt?	**Printed Material** Warren Zanes—*Petty: The Biography* (2015)
Purpose What is the t-shirt's aim in general and in terms of symbolic meaning?	Andrea Rotondo's *Tom Petty: Rock 'N' Roll Guardian*
Norms of Interpretation What common knowledge or shared understandings are required to infer meaning from the t-shirt?	**Visual Material** Peter Bogdanovich—*Running Down a Dream* (2007) Documentary Film

Touring the Great Wide Open *1991 Tour T-Shirt*

In 1991, Tom Petty and the Heartbreakers set out on a three-month American tour to promote the release of their eighth album, *Into the Great Wide Open*. The tour started on August 29th at Fiddler's Green, Denver and ended at the Oakland Arena in Oakland, California on November 24th. In early 1992, the tour reached Europe, visiting Norway, Sweden, Germany, Ireland, UK, Switzerland, France, and Belgium. At this point, Petty was at the height of his career following the 1989 success of *Full Moon Fever*. However, it was also a time in which tensions were running high in the band as a result of Petty's solo ventures.

According to Petty, *Into the Great Wide Open* was an album of reflection "about being young and old," about looking at the promises of adolescence and what can become of dreams later in life. Rotondo considers its main theme to be the battle between staying true to oneself or giving in to temptation (166). Although the American Dream of open land and freedom had become a myth by the mid–20th century (Caldwell 123), through *Into the Great Wide Open*, Petty rebuilt the idea of "withdrawing from the great world and beginning a new life in a fresh green landscape" (Marx 3). In this way, the album represented an aural compass that guided those who were lost on the path of life. The t-shirt designed for the tour explicitly highlights this message.

Made of grey cotton, the t-shirt shows an image of a Golden Retriever walking across a prairie. In the distance, behind the prairie, is a forest. The image offers a conceptual representation of the original American Dream,

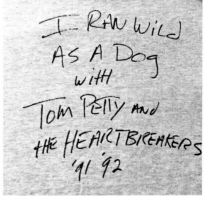

Left: This t-shirt design for 1991 *The Great Wide Open* tour offers a conceptual representation of the original American Dream. *Right:* The back of the t-shirt for the 1991 *The Great Wide Open* tour (photograph by Paul Kelly).

the dream of a place built on the shoulders of robust individualism "where the bonds of custom are broken and unrestraint is triumphant" (Turner 38). Here, the Golden Retriever symbolizes the prospect of freedom; it is looking back over its shoulder to the past while strolling on towards the future with the hope of a new beginning. The choice of the Golden Retriever is significant as, when conceptualizing the modern American Dream of a happy family with a picket-fenced house, the family is almost always accompanied by this type of dog (Heissenhuber Jr.). The Golden Retriever's placement in this image suggests that it is turning its back on the new American Dream in search of its original and uncorrupted form. Despite its strong message about the American Dream, the Golden Retriever simultaneously reveals a subtler directive about Petty and his band. It was on the *Touring the Great Wide Open* tour that Scott Thurston was first drafted in. Petty viewed him as a "good buffer" between the rest of the band that represented a new and more optimistic direction. Thus, the dog can also be considered to be a symbol of Petty himself, who yearns to continue to use his music to pursue the original American Dream of happiness and prosperity.

Further significance is added to the image of the Golden Retriever when combined with the writing on the back of the t-shirt. Printed in a style that resembles hand-written permanent marker, it states, "I ran wild as a dog with Tom Petty and the Heartbreakers '91 '92." This choice of words directly links the person who has bought the t-shirt with the image of the dog on its front, thus suggesting that buying the t-shirt is accompanied by a commitment to risking it all in search of a better life. Furthermore, the phrase conjures up a shared experience with Petty in which the date acts as visual proof that the event has taken place, while the faded lettering and hastily formed letters bring immediacy and personalization to the writing (Sassoon 76). The statement also makes a reference back to Petty's song *Dogs on the Run*, a song whose lyrics clearly recount the trials and tribulations that come with the quest for the American Dream. Sperber and Wilson argue that readers use their pre-established knowledge to make sense of a text and understand its purpose (144). In reading this statement, Petty fans are likely to draw upon the lyrics of *Dogs on the Run* and link Petty with the image of the Golden Retriever. This interpretation brings additional meaning to the dog's position, as now, it can not only be said to be looking metaphorically back at the past, but also physically looking to the back of the t-shirt. In this way, the Golden Retriever as Petty is checking whether his fans are still with him and are going to continue to follow him on this new journey "into the great wide open." This grants the image with a pseudo-biblical dimension with Petty as the Messiah leading his people to the Promised Land.

The image on the t-shirt's front is printed within a circular frame, which acts almost as the window of a vehicle that looks out onto a passing landscape.

Kress and van Leeuwen argue that the circle represents the unbroken completeness of time (55). Thus, its employment in this image suggests the possibility that, like all things, the American Dream will go full circle and return once more to a simple dream of happiness over a material dream of wealth. As the circle is also associated with the organic world of nature and creation (Kress and van Leeuwen 36), its shape further accentuates the main message of the image. The way in which "Touring the Great Wide Open" is arranged in a semi-circle at the top of the image is also significant, as the writing has a "typopictoriality" (qtd. in Stöckl, 24)—a term used for when letters form visual signs which resemble objects—that physically represents the "great wide open." Here, the typeface is expanded with large spaces between each word. Van Leeuwen argues that this choice relates to our experience of space and is used to positively reflect the importance of having room to breathe and move (148). This idea is strengthened by the fact that the trees and sky of the image blur into the blue border, thus blending words and image together to create simultaneous meaning.

The banderoles on the side of the image and the name of the band at the bottom also show overlapping, which demonstrates that the words and image are intended to be seen as connected. The overlapping of the date emphasizes that the search for the American Dream must be undertaken today, while the overlapping of the band name highlights Petty's involvement in the quest. The yellow font of Petty's name also matches that of the Golden Retriever and the prairie, which further highlights his involvement. The fact that yellow has long been recognized for its "disturbing influence" (Kandinsky 37) and "intellect, ideas and a searching mind" (Lacy 36) also emphasizes Petty's leadership over his fans and the promise ahead.

Dogs with Wings *1995 Tour T-Shirt*

The *Dogs with Wings* tour took place in 1995 in support of Tom Petty's solo album *Wildflowers*. It consisted of a massive eighty-one tour dates across the U.S., as well as Vancouver and Toronto in Canada. The tour started in Louisville Gardens in Louisville on February 28th 1995 and ended eight months later in Lakefront Arena, New Orleans. The *Dogs with Wings* tour was the first to feature new drummer, Steve Ferrone, who had replaced Stan Lynch.

The *Wildflowers* album is often said to be Tom Petty's masterpiece. Written at a time in which his marriage was on the rocks, the album presented vivid stories about characters down on their luck and looking for a way to survive. "That's the divorce album," Petty stated in an interview with Warren Zanes, "It just came before I left." Reflecting Petty's own state of mind at the time, the songs constantly stress the need to cure self-doubt with optimism and make the necessary changes to live one's life with conviction—beliefs that are central to the American Dream. The importance of shooting for the stars is reflected in the t-shirt designed for the tour, which emphasizes hope and the possibility of achieving the American Dream if only one is willing to look for it.

The t-shirt is made of white cotton and, fitting with the title of the tour, shows a flag bearing an image of a dog with wings. The Chesapeake Bay Retriever, known as Leaper, is bounding upwards towards the golden crown in the sky. The image references the lyrics of *It's Good to Be King*, which state that Petty will become King when dogs get wings. Although "when dogs get wings" bears a similarity to the well-known idiom "pigs might fly," in this case, through self-belief, the impossible has actually become possible. According to Petty, this theme was central to his thinking at the time: "People get so obsessed with that drive to be king, as if that might solve their problems. Maybe a man's king when he's fallen in love and raised a family. Maybe that's the greatest reward there is in life and strangely enough, available to anyone." In this way, Petty is arguing that the barriers in life that we face are often cre-ated by us and, as such, we are the only ones who can over-come them. We must be more like the Chesapeake, who is not afraid to take a chance on the American Dream. The Chesapeake is a dog that is often described as having high intelligence, a happy dis-position, courage, and a will-ingness to work (American Kennel Club 36). These qual-ities may have influenced the decision to choose this breed of dog over another.

The wings of the Chesa-peake are also significant, as winged animals have long been recognized as symbols of aspiration and intelligence (Cirlot 374). Wings also sig-nify mobility and enlighten-ment and can be seen as a form of spiritual evolution.

The tour t-shirt for *Dogs with Wings* tour in 1995 (photograph by Heidi Wright).

Thus, the winged dog provides viewers with an avatar that represents a metaphor "for our personal and collective progress through life and history" (Medhurst 137). It embodies a figure that is aspiring for a universe that is similar to ours, yet grander, in which one is able to discover lessons of self-identity and knowledge of their existence. The use of gold (on the wings and the crown) adds strong value-laden meanings to the image, as the vision of America as the golden land of power and wealth is a myth that derived from the Pilgrim Fathers and the original American Dream (Pohl 87).

The fictional flag on which the dog features can be seen as a representation of a utopia that exists in the mind of viewers and to which they can escape. Flags belong to a semiotic domain in which the meaning of signs is fixed by precise rules (van Leeuwen 5). Thus, the horizontal bend across its middle that separates a green and blue triangle is significant. According to the Dictionary of Vexillology, green is a symbol of prosperity and fertility, while blue signifies determination and liberation. These qualities are essential to the American Dream and are used within the t-shirt to emphasize its key message. The green and blue colors also represent the dichotomy of earth and sky. The appearance of golden stars on the blue triangle further emphasizes this distinction and gives additional meaning to the Chesapeake who is elevated in the air. The five-pointed star is a common feature of flags and is often employed as a symbol of unity. Within this image, its usage suggests that dreams are more achievable if we work together. Samuel sees this as an important part of the American Dream: "It is a comforting belief that counters the many obstacles and limitations we all face on a daily basis. The idea that each of us can realize whatever it is we hope to in our lives is reason enough to get up in the morning and do whatever we have to in order to try to make that happen." The position of the crown between the "earth" and the "sky" marks a return to Petty's statement about *It's Good to Be King* that one must be realistic and recognize that being a king can simply be about having a happy and healthy family rather than wealth and prosperity. The American Dream is an optimistic, motivating force that propels people to achieve and accomplish things that they may otherwise not strive for.

Outside the borders of the flag, "Tom Petty & the Heartbreakers" and "Dogs with Wings Tour" are printed in an abstract red font. This stylized font is repeated on the back of the shirt, this time in blue. The repetition acts as a framing device that provides a "visual rhyme" (van Leeuwen 12) that brings connectivity, cohesion, and a sense of unity to the t-shirt. The combination of red and blue is thought-provoking, as both colors are deeply wired in our subconscious in terms of their opposing meanings—red as danger, revolution and fire, and blue as calm, water and peace (Kress and van Leeuwen 348). When combined together, they reflect a person's quest for the American

Dream from the initial fear and apprehension at making a drastic life change followed by the reward and benefits reaped once it has been achieved.

The back of the t-shirt shows a more conventional tour t-shirt design, with the list of cities visited printed in blue capital letters in two columns. The spatial layout of the text is invaded with five green and red dogs with wings of various sizes, as well as stars. Their sporadic arrangement overlapping the writing blends the two messages, directly linking the fans who attend the concerts with the Chesaspeakes, therefore encouraging them to pursue their dream even if it may seem out of reach. Texture also plays an important role, as most of the lettering and

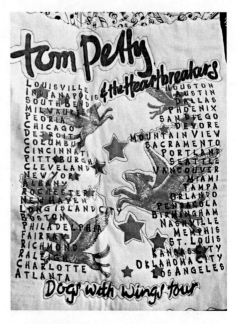

T-shirt back for *Dogs with Wings* tour in 1995 (photograph by Heidi Wright).

the dogs are stitched on top of the original cotton fabric to create a 3D layer. Not only does this give the dogs an animate quality, bringing them to life, but the padded fabric also resembles that of a quilt. The quilt's association with beds and dreams, as well as its intimate connection to the everyday life of the 18th century Dutch and English settlers in America, further emphasizes the original notion of the American Dream.

The Last DJ *2002 Tour T-Shirt*

Although *The Last DJ* album was not yet released, in 2002, Tom Petty and the Heartbreakers decided to set out on a two-legged tour spread over six months. The first part began at the Van Andel Arena in Grand Rapids on June 27th and ended at the Chronicle Pavilion in Concord on September 1st. After the release of *The Last DJ* on October 8th, the band embarked on part two, starting on October 15th at the Grand Olympic Auditorium in Los Angeles and finishing at the Fleet Center in Boston on December 13th.

The Last DJ album is often characterized as an indictment of the greed present in today's music industry, but Petty asserts that it was a commentary on the issue of American greed in general (Rotondo 218). In other words, the American Dream had turned sour, becoming more about the quest for material wealth than the pursuit of happiness. "It seems our whole American culture, if that's not an oxymoron, has become almost dangerous," Petty lamented in an interview with *The Gainesville Sun*. "It's this notion that we need to make all the money that is possible, of grabbing every cent. This attitude permeates every phase of life now. It's just so unhealthy." These frustrations are clearly manifested in the t-shirt that was designed for *The Last DJ* tour.

Made of black cotton, the t-shirt features a large black and white screen-print photograph on its front of Petty's Rickenbacker guitar leaning against a chair on top of a Persian rug. Underneath the image, almost reading like an advertisement, is the strapline "Sell your computer buy a guitar." Here, text and image stand together as separate but interdependent parts of a single whole in a complementary relationship, which Barthes terms "relay" (41). Their proximity, similarity and continuity provide a "visual beat" (Zakia 39) that establishes equilibrium and facilitates the connections between each element. Rather than telling a narrative, the image is conceptual; it shows a cynicism at the slow corruption of the American Dream in the face of capitalism, and specifically aims to encourage viewers to achieve something with their lives. By using the recognizable image of Petty's guitar, it implies that his success began with a simple six string, thus urging viewers that the same

T-shirt design for *The Last DJ* tour in 2002 (photograph by Melissa Busch).

could be possible for them if they are willing to believe in the two fundamental and foundational underpinnings of the original American Dream—individualism and work ethic.

According to Caldwell, the American Dream has become eroded by people looking for short term solutions and "get rich quick" schemes, and seeking self-realization in shallow entertainment and the cult of personality (48). Although the t-shirt's slogan clearly criticizes consumer society, there is a slight irony in the fact that one material item (the computer) is being replaced with another (the guitar). In a world in which success is now measured by material wealth, these two elements are juxtapositioned to convey the message that it is not wrong to have material goods, but we should make use of them to change our lives for the better rather than as a simple means of escapism. This was an integral belief of Petty's and runs throughout the interviews that he conducted at this time: "TV, I've quit watching it. People are already living their lives virtually, which ain't good." Through the message on this t-shirt, Petty reluctantly recognizes that, although the American Dream has changed, people have the potential to use material goods for meaningful purposes to achieve their goals.

Within the image, the rug, wires, chair and other guitar all act as "circumstances" that work together to "build up the material reality of the possible world" (Halliday 30), adding meaning and validity to the message (Cheng 172). By drawing upon their sociocultural knowledge of to whom the guitar belongs and Petty's consistent use of Persian rugs on stage, viewers are able to infer that the voice of reason belongs to Petty himself. Thus, the image acts as a riddle with a ready-made solution that can only be solved by fans who are "in the know." In this way, the tour t-shirt retains its status as an exclusive item of merchandise that is not for outsiders.

The fact that Petty is the person speaking is confirmed by his signature on the pickguard of the guitar. Jacoby calls the signature "the psychological visiting card of a person" (qtd. in Sassoon 76), as it develops as a personal hieroglyph that presents the writer and their character to the world. Here, Petty uses his signature as a seal of authenticity and, when coupled with the handwritten style of the strapline, it serves to create a bond with viewers. The use of direct speech written in an imperative form acts as candid advice from Petty, allowing no room for debate. His position as a respected figure of authority grants him the right to speak his mind and makes the advice more likely to be accepted by the targeted viewers—his fans. Block capitals also highlight the gravity of the message, as this style of writing is often associated with a raised tone of voice.

The choice to render the photograph in black and white rather than polychrome is significant, as the low modality and saturation of these colors is recognized as having a greater truth value and level of realness

(Hodge and Kress 124). It also emphasizes nostalgia for a better past in which young people had a dream and chased it rather than becoming caught up in virtual reality and consumerism, what Lerner describes as "the new soil in which America has found its roots" (100). Kress and van Leeuwen also note that most viewers see a direct correlation between low saturation and moodiness (356). This symbolic

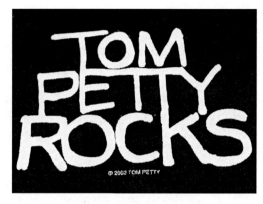

T-shirt back for *The Last DJ* tour in 2002 (photograph by Melissa Busch).

meaning reflects the frustration that Petty feels at the "commodification of individualism" (Cowen 49). The distorted view of the image is also meaningful. Displaying it in a landscape, as opposed to a portrait, position requires greater effort from viewers to interpret. From this angle, the guitar seems to be floating in the air, its neck acting as an arrow that orientates viewers, directing them to the verbal message below.

The back of the t-shirt simply bears three words—Tom Petty Rocks—written in white block capitals in a crawl text style that shows each line getting larger, thus accentuating its message. The letters show close connectivity, with the T of "Petty" and the K of "Rocks" overlapping and merging together. Kress and van Leeuwen suggest that overlapping emphasizes the importance of a person, as they cannot be confined to one spatial position (214). The polysemy of the word "rocks"—meaning "to be very good" or "to play rock music"—is also drawn upon to emphasize two of Petty's qualities. These typographic and lexical choices serve to authenticate and underline Petty as a role model. The t-shirt's expressive message requires fans not just to support Petty, but also to agree with his ideas. In buying and wearing the t-shirt, fans are also committing to an agreement with the sentiments expressed.

While the image of Petty's guitar could be seen to contradict his main message, given that the new American Dream views the "images and symbols of success as more important than the actual achievement" (Caldwell 26), when combined with the accompanying text and the context of use, it stands as a visual testimony to the hard work, dedication, and determination that Petty put in to reach the stage he is at today and ultimately, achieve his American Dream.

Conclusion

Throughout his some forty years in show business, the American Dream was a central theme of Petty's work. While its portrayal in song lyrics has long been recognized, this is the first study to turn attention to the tour t-shirt and the way in which image, color, typography, and materiality were used to convey meaning. Petty's tour t-shirts read like a history of the American Dream, taking fans from the mystique and hope of frontier life (*Touring the Great Wide Open*) to the boundless possibilities of success and happiness (*Dogs with Wings*) through to the corruption of materiality and consumerism (*The Last DJ*). Petty used the tour t-shirt as a microcosm of the general concerns that existed amongst people in American society. Whether through his symbols of the Golden Retriever, Chesapeake or Rickenbacker, his voice was always embedded within, urging fans to be realistic, while offering them hope. "I like things left ambiguous to some degree," Petty once stated in reference to his song lyrics. The same can be said for his tour t-shirts. Their beauty lies in the fact that fans can draw whatever mean they wish from them, whether it is simple proof that they attended the concert or a more spiritual connection with its metaphorical messages.

The eternal appeal of Petty's tour t-shirts mean that, although we will, sadly, never get to attend another Petty concert, his enduring and endearing personality will forever live on through the unique designs that he created. They form an unbreakable bond between fans that shared the live experience together; those who had literally been there, done that and got the t-shirt to prove it.

John F. Kennedy once said that "the problems of the world cannot possibly be solved by sceptics or cynics whose horizons are limited by the obvious realities. We need men who can dream of things that never were." Petty was one of these men. Perhaps that is why his loss is felt so greatly; it is not only a loss of an enormous talent but a loss of the American Dream.

*Special thanks to Paul Kelly, Heidi Wright, and Melissa Busch
for the Tom Petty t-shirt images.

Works Cited

Adam, N. and Martin Wild. "Applying CD-ROM Interactive Storybooks to Learning to Read." *Journal of Computer Assisted Learning*. Volume 13, Issue 2, 2003, pp. 119–132.

American Kennel Club, Inc. *The Complete Dog Book*. New York: Ballantine Books, 2006.

Anticonformity USA. "The History of the T-Shirt." http://www.anticonformityusa.com/why-t-shirts.

Bangs, Alan. "Interview with Tom Petty, Hamburg Rockpalast." *Petty Archives*. 24 April 1999. http://thepettyarchives.com/wp-content/pdfs/interviews/1999-04-24_TomPetty.pdf.

Barthes, Roland. *Image-Music-Text*. Waukegan, IL: Fontana Press, 1977.

Blanden Jo, Paul Gregg, and Stephen Machin. *Intergenerational Mobility in Europe and North America*, London School of Economics, 2005.

Burn, Andrew and David Parker. "The Skater and the Old Man: Multimodal Design and Moving Image Production." *Analysing Media Texts.* Edited by Andrew Burn and David Parker. New York: Bloomsbury Continuum, 2003. pp. 13–30.

Caldwell, Wilbur W. *Cynicism and the Evolution of the American Dream.* Lincoln: Potomac Books Inc, 2006.

Cavallo, Dominick. *A Fiction of the Past: The Sixties in America*, Basingstoke, UK: Palgrave Macmillan, 1999.

Cheng, Fei-Wen. "Scaffolding Language, Scaffolding A Writing: A Genre Approach to Teach Narrative Writing." *Asian EFL Journal*, Volume 10, 2008, pp. 167–191.

Cirlot, Juan Eduardo. *A Dictionary of Symbols.* North Chelmsford, MA: Courier Corporation, 1971.

Cosyns, Simon. "People Think They're Nothing If They're Not a Kardashian, Says Tom." *The Sun.* 25 July 2014. https://www.thesun.co.uk/archives/news/999743/people-think-theyre-nothing-if-theyre-not-a-kardashian-says-tom/.

Cowen, Tyler. *What Price Fame.* Cambridge, MA: Harvard University Press, 2000.

Dixon, Richard. "Materialism—Corruption of the American Dream." *Wessex Scene.* 12 February 2012. https://www.wessexscene.co.uk/opinion/2012/02/12/materialism-corruption-of-the-american-dream/.

Djonov, Emilia and Theo van Leeuwen. "The Semiotics of Texture: From Tactile to Visual." *Written Communication.* Volume 10, Issue 4, 2011, pp. 541–564.

Farber, Jim. "Petty Rips Today's Pop Culture." *The Gainesville Sun.* 9 Oct 2002. http://www.gainesville.com/news/20021009/petty-rips-todays-pop-culture

Fonarow, Wendy. "Ask the Indie Professor: What Does Your Gig T-Shirt Say About You?" *The Guardian.* 4 October 2010, https://www.theguardian.com/music/musicblog/2010/oct/04/ask-indie-professor-t-shirt.

Gregorio-Gardeo, Eduardo. "British Men's Magazines' Scent Advertising and the Multimodal Discursive Construction of Masculinity: A Preliminary Study." *Estudios Ingleses De La Universidad Complutense.* Volume 17, 2009. pp. 9–36.

Halliday, Michael. *An Introduction to Functional Grammar.* New York: Routledge, 1985.

Hanson, Sandra L. and John Zogby. "The Polls—Trends: Attitudes About the American Dream." *Public Opinion Quarterly,* Volume 74, Issue 2, 2010, pp. 570–584.

Heissenhuber, Steven, Jr. "The Misconception of the American Dream: What It Is, What It Isn't." *Turning Point.* 9 September 2017, https://www.turningpoint.news/misconception-american-dream/.

Hodge, Robert and Gunther Kress. *Language as Ideology.* New York: Routledge, 1993.

Hymes, Dell. "Toward Ethnographies of Communication." *Language and Social Context.* Edited by Pier Paolo Giglioli. New York: Penguin Books, 1972 pp. 21–44.

Jewitt, Carey. "The Move from Page to Screen: The Multimodal Reshaping of School English." *Journal of Visual Communication*, Volume 1, Issue 2, 2002. pp. 171–196.

Jewitt, Carey, and Rumiko Oyama. "Visual Meaning—A Social Semiotic Approach." *The Handbook of Visual Analysis.* Edited by Theo van Leeuwen and Carey Jewitt. SAGE Publications, 2001. pp. 134–156.

Kandinsky, Wassily. *Concerning the Spiritual in Art.* Mineola, NY: Dover Publications, 1977.

Kennedy, John F. "278—Address Before the Irish Parliament in Dublin." June 28 1963. http://www.presidency.ucsb.edu/ws/?pid=9317.

Kitson, Lisbeth. "Reconceptualising Understandings of Texts, Readers and Contexts: One English Teacher's Response to Using Multimodal Texts and Interactive Whiteboards." *English in Australia.* Volume 46, Issue 3, 2011. pp. 76–85.

Kress, Gunther. *Multimodality—A Social Semiotic Approach to Contemporary Communication.* New York: Routledge, 2010.

Kress, Gunther and Theo van Leeuwen. "Colour as a Semiotic Mode: Notes for a Grammar of Colour." *Visual Communication*, Volume 1, Issue 3, 2002, pp. 348–368.

Kress, Gunther and, Theo van Leeuwen. *Reading Images—The Grammar of Visual Design.* New York: Routledge, 1996.

Lacy, Mary Louise. *The Power of Colour to Heal the Environment.* Rainbow Bridge Publications, 1996.

Lerner, Max. "The Triumph of Laissez-Faire." *Paths of American Thought*. Edited by Arthur M. Schlesinger, Jr., and Morton White. Boston: Hougton, Mifflin & Company, 1963.

Marx, Leo. *The Machine in the Garden: Technology and the Pastoral Idea in America*. New York: Oxford University Press, 1964.

Medhurst, Martin J. *The Prospect of Presidential Rhetoric*. College Station: Texas A&M University Press, 2008.

O'Hagan, Lauren. *Class, Culture and Conflict in the Edwardian Book Inscription: A Multimodal Ethnohistoric Approach*. Unpublished Ph.D. thesis. Cardiff University. Forthcoming.

Pohl, Jana. *Looking Forward, Looking Back: Images of Eastern European Jewish Migration to America in Contemporary American Children's Literature*. Amsterdam: Rodopi, 2011.

Rank, Mark Robert, Thomas A. Hirschl, and Kirk A. Foster. *Chasing the American Dream— Understanding What Shapes Our Fortunes*. New York: Oxford University Press, 2014.

Rotondo, Andrea. *Tom Petty—Rock 'N' Roll Guardian*. London: Omnibus Press, 2014.

Rowsell, Jennifer. "'The Mood Is in the Shot': The Challenge of Moving-Image Texts to Multimodality." *Text and Talk*. Volume 34, Issue 3, 2014, pp. 307–324.

Rowsell, Jennifer and Lisa Chen. "English Studies Through a New Literacy Studies-Multimodal Lens." *The Routledge Companion to English Studies*. Edited by Brian Street and Constant Leung, New York: Routledge, 2010. pp. 464–475.

Sassoon, Rosemary. *Handwriting of the Twentieth Century*. New York: Routledge, 1999.

Saville Troike, Muriel. *The Ethnography of Communication*. Hoboken: Wiley-Blackwell, 1982.

Schoemer, Karen. "In Search of the Foundation of Youth." *Pop Music*. October 6 1991. http://www.nytimes.com/1991/10/06/arts/pop-music-in-search-of-the-foundation-of-youth.html?pagewanted=all.

Schruers, Fred. "Tom Petty." *Rolling Stone*. July 8–22 1999. pp. 88–94.

_____. "Tom Petty on the Road: This Is How It Feels." *Rolling Stone*. May 4 1995. pp. 48–54.

Sørensen, Af Lars. *A Multimodal Approach for Advertising for Professionals in the Film, Television and Photography Business*. Unpublished MA Dissertation. Aarhus University. 2011.

Sperber, Dan. and Dierdre Wilson. *Relevance: Communication and Cognition*. Hoboken: Blackwell Publishing, 1995.

Stenglin, Jim. *Packing Curiosities: Towards a Grammar of Three-Dimensional Space*. Unpublished Ph.D. thesis. University of Sydney. 2004.

Stöckl, Hartmut. "Beyond Depicting. Language-Image-Links in the Service of Advertising." *Arbeitenaus Anglistik und Amerikanistik*, Volume 34, Issue 1, 2009. pp. 3–28.

_____. "Typography: Body and Dress of a Text—A Signing Mode Between Language and Image." *Visual Communication*, Volume 4, Issue 2. 2005. pp. 205–214.

Truslow Adams, James. *The Epic of America*. New York: Simon Publications, 1931.

Turner, Frederick Jackson. *The Frontier in American History*. Huntington, NY: Robert E. Kieger Publishing Co. Inc., 1976.

van Leeuwen, Theo. *Introducing Social Semiotics*. New York: Routledge, 2005.

_____. *Speech, Music, Sound*. London: Macmillan, 1999.

_____. "Towards a Semiotic of Typography." *Information Design Journal*. Volume 14, issue 1, 2006 pp. 139–155.

van Leeuwen, Theo and Emilia Djonov. "Notes Towards a Semiotic of Kinetic Typography." *Social Semiotics*. Volume 25, Issue 5, 2015 pp. 244–253.

Walsh, Maureen. "Multimodal Literacy: What Does It Mean for Classroom Practice?" *Australian Journal of Language and Literacy*. Volume 33, Issue 3, 2010, pp. 211–239.

Zakia, Richard. *Perception and Imaging*. Waltham, MA: Focal Press, 2002.

Zanes, Warren. *Petty: The Biography*. London: St Martin's, 2015.

Fashioning a Rock Star

Petty's Clothing Choices and Their Connections

MEGAN VOLPERT

The legacy of Tom Petty's musicianship is fairly clear; he was perhaps America's last great rock star. The considerable influence of rock stars is not limited to their published works of music. They also wield a personal brand to impact politics, humanitarianism, and other fields of social culture. Of necessity and often with great deliberation, rock stars use clothing choice to establish their ethos, which in turn provides a kind of philosophy of style to move their audiences. As a fashion icon, Petty is often parodied and dismissed in the same breath. Whether looking at the top hat or the velvet jacket, we know a piece of his wardrobe when we see it.

This essay will analyze Petty's most recognizable attire and suggest how his clothing choice is connected to the interests of his musicianship, from his collaboration with other important figures in the history of rock music to his admiration for younger bands that would shape the future of the genre. Throughout the phases of his career, Petty has often delivered his thoughts on attire directly in songs or in the design of promotional materials, so this essay will additionally consider those. By examining Petty's attention to vestment, we can better appreciate the full picture of his success and reflect on the true implications of his rock stardom.

Imagery and Ideology

"Heeeeey, Tom Petty!" I could pay for drinks all around if I had a dollar for every time I've heard this at a Halloween party. Can you guess what I was

99

wearing? It was an oversized green top hat and a purple velvet jacket that ended at mid-thigh. I regularly attend costume parties as the Mad Hatter. Without fail, a majority of people at these parties will skip right over the Lewis Carroll reference from his exceedingly famous 1865 children's book, *Alice's Adventures in Wonderland*, in favor of Petty's costume in the 1985 music video for "Don't Come Around Here No More." What causes this frame of reference?

Although Carroll's original work was illustrated, the image of the Mad Hatter has shifted repeatedly over time as new adaptations of the beloved story emerge. "Don't Come Around Here No More" is not whatsoever a song about Carroll's work, yet the video's portrayal of it does stick in the mind. Among all the available images of the Mad Hatter, Petty rightly discerned that the outfit was the key and that such a costume could be boiled down to jacket and hat. These two items present such a complete signifier that it barely even matters what color they are. They are maroon in the video, and yet my green and purple items that hold far more closely to widely popular film adaptations of the book still read as a Petty reference. As one partygoer defended, "well, I know Petty is one of your big influences."

The other guests who misread my costume are perhaps generally more likely to be knowledgeable in the area of rock music than children's literature. Elements of the rock and roll lifestyle have always been transmitted first and foremost through the ear, but we can certainly say that musicians make wardrobe choices that allow the seen to bolster the heard. Many genres of popular music are associated with particular clothing, whether it is punk leather jackets or grunge flannel shirts or disco sequins. These genres carry differing ideologies, and fans are only too happy to sport a complete look—from the thoughts in our heads to the tunes in our ears to the shoes on our feet. The power of images is that they can activate precisely this tangle of the music, the musician, and our love of the ideas embedded within both.

In 1980, French philosopher and semiotician Roland Barthes examined this phenomenon with *Camera Lucida*, wherein he identifies the two parts of a photograph as studium and punctum. The studium is the surface, which is comprised of bits and pieces of objectively discernible photographic elements. We can agree upon what Petty wore in any given picture, note where and when it was taken and by whom. Punctum is our subjective response to the image. It is "that accident which pricks me (but also bruises me, is poignant to me)" (27). The sensation is both fleeting and elastic. "However lightening-like it may be, the *punctum* has, more or less potentially, a power of expansion. The power is often metonymic," Barthes wrote (45). A metonym is a rhetorical figure of speech where a thing is called not by its own name, but by the name of some other thing with which it is closely associated, such as referring to the American film industry simply as Hollywood. As a metonym, the article of clothing comes to stand for the principles of the person; this is the basis of what we call style.

Petty's style was complex and did not necessarily aggregate into a cohesive whole. It can be understood as a multiplicity of elements rather than a singular trademark. This is in contrast to one-note stylistic hallmarks, such as the cowboy hat on Garth Brooks or the face paint on Gene Simmons. Petty's most notable fashion choices offer a mix of regal and proletarian, stark and subdued, ancient and alien. The clothes convey something altogether ornery that refuses easy categorization, and in this above all, they convey the spirit of the person who wore them. Barthes says, "Whatever it grants to vision and whatever its manner, a photograph is always invisible: it is not it that we see. In short, the referent adheres" (Barthes 6).

The personality of the rock star will come through in the photographs. There are obviously a great many images of Petty, and not all of them are necessarily worth isolated analysis, but Barthes thought that culture could sift through these piles and in time yield some images that we can say are iconic because of the way we agree upon their punctum beyond the studium: "Among those which had been collected, evaluated, approved, collected in albums or magazines and which had thereby passed through the filter of culture, I realized that some provoked tiny jubilations, as if they referred to a stilled center, an erotic or leveraging value buried in myself (however harmless the subject may have appeared)" (16).

This is an excellent description of influence—the way signs, such as a green top hat and purple velvet jacket, circulate the referent around the party, ultimately achieving significance through the feelings of the other partygoers. Although Petty is the man in these images, he also had referents of his own. His wardrobe choices were not spun from thin air. It is necessarily true that his closet was a product of the same influences as his music. Everything is of a piece as a matter of punctum, which "is a kind of subtle *beyond*—as if the image launched desire beyond what it permits us to see: not only toward 'the rest' of the nakedness, not only toward the fantasy of a *praxis*, but toward the absolute excellence of a being, body and soul together" (59).

When we put the soul of rock and roll in a room with a camera, Barthes says, "in front of the lens, I am at the same time: the one I think I am, the one I want others to think I am, the one the photographer thinks I am, and the one he makes use of to exhibit his art" (13). As a rock star, Petty was responsible for producing images conducive to commerce, but he had a long history of struggle against those corporate obligations. He appeared on the cover of *Rolling Stone* #348, in July of 1981, ripping a dollar bill in half accompanied by the headline "one man's war against high record prices." Yet he wore a classic white oxford shirt with a black blazer and tie, the definition of an anonymous business suit. The cover art for the record in question features

Petty in front of a vinyl bin clearly priced at $8.98 instead of the $9.98 that MCA had hoped to charge for *Hard Promises.*

Not every musician has such strong visual acuity. One could surely examine the visual representations of any given rock star and yield some solid results in approaching their personal character and philosophy of life. But there is consistent evidence to suggest that Petty participated in the construction of his own images with somewhat more deliberate flair and intentionality than the average rock star. Upon the rather religious experience of meeting Elvis as a young boy, the first thing he talked about was that white jumpsuit and pompadour. As a teenager, Petty would describe movies scene by scene to his bandmates for hours. His first wife, Jane, looked so much like him that they were often mistaken for siblings when they were in their twenties. The early success of MTV was made possible at least in part by Petty's stunning approach to video as a medium for delivering music when he was in his thirties. In his interview for *I Want My MTV: The Uncensored Story of the Music Video Revolution,* he recalls having balked at suggestions for imagery that were sexually exploitative of female extras (307) and confirms that he exercised a significant amount of creative control over how he was visually represented in videos throughout the four decades of his career (95).

He grew up looking at images of Bob Dylan and George Harrison and was later befriended by both men. He sought musical collaborations with Jeff Lynne and Stevie Nicks that bled into his visual sense. He inspired the next generation of rockers, with Kurt Cobain eventually appearing on the cover of *Rolling Stone* #628 in a t-shirt that said "corporate magazines still suck," eleven years after Petty's dollar bill stunt. As much as Petty's fashion choices hold the weight of our feeling as his fans, they must also, of course, tie back to his own feelings—to the punctum he himself felt while gazing at images of those whose music careers he admired. His garb shows their influence.

Hats

Petty did not need to wear hats. He began growing his hair shaggy and long as a young teen, much to the chagrin of his father and his teachers. Gainesville, Florida, might have been a college town in the early Sixties, but it was still very much the South and you did not want to be beaten up for looking too much like a hippie. His hair was such a bold statement of outsider status that it seems a bit silly and even counterproductive to cover it with a hat. At his death at the age of sixty-six, Petty still had a full head of hair hanging down to his shoulders. Maybe it was a little thinner and had streaks of gray, but it was neither receding from his forehead nor balding on top behind. Unlike Brett Michaels, for example, whose ever-present bandana is accompanied by a whiff of aging desperation, Petty never wanted a hat to hide anything.

He had been donning the occasional top hat at concerts since at least 1978, when legend has it he was given one by a fan at a show. His most famous deployment of the top hat was for the "Don't Come Around Here No More" video, but he had already worn a black one in the video for "You Got Lucky" three years earlier. He would sport a variety of hats beyond the topper. There were some fedoras and trilbies associated with his time in The Traveling Wilburys around 1989, his return to work with the Heartbreakers in the early Nineties, and with his promotion of the *Mojo* album in 2010. There is a single recorded instance of him wearing a baseball cap during publicity—with a Confederate flag on it for the *Southern Accents* documentary in 1985, a symbol he would later take pains to publicly reject as inappropriate—but the main thread of his interest in tall hats ran across several decades. Why the interest in tall hats?

Petty was 5'9" and did not need to exaggerate his stature, as opposed to a performer like Stevie Nicks, who is 5'1" and may like to give the impression of a more imposing figure. At any Nicks concert, you can find hordes of women emulating her simply by wearing two items: a black dress flowing with witchy chiffon layers and a top hat. She has been wearing top hats since at least 1975, and it is to her early influence that many people credit Petty's interest in the look, but pianist Leon Russell was also very fond of them as early as the *Mad Dogs & Englishmen* tour of 1970. Russell was cofounder of Shelter Records, with whom the fledgling Heartbreakers first signed a contract, and Petty wrote songs for Russell in the mid–Seventies.

A top hat is for a person of refinement. With its faint echo of royalty and its connotation of seriousness, the tall hat is a marker of a successful gentleman. Several rock and roll figures, most prominently Slash and Alice Cooper, engage in an ironic deployment of the top hat that nods to this prestigious heritage while simultaneously contrasting it with fierce guitar attack and shocking persona. Nicks' hat is supposedly an antique, dating back to the Twenties and possessed of its very own stage hand when she takes it on the road to wear during "Go Your Own Way." This narrow field of repetition constitutes much more scrupulous and specific usage, which does not quite fit with Petty's distinguished vagabond image.

His usage is closer to an homage to Russell, whose immense talent stood in contrast to his haphazard lifestyle and who used his top hat to signify a kind of louche, insouciant grace. Petty's ability to channel this type of unruffled charm snowballed into oversized menace for the Mad Hatter video concept; a giant hat managed to lend credibility to the idea that his character would eat Alice as a cake—to him a hilariously surreal idea, but to Tipper Gore and the censorious Parents Music Resource Council it was the stuff of nightmares. The gravity attributed to the hat in either interpretation cannot be denied.

Jackets

Some part of Petty's torso appears on the cover art for each of his first five studio albums. For the 1976 debut, he sported a classic leather biker jacket with a line of bullets peeking out from the left lapel. Combined with his narrowed eye contact and smug side-smile, this photo immediately conveyed a tough image. When radio and concert promoters could not quite figure out how to label the music of the Heartbreakers, they relied upon images like this to lump Petty in with the punks first and then with new wave shortly thereafter. John Lydon of the Sex Pistols and Debbie Harry of Blondie wore similar jackets.

In trying to steer away from these comparisons in 1978, the entire band appeared on the cover of *You're Gonna Get It!*, all of them jacketless except for Petty. While they were in vests and button-downs, Petty had on a turtleneck and velvet jacket. The blue wash on the photo preserved that hard-edged appeal of a leather jacket, but the richness of the fabric also added a strongly regal connotation. With his crossed arms and unsmiling eye contact, he announced himself as standing firmly a cut above musical fads. When that album did not sell as well as expected, subsequent covers retreated to more traditional territory.

The iconic 1979 cover of *Damn the Torpedoes* featured Petty with less squinty eyes and a toothier smile in a pink t-shirt and slim black blazer. In 1981, the album cover features\d a brown leather jacket, more casual and less threatening than the black one on the debut album. In 1982, for *Long After Dark*, the black leather jackets returned, though the ominous quality conveyed by bullets on the original was this time managed simply by applying a red wash to the photo. Petty's relatively extensive use of leather jackets in promotional material, especially in the first decade of his career, did not translate to his fashion choices for performances at least in part because leather is simply too sweaty under stage lighting.

But he did generally wear a jacket to perform for four decades, and especially in the late Seventies through the early Eighties, would sometimes choose a suit with pants to match. Art work for the compilation albums shows this. The cover of *Pack Up the Plantation: Live!* from 1985 featured his so-called space suit, which was black with a silver shawl collar and had colorful planets dotting it all over besides rocket ships taking off up the sleeves. He often wore it during the *Southern Accents* tour, showing his surrealist sense of hilarity and a defiant streak against the pressure to pander to his audience with more Southern-influenced attire. This jacket is on display at the Rock and Roll Hall of Fame in Cleveland.

On the 2000 *Anthology: Through the Years* album, he performed in a stark black and white awning-striped shirt. Although this photo itself involved no jacket, it points toward Petty's longtime love of jackets or suits with wild stripes. He wore an even more thickly striped black and white jacket in concert as early as 1977. He had pencil-stripe jackets dating back to shows before he signed with Shelter, and unbalanced barcode-striped jackets as late as the early Nineties. On *The Live Anthology* of 2009, he was featured in a velvet jacket in the ink-drawn cover portrait. Petty had two very well-known velvet jackets in his regular concert rotation throughout the Eighties: one in sea foam green with forest green cuffs that is featured in his Red Rocks Hall of Fame portrait, and one in violet that lead guitarist Mike Campbell would also sometimes wear in performance.

Beginning in the late Nineties, Petty primarily wore one of two jackets on stage. One was a brown suede number with foot-long fringe on the sleeves, chest and hem. The other was a rotating series of mostly olive green but sometimes black canvas army jackets with miscellaneous generic patches on them. Canvas, suede and velvet are all fabrics with a soft hand-feel. While the stand-out velvet and suede jackets cast Petty as a sort of royal and imposing figure, the army jackets were highly practical gear for the everyman. All three types of jackets could convey that he was holding fast to his fighting spirit in a rather ageless way.

Though his choice of jackets, Petty was consistently projecting the image of an outsider who was not trying too hard to fit in. Though he kept having to go back to leather jackets in promotional cover art, his could exercise more control over his stage style and he generally was interested in jackets that were a little loud or even silly. This is very much in keeping with the jacket choices of one of his biggest influences who eventually became a dear friend, George Harrison. Petty was inspired to pick up a guitar in the first place thanks to the Beatles and the two men had met for the first time in 1974, though they would not collaborate until the late Eighties. During the eight years of his work with the Beatles, Harrison was, of course, required to put on whatever all the lads wore for album covers, from the straight-laced black jacket or turtleneck looks on the early albums to the cartoonish satin soldier and animal costume getups on the later albums.

These standardized looks evaporated in his personal life and in his later career as a solo musician. In the mid–Sixties, Harrison could be seen in a purple velvet jacket with a contrasting awning-stripe. He also wore a paisley floral jacket with black background whose color scheme is quite an echo of Petty's later space suit. They were both fond of fabrics that draped and patterns loud enough to turn heads. In his solo career, Harrison increasingly wore denim jackets and work shirts just as Petty turned toward canvas army jackets. Whether using the lushness of velvet to elevate their image to the point of kingly absurdity or using common workwear to defeat the trappings of their stardom, they had a shared sense of humor that certainly applied to wardrobe decisions from the beginning of their friendship in 1987.

Sunglasses

Sunglasses are standard fare for a majority of rock stars and the decision to hide one's eyes is practical on a number of levels. At a minimum, they cover those windows to the soul in a way that puts some deliberate distance between stardom and fandom. It is more difficult to read someone's facial expressions for hints of surprise or anger, so sunglasses aid a rock star in appearing more cool, more collected and professional. More cynically, sunglasses increase the likelihood that a rock star can pass incognito in public, or show up somewhere high as a kite in a manner that hides dilated pupils or red eyes. Most cynically, ugly faces do not sell records, and sunglasses can cover up a lot of an ugly face. That was the basic strategy of Electric Light Orchestra's Jeff Lynne, who Petty was interested to recruit as a producer in the late Seventies, although they would not join forces until the late Eighties.

All three of these utilizations essentially constitute an assertion of privacy. Though much of his audience may consider Petty a handsome man, he undoubtedly did not conform to industry stereotypes of male rocker sexiness at any point in his career. So little did he care about trying to be a heartthrob that his bandmates agreed calling themselves the Heartbreakers would be a good little joke about their unusual looks. Petty also admitted to a few phases of drug use: marijuana in the Seventies, cocaine in the Eighties, and heroin in the Nineties. A bit of eye cover would have been useful in glossing each of these.

But the main distancing function of sunglasses is what interested him most. The need for this distance was an earned distinction. Only a truly famous rocker needed sunglasses. When Petty accepted his MusicCares Person of the Year Award, he relayed an anecdote about what it was like in the beginning, to be sitting among the greats jamming at Leon Russell's house. Feeling a bit small in the presence of the infamous pianist, two Beatles and legendary sessions drummer Jim Keltner, Petty slipped on his sunglasses. Russell mocked him for it, saying he had not paid enough dues to warrant wearing shades indoors and at night. At the end of his telling at the ceremony in 2017, Petty donned a pair of sunglasses at the podium to signify his status as an elder statesman.

The style of his sunglass frames changed with the times. In the Seventies, he mainly wore aviators or styles with similarly fuller coverage. In the Eighties, he wore Lennonesque rounded glasses and a pair of oval ones in the "Don't Come Around Here No More" video that became part of its iconic look. In the Nineties, he went back to fuller coverage, squarish frames or wayfarers, and swung back to his Seventies preferences at the turn of the century. While Jeff Lynne preferred mirrored lenses that reflected audiences and cameras back on themselves, Petty always went with brown or gray tints instead. More often than not, his tints employed enough transparency so that his eyes could still be viewed quite plainly behind them.

Photos of Lynne without sunglasses are so rare that they are collectibles among his fans. Though Petty could be reclusive and did employ sunglasses to afford himself some privacy, there was a particular type of occasion for which he never wore sunglasses: cover stories for *Rolling Stone*. Though he'd been reviewed or profiled in the magazine a number of times, his first cover shoot was issue #311 in February 1980. He wore a loud-print snap shirt, undershirt and jeans, no sunglasses. He made the cover again July 1981, ripping up that dollar bill and staring mischievously into the camera for issue #348, a feature on his battle to keep album pricing low. In 1991, for issue #610, he wore a hat without sunglasses and smiled sweetly at the camera. An alternate take from that same shoot—with a little less smile and a little more shadow around the eyes—was chosen for the cover of issue #1299, on Petty's memorial. In 1995, for issue #707, he was laid back in a flannel shirt, looking comfortably at the camera. This same photo was reissued on the cover of the magazine's 2014 special collector's edition on his work.

Even as Petty seems to take some of his sunglass cues from Lynne, he makes this constant exception for major interviews, pointing to an earnest effort to answer questions transparently instead of automatically. Petty generally resented promotional work and thought of it as getting punished for making albums, yet he wanted to deal as honestly and openly with journalists as he felt able. In this regard, he more closely paralleled Bob Dylan's sunglass strategy. We will consider Dylan's influence more substantively when examining Western wear later in this essay, but it is useful to note that in July 1986, the cover of double-issue #478/479 featured both Petty and Dylan smirking right at the camera. Dylan is seldom seen without sunglasses in public, even wearing them to accept his Medal of Freedom from President Obama. Yet across more than a dozen covers for *Rolling Stone* for which he actually posed—as opposed to his inclusion on covers via archival photos—he only opted for sunglasses in two of them. When these two stars gave an interview, thorny and fraught though the process may have been, they wanted the resultant publicity to be at least marginally intimate and worthwhile to all concerned. This necessitated some extra eye contact.

Shirts

As someone who wore jackets or vests much of the time, Petty generally tended to prefer collared shirts over tees as being more suitable to complete the look. On stage, it was the outerwear that showcased much of the flashiness in his personality. The shirts underneath were usually dark and solid colored, fading away against the comparatively louder layers on top. But there were windows during his career where he did go around in just a shirt and for the most part these shirts were either Western or flannel.

Flannel shirting is about the warmth and suppleness of the fabric. In that sense, it finds a common resting place within the symbolism of Petty's choice of jacket fabrics like suede and velvet. Many people use flannel for an outer layer, so it also presents a bit of middle ground both emotionally and physically, adding a protectiveness that is beyond the usual collared shirt but less than that of a proper jacket. Western shirting is more about tailoring details than fabrics, but with its reliance on wrinkle-free polyester geared toward a sort of weather-beaten look, it can also been seen as emphasizing this idea of softness. Flannel shirts are most often associated with the grunge music of the 1990s, and we will consider Petty's embrace of this important rock sub-genre later in this essay when we look at shoes.

Perhaps especially from the back row of a concert venue, the snap closure and contrast stitching or piping on a Western shirt make for a shiny, lively stage figure. As the light hits these elements on a shirt, it helps define the movements of the body within the shirt more completely than a solid-color shirt with regular buttons. This would be especially valuable to heighten a stage presence when one's movements are otherwise quite minute or restricted, such as during a sit-down set or solo acoustic number. Petty tended to wear flannel or Western shirts when he was separated from his identity as one of the Heartbreakers, in precisely those performance conditions.

He returned to these shirts across three decades, each time he released a solo album. When *Full Moon Fever* came out in 1989, he was newly steeped in the influences of his supergroup, The Traveling Wilburys. Three of his four bandmates—Dylan, Harrison, and Roy Orbison—all frequently enjoyed Western shirting. Despite the immense talent of these individuals, their shirts convey a feeling of simplicity and the old-fashioned. This is in keeping with the stripped down rock of that first solo album whose number one single, "I Won't Back Down," originally frightened Petty because he thought the obvious, straightforward nature of its lyrics was too naked, too unadorned by metaphor or artistry. It's hard to imagine Petty performing without his shirt on.

He continued to go back to these shirts for solo work in 1994 and 2006, on *Wildflowers* and *Highway Companion*. The iconic Robert Sebree photo of Petty in the studio sitting down in a pair of jeans to record *Wildflowers* does not feature a Western or a flannel, but instead goes with a classic black collared shirt with black buttons. It's a man in black echo of Johnny Cash. Immediately after *Wildflowers*, Petty would back Cash for his *Unchained* album, which won a Grammy for Best County Album and was originally titled *Petty Cash*. The *Highway Companions* recording was done with Rick Rubin's American Recordings label, which had been responsible for the resurgence of interest in Cash's work. The cover art by surrealist Robert Deyber foregrounds a monkey and an astronaut holding hands beneath a towering rocket ship, tiny presences in a vast desert scene reminiscent of the setting of the "You Got Lucky" video. He was getting back into an extended Western groove, with the Wilburys box set released in 2007 and then a return to his countryfied Mudcrutch roots in 2008.

Shoes

Like the majority of classic rockers, Petty most frequently wore chelsea boots on stage. Unlike others of his generation, however, the attire we have covered so far shows that he was not interested in cultivating a singular look for his brand, but instead would move in and out of phases in a way that was somewhat more forwarding-looking and less static than his peers. Classic rock certainly does have a particular image that is not attributable to a single artist. By contrast, Petty's footwear choices highlight the fact that he searched for influences among the next generation and emerging genres of music, not only among the heroes that had gone before him.

Publicity stills and candids captured on the street reveal that he liked to wear Converse tennis shoes. The Chuck Taylor All-Star low-tops are easily distinguishable by their white cap toe and brown rubber treads. Chucks have been around since the 1920s, first as a basketball shoe but eventually proliferating among musicians and the culture at large. Many candids of Petty feature Converse shoes, from an unlaced, purple pair that he wore court side at L.A. Lakers games to a laced, red pair that he wore with a black and white suit to meet Barack Obama at the White House. Most commonly, in publicity, he wore the traditional black Chucks, laced or unlaced and occasionally with a Jack Purcell smile toe, that can be seen in many of his posed photos beginning in the early 1990s.

Chucks are widely associated with subgenres of rock that have less mainstream appeal than Petty's body of work. In the 1970s, they were a staple for punk bands like the Ramones and the Clash. Petty did not wear Converse then, as he was already troubled by getting lumped in with punk acts. In the 1990s, Chucks were affiliated with the emergence of grunge rock courtesy of bands like Nirvana, Hole, and Pearl Jam. Kurt Cobain and Eddie Vedder were rarely seen in any other kind of footwear. Petty often professed his interest in Cobain's work and ultimately even attempted to hire Dave Grohl to drum for his band after the dissolution of Nirvana and the dismissal of Stan Lynch from the Heartbreakers. In 1994, Grohl drummed for them when they appeared as the musical guest on episode 372 of *Saturday Night Live*. Courtney Love continues to tell stories about Petty's career that express admiration for his rebellious attitude and Eddie Vedder has long covered Petty's material at shows as well as having occasionally shown up as a guest at Petty's own concerts.

This willingness to look forward as well as backward speaks to the fluidity with which Petty chose a wardrobe that sustained his evolving sense of self. He was willing to visually align himself with younger artists whose mission he understood, rather than seeking only those shoes that would compile his image alongside other classic rock acts as merely more of the same. Nor was he simply trying to portray himself as still young and hip. Petty was never aiming to be on trend or of the moment in the first place. He choose things that had enough energy and were versatile enough to grow along with him.

Merchandise

It is difficult to say how involved Petty may have been in the design of his own merchandise, but certainly the items of clothing emblazoned with his name and likeness must have conformed to some extent with his personal brand in a way that he approved. Looking at his tour tees over the years, patterns easily emerge. The preferred color scheme on the Heartbreakers was black, tomato red, and beige. Black and red are the mainstay of rock merchandising, but to use beige as the offset color evokes a feeling of inclusivity and smoothness that is everlasting when compared to other parallel offset options like a high energy yellow that would grow dated or a blue that would be a little too on the nose of Americana. Beige rather blandly offends no one and has a timeless quality, as does the band's consistent choice of a highly readable and basic all-caps sans serif font.

The concert tees most commonly featured Petty's likeness or the band's logo. Most of the likenesses were straight off the album artwork, but occasionally there was a live performance shot. The logo itself depicted Petty's Gibson Flying V guitar, as well as the band's namesake banner colored in rainbow ombre with a left-to-right, purple-to-red inversion instead of the usual other way around. The Flying V reads as a reference point for any rock style from the 1950s blues of Albert King to the 1980s heavy metal of Metallica, and was thus as inclusive as beige.

The rainbow ombre showed off a more independent streak, riffing on the artwork affiliated with thought-provoking or highly individualistic musicians of the 1960s and 70s, including psychedelic bands like Pink Floyd or jam bands like the Grateful Dead. Petty's merchandise often mimicked the look of concert posters from this era or even earlier, deploying three-color ombre schemes most notably for *Full Moon Fever* and the fortieth anniversary tour. Overall, the merchandise aimed for a sort of perennial familiarity by combining the most open signifiers from each era of music that influenced Petty's career. These symbols were insistent in their traditionalism, but also unique for their combined deployment, masterfully designed to speak across generations to influences past and future.

Songs

Though determining precisely how much control Petty had over his own clothes or his band's merchandise is tricky, we can say with certitude that he had absolute control over his song lyrics and that he often wrote lyrics containing direct expression of a philosophy of style. Petty clearly understood how style translated to influence, and he revisited this subject with consistency across four decades.

Petty's fondness for the Byrds led him to cover their Sixties hit "So You Want to Be a Rock 'n' Roll Star," which famously made fun of the importance of a pop star's impeccable hairdo and too-tight pants as emblems intrinsic to the brand. In the late Seventies, he categorized lipstick and rouge as a type of hiding in "Mystery Man." Accessories and scents worn in public are part of an incognito glossing of the personal, and rather than criticize these maneuvers of social distancing, Petty sang them a love song. In "Louisiana Rain," the chorus emphasizes how much shoes make the man because once that downpour soaked through them, he would be forever changed inside.

In the early Eighties, he meditated at length on fashion culture in England with "Kings Road," so named for the west London street that made Vivienne Westwood famous, among many other Chelsea designers. Petty described this place as a multicultural mecca of gender-bending acceptance, more forward-looking than New York or West Los Angeles. His tone is one of delighted bewilderment and open exploration, similar to his fond memories of a girl in "The Same Old You" who took no prisoners while wearing platforms and David Bowie's haircut. Later in the Eighties, he referenced Union soldiers exclusively by the blue color of their uniform jackets in the final verse of "Rebels." In "Spike," he expressed admiration for a teenage boy whose sole distinguishing characteristic was that he wore a dog collar to a Gainesville dive bar, undaunted by the merciless needling of the bikers there.

In the Nineties, he invented the story of a promising young rock star for "Into the Great Wide Open" that lampooned his own past challenges with a leather jacket and chains that made noise when he moved, not unlike the Byrds cover, though perhaps a little less upbeat in its conclusion. In "All of Nothin'," polishing the medals of a father's uniform stood in for a lifetime of coercion, domination, and subsequent resentment. Then of course, there was the iconic party dress from "Mary Jane's Last Dance." It was a song about an ephemerally great evening with a sexy stranger, which the video transformed by moving the party to a morgue and costuming Kim Basinger in a wedding dress. Everyone remembers the dress because it pointed—even somewhat against the grain of that short-lived encounter in the lyrics—toward the creepy deepness of their connection; few remember that the music video focused on Petty's morgue assistant character taking the time to put it on her. His emphasis was tuned to the satisfaction implicit in the ritual act of putting on these clothes.

In the Aughts, Petty continued to sing about what symbols he would and would not wear as a matter of moral choice. In "Joe," he impersonated a sneering music promoter intent on making quick pile of money off a virgin whore archetype who was willing to undress on stage. Her nakedness was the proof that she had been exploited by the industry. In "Square One," he reflected on how hard it still seemed to make the ends of his varying obligations meet. The weight of his responsibilities was analogized as clothing he didn't want to wear. On 2010's "U.S. 41," he referred to his grandfather by the color of his coat—green, which draws a straight line from his family's work history to his own velvet upgrade while performing on stage.

Conclusion

Fashion magazines and style bloggers paid an unusual amount of attention when Petty passed away. *Vogue* offered homage with a slideshow of favorite looks and *Elle* called him "the fashion icon we didn't deserve," giving some historical analysis that Petty "epitomized the rawness and eccentrism that the fashion industry has been chasing ever since." *Cheatsheet's* Jesse Quinn declared that "his style was as iconic as his music." We can say Petty's clothing choices were iconic precisely because he did not harden his wardrobe into the flat stereotype of rock star branding.

Barthes argues that this is how the images that remain of Petty can truly become impactful: "Ultimately, Photography is subversive not when it frightens, repels, or even stigmatizes, but when it is *pensive*, when it thinks" (38). Indeed, one of the many ways that Petty subverted expectations was through his thoughtful approach to clothing. Though he did have some foundational looks, he shifted between them based on his musical influences of the moment and the creative projects he was working on at particular times. He took a chameleonic approach, phasing in and out of looks as a reflection of his moods and as a response to his industry. This is why we should view his legacy not only in light of the albums he made, but in the context of the photographs that clearly demonstrate the extent to which he was one of a kind. "The important thing is that the photograph possesses an evidential force," wrote Barthes, "and that its testimony bears not on the object but on time" (88–89).

The photographs are evidence of Petty's talent, and additionally they point at the endurance of his influence across time. In particular, we can look at their impact on the subsequent photography of his younger daughter, AnnaKim Violette, whom *L.A. Weekly* has also referred to as a style icon. "Unapologetically, I love costumes," she says. "But I hate the fashion industry. I don't have a standard. My low is my high, basically." Her own wardrobe is based on "a love of creating a world," she says. "It's that simple. When you're doing anything in the world, you want it to be seen as simple." Violette's Instagram has over thirty-five thousand followers. She regularly posts old photos of her father, featuring captions like "Looking good is important [sic] I blame my love of crazy clothing on my father. Petty details define my style."

After Petty's funeral, Violette posted a photo of t-shirts that were made for the occasion with the caption, "Who gets a ringer t shirt at a funeral." It's a white cotton tee with a black illustration of young Petty playing guitar, underneath which is printed "nil desperandum." Found originally in Horace's *Odes*, the Latin phrase means "never despair." It was a rallying cry in support of a skilled archer who fought on the side of the Greeks during the Trojan War. The cleverness of the Greek's giant horse shows they understood the fundamental style concept that we comprehend as we continue looking at pictures of what Tom Petty wore: what we see only from the outside may contain multitudes on the inside.

WORKS CITED

Barthes, Roland. *Camera Lucida.* Translated by Richard Howard. New York: Hill & Wang, 1981.

Harwood, Erika. "Tom Petty's Funeral, Like Any Good Concert, Had Great Merch." Vanities, *Vanity Fair,* 17 October 2017, www.vanityfair.com/style/2017/10/tom-petty-funeral-t-shirt.

Laden, Tanja M. "Annakim Violette, Tom Petty's Daughter, Is an American Girl." *L.A. Weekly,* 2 October 2017, www.laweekly.com/content/printView/2165164.

Quinn, Jessie. "8 Times Tom Petty Proved His Style Was as Iconic as His Music." The Cheat Sheet, 3 Jan. 2018, www.cheatsheet.com/gear-style/tom-petty-style-icon.html/?a=viewall.

Tannenbaum, Rob and Craig Marks. *I Want My MTV: The Uncensored Story of the Music Video Revolution.* New York: Plume, 2012.

"Tom Petty Was the Glorious Fashion Icon We Didn't Deserve." ELLE, 4 October 2017, www.elle.com.au/fashion/tom-petty-fashion-14567.

Violette, AnnaKim (@annakimwildflower). Photo of Tom Petty in black and white striped jacket. *Instagram,* 1 March 2018, https://www.instagram.com/p/BfyatouhyzA/.

_____. Photo of Tom Petty memorial tee shirt. Instagram, 17 October 2017, https://www.instagram.com/p/BaVy_wChtT7/.

Contributing to Success

Tom Petty, the Heartbreakers and Baby Boomer Behavior

REBECCA A. CATON

The stage is dark. The crowd has gathered. People chatter and mill about—ready, waiting. Cheers erupt from areas of the arena. Those close to the stage can see flashlights helping performers get to their places for the start of the show. Our breath is held hostage. The hairs bristle on our skin. We watch, eyes widening; we anticipate, hope … and pause. We are awaiting our salvation. First, a beat starts, with a chord, then a voice—and we are transported.

Rock and roll music has not always been so transformative to the masses. What has changed since rock and roll has come to center stage of the music industry? Rock and roll roots came around the mid-twentieth century and has grown from its early and experimental days to become a bedrock, a foundation, supporting much of American culture. How did it become so popular? One answer may be the Baby Boomers.

Baby Boomers were born between the late 1940s and the middle 1960s. They were born to parents who labored through The Great Depression and fought in World War II. These children learned they could be anything they aspired to be by parents looking ahead with optimism and energy. What kind of core values were instilled in the Baby Boomer generation? What historic events shaped their outlook and culture? How has the world changed since most Baby Boomers retired? In this essay, I will explore these as I put a critical eye on how the Baby Boomer generation shaped the success of and was embodied in Tom Petty and the Heartbreakers. In this essay, I will explore how the right talent, in the right time and the right place, created enduring music for generations.

Baby Boomer Attributes

What shaped the Baby Boomer generation? What significant values and traits do they possess that changed the world? The Baby Boomer cohort was the largest size birth group impacting the economy, society, workforce, culture and everything in between in the United States. They experienced a tremendous amount of change as they grew up during the golden age of television, watching Elvis, the Beatles, the Vietnam War, and contributed to significant changes in society, industry, and technology. They, as a generation, developed strong attributes in that they were adaptive, self-assured, ambitious, and questioned authority.

Thomas Earl Petty, born October 20, 1950, was the firstborn child to Earl and Kitty (Avery) Petty. Tom grew up in a volatile household with physical abuse from his father and little money to go around (Zanes 31). He described himself as a really weird kid. Engrossed in music to the point that it was strange. He found every opportunity he had to listen or learn about music. (*Tom Petty and the Heartbreakers: Runnin' Down a Dream*). Petty was enterprising and creative, soaking up as much music as he could. He would listen to music repeatedly. He worked with his peers to create bands from neighborhood kids, such as the Epics and the Sundowners. Later, after high school, Petty would go on to build the group Mudcrutch, the precursor band to Tom Petty and the Heartbreakers. Early on, he and his cohort adapted to available band talent and resources.

Moreover, Tom Petty adapted as he went through life. From moving between music groups in his youth, he adapted with the groups he was in— and the band members adapted to him. When Shelter Records was not willing to sign Mudcrutch to an album deal, rather just Tom as a solo artist, he adapted. Petty knew himself well enough that he did not want to be a solo artist; he wanted to be part of a band. Shortly after Mudcrutch broke up in Los Angeles, Petty was invited to a music session of Gainesville artists. Petty listened to the group and instinctively knew this was the group he should be working with—to work on the album deal Petty had already secured. In the documentary, *Runnin' Down a Dream*, Petty would later say of that moment, "I am sitting in the control room, listening to this band play.... I gotta steal this band ... (laugh) that was my first thought." Petty and this Baby Boomer cohort adapted to the situation and progressed to create Tom Petty and the Heartbreakers.

Raising a generation who was always told "you can do anything" certainly yields a society with self-assuredness. "The utopian promises of accessible education, social mobility, scientific progress, racial and gender equality, political rebellion, and technological innovation that accompanied the Baby Boomer life course, and spread beyond its location, created compelling expectations" (Katz 15). Tom Petty and the Heartbreakers were not immediately successful. This lack of immediate success might have been an indicator to others to pursue a different career and may have depleted any reserves of self-assuredness. This was not the case with Tom Petty and the Heartbreakers. Their first self-titled album resulted in little airtime and a top 40 single. In relentless pursuit of their dream, the Tom Petty and Heartbreakers toured in Europe, performing as an opening act and gaining overseas success. After this tour, they continued to struggle with U.S. success. While neither the first nor second albums resulted in commercial success and fame in the United States, the third album had determination. The band continued forward together. They worked with a different producer, Jimmy Iovine, and delivered the platinum album, *Damn the Torpedoes*. Although concerns with success were certainly consuming the minds of band members, their self-assuredness attributes from the Baby Boomer generation surely must have aided in the band's perseverance.

As the Baby Boomer cohort came of age, their ambition and goal-focused attributes strengthened. Ambition can be found amongst many young people, regardless of generation. However, with a like-minded group of talented friends with a strong leader, effects can be exponential. "'I think very few people are as ambitious as Tom Petty,' Mike Campbell says. 'He just has that drive, always did ... nobody's like Tom Petty'" (Zanes 80). To help realize the group's potential, Petty needed to convince the group to eliminate other pursuits and education, and instead to follow his vision. "He (Tom) got a lot of people to quit college so they could be in his band" (Jim Lenahan qtd. in Zanes 79). Petty's driving ambition pushed the group into moving forward, playing music full time.

Tom Petty's ambition continued throughout his life, sometimes to the disadvantage of others. After Ron Blair left the group in 1982, Tom needed a new bass player. Knowing the dynamics of the band changes whenever a new member joins, Tom Petty and the Heartbreakers were concerned about what the band would become. While helping Del Shannon, a friend in the music business, Petty met, listened to, and jammed with Del's bass player, Howie Epstein. Petty knew that Epstein's talent would greatly benefit Tom Petty and the Heartbreakers. After learning that Epstein was interested in joining the Heartbreakers, Petty informed Del Shannon that Epstein would be joining the Heartbreakers, amidst protests from Shannon. Both Petty's and Epstein's ambition created a rift between Petty's and Shannon's professional relationship and friendship.

Many of the Gainesville bands in the late 1960s and 1970s were independent of the older generation and questioned everything, including the status quo. "Trust no one over 30" was a well-known saying of the Baby Boomer cohort. Baby Boomers were not a group to lie down and let the older population tell them what to do. They became involved. They experimented. They made up new rules. After playing many places around Florida, the group Mudcrutch hosted a festival, outside of the traditional venues, much like Woodstock, out in the open air. To do so, they cleared out an area to host this free event where all were invited. They called it the "Mudcrutch Farm Festival" and advertised with a hand-drawn flyer and map (Tom Leaden Interview). Mudcrutch and their generation organized events their own way, independent of mainstream methods.

Independence is often considered a strength. Tom Petty and the Heartbreakers demonstrated this many times as a band. They chose to keep copyright to their songs—and battled with their record company to do so. The band also fought to keep album prices and concert tickets affordable for the fans. Not all musicians go to these efforts, and most musicians let the market and the music executives, machinery, and booking agents help determine prices. Tom Petty and the Heartbreakers stayed independent by owning their own copyright and keeping some control over some of the pricing of music and concerts.

Baby Boomers: Influences and Industry

How did this adaptive, independent, ambitious cohort experience the world? What influenced the Baby Boomers as they grew up in society? Understanding these questions offers insights into the world in which Tom Petty grew up. Rapid changes had been happening since the late 1940s. The Allies had defeated the Axis powers in World War II. Industries in America were rapidly expanding, and the Silent Generation with their Baby Boomer children were looking to the future with a positive outlook. Food, broadcasting, technology, and health science industries certainly influenced the Baby Boomers and their world.

Because of the increase in population after World War II, the food industry needed a mechanism for feeding this largest generation in recorded history. According to Lustig, author of "Processed Foods—An Experiment That Failed," "In 1965, Coca-Cola, Pepsico, Kraft, Unilever, General Mills, Nestle, Mars, Kellog, Proctor & Gamble and Johnson & Johnson hypothesized that processed food is better than real food" (212). While Lustig's words were cynical in context, the hypothesis-research idea of the food industry companies on consumers still rings true. Much of the food industry research and development growth was from post war progress. Baby Boomers, then were the research subjects for these new food-based creations. As more people worked outside the home, victory gardens and home canning declined while more food was processed in factories. Processed foods, corn syrup, and hydrogenated oils were developed, and the processed foods industry has grown ever since. Currently, the food industry grosses $1.46 trillion annually, of which 45%, or $657 billion, is gross profit. (Lustig 213).

The broadcasting industry influenced the Baby Boomers as well. According to industry author Phillip Ennis, "At war's end, the entire broadcasting industry—networks, individual stations, hardware manufacturing subsidiaries, and the full array of retail outlets—decided that the moment for the commercial exploitation of FM radio and television had come." Ennis further explains that ninety-five percent of households had a radio by 1949 (132). Young, impressionable children would learn so much from what they heard and saw. Industries could advertise food products, miracle pills, and other consumables to cure disease, discomfort or anything else that ailed a working society.

How things were broadcast also grew in technology and scope. Technology rapidly advanced—from radio to television, computing to the Internet to the smart phone. In the 1950s, the auto industry began automation, science introduced solar batteries, commercial power was introduced, and fiber optics were invented. In the next decade, Americans landed on the moon. Today, we can currently see and talk with a person's video image from the other side of the world—with a device that can fit in a pocket. Technology has significantly changed, and Baby Boomers grew up, developed and adapted with these rapid changes.

Healthcare has rapidly progressed since the late 1940s as well. In the 1950s, advancements such as the first heart-lung machine, first proposed structure of DNA unveiled, the reward center in the brain discovered, and the Salk polio vaccine used with the masses. Doctors performed the first successful kidney transplant. Now, scientists can design a drug to specifically target a person based on their DNA, and genetic disorders can be diagnosed in the womb. Baby Boomers have experienced rapid advances in health care and health care technology. For example, no longer did families have to be concerned about their children getting polio or purchasing an iron lung—a vaccine was created and readily used (some Baby Boomers still have the scar from the vaccine). Times were changing, and the Baby Boomers were growing up with this progress, just as swiftly.

This progress and these industries have a few things in common—plenty of post-war time and investment, a positive outlook for the future (after having just won World War II), and a growing work-force of cooperation to move the ideas and innovation forward. Many considered this time period "the threshold of the greatest forward movement with respect to food, health, and human progress in all history" (Wilson 215). The Silent Generation and the Baby Boomer Generation were chasing down the American Dream, which influenced how the Baby Boomers viewed and valued the world around them.

Baby Boomer Values

With Baby Boomer attributes fueling the beginning stages of the band and their world quickly advancing around them, Tom Petty and the Heartbreakers' values retained most of the band's structure throughout the years. A professional band is not a typical working environment; however, the members of Tom Petty and the Heartbreakers possessed certain work values, attitudes, and expectations which helped them continue their success. Hardwork, loyalty, and experience were just a few Baby Boomer fundamental values needed for success (Yu and Miller).

The industriousness of the band helped propel their career into epic proportions. Tom Petty and the Heartbreakers were successful when making music or touring. Over the course of a 40-year career, Tom Petty created three solo albums, thirteen studio albums with the Heartbreakers, three albums with the Traveling Wilburys, and two full albums with Mudcrutch. In addition, each member of Tom Petty and the Heartbreakers worked outside the group, collaborating and producing with countless other musicians. "We worked and we loved working," Petty said (*Tom Petty and the Heartbreakers*). At one point, earlier in this 40-year career, the band decided to produce the next album, *Southern Accents*, by themselves and on their own timetable. Unfortunately, it was less than focused. Frustration set in, and Tom broke his hand. "It was a joke. We couldn't police ourselves," said Petty; "It was hellish," said former drummer Stan Lynch (*Tom Petty and the Heartbreakers*). Things fell apart without direction and work to do. Once they utilized outside assistance to finish the album, the band was back touring. "As soon as we were back on the road again … everything was back to normal," said Petty (*Tom Petty and the Heartbreakers*). The group learned that they needed to keep propelling forward with their hard-working values.

In addition to hard-work ethics, loyalty to the band helped sustain a successful 40-year career. Along the way, some members, Ron Blair and Stan Lynch, left the band, and another, Howie Epstein, was lost to a drug overdose, a main core of the band remained in Mike Campbell, Benmont Tench, and Tom Petty. Even in the beginning, Petty was loyal to his bandmates and equally distributed the band's earnings. They were more than band members; they were friends—even family. "It's a story about a family, not tied by blood, but a shared sense of mission" (Zanes). In fact, when Tom's house was burned down by an arsonist, Tom was given perspective on life: "You realize how many friends you have … what they are worth, and how you can't burn that up" (*Tom Petty and the Heartbreakers*). When Petty went into deep depression from his marriage dissolving, fellow founding member Mike Campbell continued to write music for the group and others. "By that time, Campbell was well established as Petty's partner. He'd cowritten some of the best-loved

Heartbreakers songs ... however, [Campbell] had more to do than he'd done in the past.... Campbell was the one who remained accountable" (Zanes, 260–261). Even though Petty worked on solo albums and with other musicians, he and the Heartbreakers remained loyal to their group.

Petty and his friends' loyalties stayed strong throughout the years. Ron Blair rejoined Tom Petty and the Heartbreakers in 2002. First, Ron played for the Rock and Roll Hall of Fame induction ceremony, then stayed with the band for the summer tour, and eventually stayed with the band for subsequent albums and performances, following the death of Howie Epstein, who was Ron's original replacement back in 1982. Additionally, Mudcrutch reformed in 2007, after dissolving in 1975, bringing together some Tom Petty and the Heartbreakers members, as well as Tom Leadon and Randall Marsh of the original Mudcrutch. This rock and roll family stayed true to one another through the decades.

Although Baby Boomers questioned authority as an innate attribute, they valued experience. For Tom Petty and the Heartbreakers, they valued those that had music and performance experience. Early in his career, before the Heartbreakers band formed, Tom learned from practiced musicians through a connection with Leon Russell. Leon introduced Tom to experienced songwriters, musicians, and producers, such as Brian Wilson, George Harrison, Ringo Starr, Terry Melcher, Sly Stone, Jim Keltner, Al Kooper, and Emory Gordy (Zanes 98–100). Tom learned much from music sessions with these people, such as how studio music was created and produced, but he also learned from the performers and writers themselves. The connections formed and lessons learned from these skillful artists helped Tom gain an understanding of so many facets of the music industry. This understanding and valuing the experienced ultimately contributed to the success of Tom Petty and the Heartbreakers.

Right Time, Right Place: Leaders in a Cultural Shift

Even with the common Baby Boomers' values and work attributes, the music industry and society as a whole were changing quickly. Yet Tom Petty and the Heartbreakers survived as a band for over 40 years. The Beatles had broken up after 10 years. The 1980's continued to show huge economic growth in the U.S. MTV was opening a new genre—the music video. Tom Petty and the Heartbreakers capitalized on these changes. They contributed musically and made headlines throughout the industry.

Stylistically, Tom Petty and the Heartbreakers had a different sound than previous rock and roll bands as well as the current music trend. "We have a slogan: 'Don't bore us, get to the chorus,'" Mike Campbell said (*Tom Petty and the Heartbreakers*). Their music was uncomplicated, had distinctive progression, and with the birth of MTV, the band added memorable videos, creating a masterpiece of music and storytelling, generating a larger fan base, more concert tickets, and permeating American culture.

In creating the music video for "You Got Lucky," Tom worked with others to make a promo/intro to the video without any of the music from the song. It was a first of its kind, as no one had known of anyone else who had created something like that previously (*Tom Petty and the Heartbreakers*). In addition, the "Jammin' Me" music video from *Let Me Up (I've Had Enough)* utilized a green screen to mix visual effects both behind the band and between Petty's grabbing hands—certainly new to an audience in 1987 (Merry). Petty and the band adapted to the change in pop culture. Petty said, "And MTV—I could tell right away that was going to rule out anybody not clever enough to make a video and look good doing it. I adapted" (Fricke 65). Tom Petty and the Heartbreakers were trailblazers in music videos; they provided innovative visuals to the radio element

Tom Petty and the Heartbreakers also made headlines for being at odds with their record company early in their career. At the time of the first record deal, many artists were signing away their rights to their creative expression—their music. Many times the intellectual property owners were the music companies. Often, artists were so excited about making a deal, the details and their meaning was lost on the artist. So was the case for Tom Petty. Petty believed he was agreeing to song book production, not the copyright of the song (*Tom Petty and the Heartbreakers*). The band members were receiving a low royalty rate, which risked the financial viability and livelihood of the band. As such, Petty challenged his deal with the record company and reversed and changed some of the original deal. The news of this made headlines and many Baby Boomers of the day reveled in Tom Petty standing up to the music industry. This also paved the way for future musicians to consider their contracts before signing.

More news stories broke when Petty learned of a planned increase in the price of albums with the release of *Hard Promises*. Petty was upset over how the price increase took advantage of the fans and the success of *Damn the Torpedoes* to add more to the coffers of industry executives (*Tom Petty and the Heartbreakers*). Petty created a stir before their album came out, and the price of *Hard Promises* stayed the same. "'Certainly, I am glad I did it.... It really beat me up,' Petty says. 'My psyche suffered. And no other artist stepped up'" (Strauss 56). Although ultimately, the pricing of all music albums increased, the burden did not lie on the shoulders of Tom Petty and the Heartbreakers.

But the band did not just stand up to the music industry in the press. Tom Petty and the Heartbreakers created lyrics calling out the music industry itself. In *The Last DJ* album, the band calls attention to the music industry shaping what used to be a society listening to music for its sound and message to a sensationalist culture for the sake of celebrity. Although many concepts permeate throughout Tom Petty lyrics, *The Last DJ* focused on this dark side of the music industry, and how it manipulates the masses. Petty said, "'But the audience started to change—I saw people being fed shit and only too happy to eat it'" (Fricke 65). According to rumor, *The Last DJ* was even banned from being played on several radio stations. Still, Petty's message stayed consistent: "If they tried to offer my generation music by someone that won a gameshow, it would have been hysterical. It would have been laughed out of the room" (*Tom Petty and the Heartbreakers*). Petty, who had played with the likes of Bob Dylan, Jeff Lynne, Roy Orbison, and George Harrison, knew what music should be.

Baby Boomers' Significance Today

Baby Boomers continue to influence society today. This largest generation influences social norms, the economy, and the health care/pharmaceutical industries. This group continues to be high contributors in U.S. consumerism and seek remedies to continue fighting old age. Logic demands that an aging population will have higher needs for healthcare. It is no surprise, then, that Baby Boomer needs will continue to drive pharmaceutical company strategies, including shifts in drug discovery, development, and policy (Bender 31). The numbers in health care spending reflect the power of an aging Baby Boomer population as well. Health care has grown from 2% in 1965 to 17.9% in 2014 of gross domestic product and is estimated to reach 21% by 2020 (Lustig 2013).

Illicit and illegal drugs have also become less of a stigma because of Baby Boomers. As of now, 30 states, plus the District of Columbia, Guam, and Puerto Rico allow some form of medical or recreational marijuana use … and this number is anticipated to climb (National Conference of State Legislatures). This continues for more than just marijuana. "The prevalence of illicit drug use among older adults is expected to undergo a profound change as the Baby Boom generation ages" (Purvis 2). From 2003 to 2008, the percentage of the population 50+ has reported an increase in cocaine and hallucinogens, in addition to marijuana, and this number is expected to climb (Purvis).

Some would argue the Baby Boomers have left our society in worse shape than we were over 50 years ago. If they were taught to chase the "American Dream," then they certainly caught it. But, Stephen Brill, author of "How Baby Boomers Broke America," argues, after that "they were able to consolidate their winnings, outsmart and co-opt the forces that might have reined them in, and pull up the ladder so more could not share in their success or challenge their privacy." Brill goes on to say, "Our society is less stable than before and is less like a democracy and more of a 'meritocracy.'" The achievers of the American dream won—the others were left out in the cold, which is the great reason why we live in a divided America today (Brill). Yet we are not without hope. What we value is what can continue to unite us; valuing achievement through equality and community can balance out this instability.

And every generation has left its mark. "For Baby Boomers, a sense of individuality is a hallmark trait, one of the foundations for this generation, which prides itself on constantly doing things differently than the way they were done before" (Klie 34). One important distinctive characteristic of the Baby Boomers is their lifelong friendships. Even though Baby Boomers have fewer "friends" according to some social media standards, "*Facebook* networks of the old baby boomer cohort include a higher proportion of actual friends" (Blieszner 59; Chang 232). No social status or digital network hangups exist for this generation—social networks cannot replace a cohort of people growing up together, sharing one collective history and perspective through experience and relationships. Additionally, as if to punctuate Baby Boomer prominence and strength in friendships and oneness, a planned festival to honor Tom Petty, the Gathering in Gainesville, was planned over social media. This gathering was planned to celebrate what would have been Tom Petty's 68th birthday (Eveland).

Lasting Impact of Music

Music began flourishing for the masses during the Baby Boomers coming of age. They grew up watching and learning from Elvis and were teens to young adults when the Beatles broke in the United States. "They (Baby Boomers) created an American popular culture—particularly music—that swept the world and still dominates" (Kinsley 129). As a report investigating the decline of the traditional arts suggests, Baby Boomers defined themselves by popular music, separating from their elders with preference for the more traditional arts of classical music and ballet. Young Baby Boomers selected genres and, as they got older, appreciated the new sophistication and enhancements as the rock musicians refined their craft. Plus, by keeping to the rock genre, Baby Boomers were still separated and independent from their elders, continuing to support their anti-establishment and "trust no one over 30" slogan (Balfe 7).

The lasting impact of the Heartbreakers is partially credited to their creation of timeless, relatable music and lyrics. As Baby Boomers age, they "are they more likely to reveal their thoughts and feelings through word and deed" (Adams 70). Tom Petty and the Heartbreakers continually accomplished this throughout their career. There certainly is an art to writing lyrics where each person listening can relate as if it were her/his own story. Petty's songs emphasized dreaming about opportunities, time, relationships, determination, and optimism. Tom Petty and the Heartbreakers sustained their quality music to draw younger fans. Produce Jimmy Lovine said, "I think that he (Tom Petty) captures a side of America that is as relevant today as it was in 1978" (*Tom Petty and the Heartbreakers*). Indeed, Baby Boomers, GenXers, and Millennials attended Tom Petty and the Heartbreakers concerts together, where multiple generations of the same family enjoyed the collective experience.

As for the future, Tom Petty had said of music, "Music is probably the only real magic I have encountered in my life. There's not some trick involved with it. It's pure and it's real. It moves, it heals, it communicates and does all these incredible things" (McCormick). As multiple generations mourn the loss of Tom Petty, they continue to celebrate the music, this connectedness, with something greater. Future generations will find that Tom Petty and the Heartbreakers' music still holds that same mystical quality. "'...and you realize this music is going to be here a long time after I am gone. So I really want to put everything I can into it and make it as good as I can'" (Petty in Strauss 55). Tom knew; the music matters. As Rick Rubin said in Runnin' Down a Dream, "All the young songwriters tend to look up to Tom Petty. They feel the truth in what he's doing" (*Tom Petty and the Heartbreakers*). This truth continues to shine through and will continue to resonate with us, as human beings. This magic, this music, this truth all speak to us. And we listen.

Conclusion

Tom Petty and the Heartbreakers' influence spanned over four decades. Their success was due to many factors including extreme talent, dedication, societal influence, and their Baby Boomer qualities and values. As these Baby Boomers grew up, matured into adulthood, and experienced life, culture, and shifts in industries, they expressed the world around them lyrically and musically. These expressions reflect understandings in life that are truly universal.

And, as our concert ends, we understand we were transformed—into something pure, and magic, and real that can be shared with all.

Works Cited

Adams, Rebecca. "Baby Boomer Friendships." *Generations*, vol. 22, no. 1, 1998, pp. 70.
Balfe, Judith H and Rolf Meyersohn. "Arts Participation by the Baby Boomers." National

Endowment for the Arts, Washington, D.C. Report. February 1995. ERIC database, https://files.eric.ed.gov/fulltext/ED390726.pdf.

Bender, A. Douglas. "The Coming of the Baby Boomers: Implications for the Pharmaceutical Industry." *Generations: Journal of the American Society on Aging*, vol. 28, no. 4, 2004, pp. 26–31.

Blieszner, Rosemary and Aaron M. Ogletree. "We Get by with a Little Help from Our Friends: Aging Together in Tandem, and Meeting the Challenges of Older Age." *Generations: Journal of the American Society on Aging*, vol. 41, no. 2, 2017, pp. 55–62.

Brill, Stephen. "How Baby Boomers Broke America." *Time*, May 17, 2018, http://time.com/5280446/baby-boomer-generation-america-steve-brill/.

Chang, Pamara F., et al. "Age Differences in Online Social Networking: Extending Socioemotional Selectivity Theory to Social Network Sites." *Journal of Broadcasting & Electronic Media*, vol. 59, no. 2, 2015, pp. 221–239.

Ennis, Philip H. *The Seventh Stream: The Emergence of Rocknroll in American Popular Music.* Middletown, CT: Wesleyan, 1992.

Eveland, Keith, Keith Harben, and Melanie Barr. "The Gathering in Gainesville." https://www.facebook.com/groups/theGatheringinGainesville/.

Fricke, David. "It's Good to Be the King." *Rolling Stone—Tom Petty: The Ultimate Guide*, 2017.

Katz, Stephen. "Generation X: A Critical Sociological Perspective." *Generations: Journal of the American Society on Aging*, vol. 41, no. 3, 2017, pp. 12–19.

Kinsley, Michael E. *Old Age: A Beginner's Guide*, 2016. Internet resource.

Kirchheimer, Barbara. "A Baby Boomer Boom. Hospital Executives Are Pinning Growth on Consumer-Oriented Age Group." *Modern Healthcare* [serial on the Internet], vol. 31, no. 3, p. 28.

Klie, Leonard. "The Boomer Generation: Booming or Busting?" *CRM Magazine*, vol. 20, no. 2, 2016, pp. 32–36.

Lipschultz, J.H. "Organizing the Baby Boomer Construct: An Exploration of Marketing, Social Systems, and Culture." *Educational Gerontology*, vol. 33, no. 9, 2007, pp. 759–773.

Lustig, Robert H. "Processed Food—An Experiment That Failed." *JAMA Pediatrics*, vol. 171, no. 3, 2017, pp. 212–213.

McCormick, Neil. "Tom Petty: A Rock Star for the Ages." *The Telegraph*, 16 June 2012. https://www.telegraph.co.uk/culture/music/rockandpopfeatures/9334051/Tom-Petty-a-rock-star-for-the-ages.html.

Merry, Stephanie. "Tom Petty Made Amazing Music Videos. Here Are Nine of the Best." *Washington Post*, 3 October 2017, https://www.washingtonpost.com/news/arts-and-entertainment/wp/2017/10/03/tom-petty-made-amazing-music-videos-here-are-nine-of-the-best/?utm_term=.60edc6375272.

National Conference of State Legislatures. "State Medical Marijuana Laws." 27 April 2018. http://www.ncsl.org/research/health/state-medical-marijuana-laws.aspx.

Paulin, Geoffrey D. "Fun Facts About Millennials: Comparing Expenditure Patterns from the Latest Through the Greatest Generation." *Monthly Labor Review*, U.S. Bureau of Labor Statistics, March 2018, https://doi.org/10.21916/mlr.2018.9.

Petty, Tom. Interview by Jian Ghomeshi. Q, CBC Canada, 17 Jul. 2014, http://www.cbc.ca/player/play/2474274952.

Purvis, Leigh. "Prevalence of Illicit Drug Use in Older Adults: The Impact of the Baby Boom Generation." *PPI Insight on the Issues*, no. 41, 2010, pp. 1–7.

Strauss, Neil. "Last Dance." *Rolling Stone—Tom Petty: The Ultimate Guide*, 2017.

Tom Leadon Interview. "Tom Leadon: A Life in Music." Gainesville Rock History, http://www.gainesvillerockhistory.com/TLeadon.htm.

Tom Petty and the Heartbreakers: Runnin' Down a Dream. Directed by Peter Bogdanovich, Warner Brothers, 2007.

"Tom Petty: Behind the Music." #79 Season 1, Episode 79, 1999, 16 May 1999, http://www.vh1.com/episodes/b8lq2r/behind-the-music-tom-petty-behind-the-music-79-season-1-ep-079.

Wilson, M.L. "The Role of Libraries in War Food Education." *ALA Bulletin*, vol. 37, no. 7, 1943, pp. 211–216.

Yu, Hui-Chun and Peter Miller. "Leadership Style: The X Generation and Baby Boomers Compared in Different Cultural Contexts." *Leadership & Organization Development Journal*, vol. 26, no. 1, 2005, pp. 35–50.

Zanes, Warren. *Petty: The Biography*. New York: St. Martin's Press, 2015.

_____. "Tom Petty and the Heartbreakers: Runnin' Down a Dream." [Brochure] In: Petty, Tom, et al. *Tom Petty and the Heartbreakers: Runnin' Down a Dream*. Warner Bros. Records, 2008.

Pretty Woman, American Girl

*The Female in American
Popular Music, 1960–2000*

PAMELA P. O'SULLIVAN

Women have been the inspiration for songs from the earliest years—as lovers, cheaters, mothers, daughters, housewives, harridans, whores and holy women. With the explosion of American youth culture that began in the 1950's and manifested itself in the changing music scene, one might expect that the portrayal of women would change as well. However, in the majority of popular tunes that streamed out of the still relatively innocent 50's, into the freedom and rebelliousness of the 1960's, women were dealt with from pretty much the same perspective. A major exception to this generalization is the songwriting of Tom Petty, whose female protagonists were, in his spare yet eloquent phrasing, portrayed as individuals.

Popular music—meaning broadly, music that was written by and for a general audience—had been on a whirlwind journey since the early years of the 20th century; the ability to record sound for playback whenever one desired provided much of the fuel. Add to that more rapid transportation of both information and people, factor in the rapid changes in society and culture in general, and you have a solid basis for the rapidly evolving musical scene. By the 1940's, youth culture was beginning to come into its own, and the following decades only cemented and aided the growth of that culture. Popular music as a phenomenon is generally agreed to have originated in the 1950's, as youth-oriented singers and groups produced recordings and travelled the country playing to large audiences. It was a fusion of forms and cultures, "race" music like rhythm and blues, as well as jazz, bluegrass, gospel and folk.

Thematically, popular music covered a wide range as well, but songs about love and its object, either men singing about women or women about men, made up a large portion of the recordings. As in other areas of culture, women in song were often seen in the stereotypical roles mentioned above. Youth and beauty were celebrated. Women were the problem and the answer to the problem. They were to be taken care of, sometimes played with or cheated on, expected to often to forgive and forget, or wait patiently at home. They could be cruel and fickle, despite the pleadings of singers like Elvis Presley. They could be angelic, as in "Teen Angel," first recorded by Mark Dinning in 1959 (IMDB).

American life changed significantly after World War II. During the war, women had held the home front, many of them working factory jobs that previously were the province men. Many women were not content to be relegated again to the more confining role of housewife.

It was also a period of relative prosperity in the United States, as the privations of the Great Depression and the strict rationing of wartime faded into the past. An entirely new lifestyle was taking shape, not in the cities this time, but in neighborhoods and housing developments just outside those cities—the suburbs. Suburban life was idealized by the builders and planners behind it. Contemporary ranch homes, clean, bright and filled with all the latest time-saving devices from electric stoves to capacious refrigerators; a bedroom and closet for each person. Wide, green expanses of lawn, backyard pools and patios; it was all made possible by another contemporary phenomenon, the American love affair with the automobile. Even the popular colors for decorating were optimistic, from pale aqua and mint green to pink. One can still find original pink bathrooms in older suburban homes that have not been updated.

In addition, and not surprisingly, this time period also produced a large uptick in the number of births nationwide, nicknamed "the baby boom" by a number of authors and sociologists. Both the telephone and television shaped the way people communicated and thought. Radio, which through the 1940's and into the 1950's, provided a wide variety of non-music programming, found its dramas and comedies usurped by the magic screen. As the decade wore on, more stations changed to a youth-driven format of popular music.

Even as the American people bought in to this utopian vision, other social and political factors were in play. The Cold War, the Korean Conflict, "witch hunts" of varying kinds—against comic books, for one, and the phenomenon of McCarthyism contributed to a more conservative general outlook for many. Fear of the spread of Communism and of nuclear war were fed not only by news reports but by films such as *The Day the Earth Stood Still*, which warned of a dire fate for humanity should they not learn to forego violence and war. Every area of science seemed to be a competition between the United States and Russia, even extending beyond the confines of this planet in the race to outer space.

Sexual standards were outwardly very restrictive; in this area, as in so many others, there was an obvious double standard. Girls who were perceived, correctly or not, as being promiscuous were social pariahs, whereas boys who made their "conquests" were seen as more manly. Pregnancy outside of marriage was still a major taboo, often resulting in a young girl taking an extended trip so that the pregnancy and birth could be concealed, the child being given up for adoption. Yet, male recording artists could sing of passion and longing, even to demanding that the love interest give in, as Elvis did in "It's Now or Never."

At the dawn of the 1960's, the country was poised at an unimagined gate which would shake up social and political culture to an unforeseen degree. A convenient placeholder for the point of change is the assassination of President John F. Kennedy in 1963. In many ways, his ascension to the White House was the pinnacle of 1950's American culture, an idealized vision perceived in the description of his presidency as "Camelot." The changes were already underway, however—the *Kinsey Report*, first published in 1948 and the availability beginning in 1960 of a reliable oral contraceptive for women, coupled with an increased awareness by young women of their own worth, started the "sexual revolution." Young people also were increasingly concerned about the direction that the government was taking and started to protest and demand change. By the mid–1960's, the country had also come under the influence of the British invasion, led by the Beatles. This affected not only music but fashion; as boys' hair became longer, girls' skirts became shorter.

Music during this time period was changing rapidly. Many genres and styles, from the synchronized dancing and harmonies of groups like the Ames Brothers or girl groups like the Andrews Sisters, gave way to a variety of musical styles that became rock and roll.

Some things, however, remained the same, including the female role in song. Ricky Nelson's "Travelling Man" had a girl in every port, while The Supremes begged "Stop In the Name of Love." This era in music also continued a trend from the 1940's, the "Heartthrob," a male singer who caused the girls to swoon—Bobby Rydell, Fabian, Ricky Nelson and, of course, Elvis to name just a few.

In addition to swoon-worthy vocalists, there were many popular singing groups, quite often consisting of four singers. A number of those who rose to fame were female groups—The Supremes, The Shirelles, The Angels, The Andrews Sisters. Like the male singing groups of the period, they often relied on tight harmonies and synchronized dance moves. However, as the 1960's dawned, a different kind of group was gaining in numbers and popularity. The biggest difference was that the members played their own instruments in addition to singing.

Although they did not hit the shores of the United States until 1964, the Beatles embodied this musical style—guitars, bass, drums, and singing. American groups like the Beach Boys and Paul Revere and the Raiders helped to set the pace on this side of the Atlantic.

Returning briefly to girl groups, they remained a staple through the 1960's, although for the most part they relied on back-up instrumentalists. Some of them spawned highly-successful lead singers, like Diana Ross. Their styles and songs were unique to each group, and they tackled hard topics such as unwanted pregnancy, the "double standard," abuse and abandonment, but for the most part, they stuck very close to the stereotypical female role. For example, when The Angels sang "My Boyfriend's Back," it's clear that the narrator needed male intervention to restore her "reputation."

The Exciters' recording of "He's Got the Power" may initially sound romantic, but listening more closely to the lyrics suggests that the power is physical—and abusive. The Lovelites, in their track "How Can I Tell My Mom and Dad" tackle a topic that was still timely in the mid–1980's, when Madonna released "Papa Don't Preach." The anguish of an unexpected pregnancy, made more difficult by the disappearance of the boy in question in the first song, perfectly captures the double standard mentioned above,

Tom Petty grew up in the midst of all of this, a child who, by his own admission, did not quite fit in, at least the way his father wanted him to do so. His mother, on the other hand, was supportive, as he states in the biography by Warren Zanes. Of course, Petty's family also did not fit the ideal of the 1950's/early 1960's portrayed by June, Ward, Wally, and Beaver Cleaver. A meeting with Elvis Presley, and the experience of seeing the Beatles on the Ed Sullivan Show, cemented Petty's determination to use music as a way out of Florida (Zanes).

The first album released by Tom and the Heartbreakers included the song that, for many, is one of the defining songs of his career as well as a perfect encapsulation of both his songwriting skill and his capacity to treat women as fully realized people rather than one-dimensional stereotypes. From the first notes floating out from the subtle hiss of needle against vinyl, "American Girl" became instantly recognizable—the introductory guitar chords lent a sense that something good was coming, and the song did not disappoint. It was, in two spare verses, a complete story.

Other songwriters had written about a woman—think of Van Morrison's brown-eyed girl, or the Beach Boys "California Girls," or Roy Orbison's "Oh Pretty Woman." "American Girl" was storytelling stripped down to the bare bones, and it sounds as fresh today as when it was first released in 1976. I think it no coincidence that when released as a single, the B side of the single was "The Wild One, Forever"—a more intimate story of a one night stand that profoundly affected the narrator for the rest of his life.

"American Girl" strikes every chord dead on, from the promises and high expectations of American youth in general, to the iconic aural note linking the flow of traffic on the highway to the sound of waves against the shore and the pain of broken promises. Then it slides easily into that chorus so deceptively simple and yet so intimate. Slow it down. Take some time. Is he talking about the story, or something else?

It was also highly relatable. Everyone knew—or was—an American Girl. She was the girl next door, but without all the trappings of fresh-faced innocence. She was the American Dream personified, but devoid of physical description. She was Every American Girl, on a quest that only she could understand, but as we listened to the song, we knew what she was looking for as well.

Fans want to read meaning into song lyrics when they can, and "American Girl" got the full fan treatment. The song was linked to the supposed suicide of a co-ed at the University of Florida in Petty's hometown of Gainesville. Petty debunked that theory quite firmly in *Conversations with Tom Petty*, released in 2005 (Zollo).

In looking at Tom Petty's overall portrayal of women in his songwriting, an aspect that is immediately discernible is his respect for women. Even when the narrator loses in the game of love, he does not speak disrespectfully of the woman involved. When ones looks at the lyrics to "Even the Losers," the narrator is aware that he made some impression on the object of the song. The irony is apparent if you assume the narrator and songwriter to be the same person; the outcome might have been different if she had an inkling of who he would become.

There are many popular songs that talk about the outsider, the bad boy, the boy from the wrong side of the tracks, but it is more common that the family objects to the romance. From Firefall's "Wrong Side of Town" to Billy Joe Royal's "Down in the Boondocks," to the Beach Boys' more youthful yearnings in "Wouldn't It Be Nice," differences in social or economic status, or the wish to be old enough to be together like adults, resonate with many listeners. Tom Petty's music, however, started from a more mature point of view, with songs like "She's a Woman in Love (It's Not Me)."

After Petty's untimely death in 2017, Scott Mervis wrote a tribute in the Pittsburgh Post-Gazette. In it, he quotes former DJ Steve Hansen as saying that, in a landscape flooded with "sappy love ballads," a la Fleetwood Mac, Petty's lyrics were straightforwardly about sex (Mervis).

While I do not entirely agree with that assessment, it does contribute to the point that Tom Petty's economy of words was in contrast to most other groups out there at the time. If one looks at classics from the previous decade, such as the Beatles' "She Loves You (Yeah, Yeah, Yeah)," or "I Want to Hold Your Hand," Petty's songs from the first Heartbreakers' album forwardly demonstrate a realistic sensibility, closer to Meatloaf's "You Took the Words Right Out of My Mouth" or Alice Cooper's "You and Me."

The second album from Tom Petty and the Heartbreakers, *You're Gonna Get It*, contained several cuts that clearly show Tom's treatment of women is often more mature and more subtle than other songwriters. The song "Hurt" is very straightforward, but without begging for another chance or putting down the woman for what she did. "Listen To Her Heart" is an unabashed declaration that the woman he loves will not be swayed by outside influences. The opening line sums up perfectly the kind of thing that could influence a more shallow woman; had Petty bowed to pressure to replace the word cocaine with champagne, the song would have lost a great deal of its impact. He is confident in the relationship, confident of the strength of the woman's faithfulness.

The third album, *Damn the Torpedoes*, was released in 1979. It includes an unabashedly romantic song that is quite different in style from any Petty had done previously. "Here Comes My Girl" celebrates the incredible confidence and support of a loving relationship. It's tempting to look at songs such as the one mentioned above and try to relate it to the songwriter's life at the time. Tom generally did not talk about his songs in those terms. He was, in many ways, a very private person, and did his best to keep his family life out of the limelight. Nevertheless, the song adds to the overall development of female characters in Petty's lyrics.

The fourth album, *Hard Promises*, demonstrates an ongoing consistency in the way he treats women and relationships in song. "The Waiting" became an often-played hit, capturing perfectly the initial, heart-pounding, yearning stage of falling in love. At the opposite end of the spectrum is "A Woman in Love (It's Not Me)." In this cut, while the narrator laments the woman he loves giving her heart to another, less worthy man; the narrator recognizes that he cannot do anything to prevent her eventual heartache, but also, at the end, admits that he never could figure out what she wanted. This stands in stark contrast to songs like R.B. Greaves' "Take a Letter, Maria" or even The Eagles' "Lying Eyes."

However, the last song on that album, which received little or no air play, "You Can Still Change Your Mind," is a lovely ballad that showcases Petty's talent with lyrics. It is a strong yet subtle plea to his woman to hold on for a little longer for things to be all right, that she has it within her power to overcome whatever negative or difficult circumstances they are facing. Songs like this one have an intimate feel to them, a little like a lullaby comforting and calming, and clearly indicate agency for women in Petty's lyrics.

About a year later, the band released their fifth album, *Long After Dark*. One of the big hits from that album is "You Got Lucky." This song takes a slightly defiant tone as the narrator tells a woman that she was lucky that he chose her, and it will be her loss of she decides to leave. However, despite the tone, the singer never resorts to any down and dirty blame; he does not, for example, tell her as Bon Jovi does, "You Give Love a Bad Name."

Southern Accents, released in 1985, contains fewer songs about women and relationships. "Don't Come Around Here No More," which is recognizable to the MTV generation due to its hallucination-themed video with its "Alice In Wonderland" theme, is more of an anti-love song directed at someone acting like a stalker. However, the closing track on side 2 is another testament to Petty's ability to wish an ex-lover well, years after a break-up.

It is quite evident, looking back over the first decade of Petty's albums with The Heartbreakers, Tom's respect for women, his ability to see them as fully realized humans rather than stereotypes, stayed consistent. It is a remarkably mature view for someone relatively young in the music business, especially when one takes into account the entire popular music scene of the late 60's to early 80's. Despite the growth of the Feminist Movement and the rise of many powerful female singers, from Helen Reddy to Cher, Madonna, or Whitney Houston, many lyrics still portrayed women as sexual objects. Unlike songs from the 1950's and early 1960's, which employed euphemism and romantic lyrics along the lines of Elvis's "Love Me Tender," groups like Guns N' Roses took songs like "You Could Be Mine" to a more explicit level, which conflates love with abuse.

Let Me Up (I've Had Enough) released in 1987 featured a larger proportion of songs co-written by Petty and Mike Campbell. The album also has an overall feeling of disillusion and the ending of relationships. "Runaway Trains," "The Damage You've Done," and the title track all have this same vibe to them. However, one track stands out to me: "It'll All Work Out" is another one of those lullabye-type quiet ballad, but this time, the narrator laments his failure to carry out his obligation in the relationship. The title is a phrase more of resignation than of hope.

By 1991, Tom's personal life was in shambles, but *Into the Great Wide Open* showed little indication of that. One cut on the album, slightly reminiscent in its sparse writing, is "Too Good To Be True"; the object of the song, a woman who seems to have attained her dreams, leaves the narrator in the end realizing that whatever "it" was, was too good to be true. "All the Wrong Reasons" tells of a woman who, when things go wrong, determines that she wants to have it all, but nothing works out. In this song, there is no blame assigned, merely the refrain that lives went wrong due to mutual misunderstanding and bad luck. Despite a different theme and entirely different sound, the song hearkens back to "American Girl." "Built To Last" is a hopeful and ultimately positive song. In it, the singer talks about a love that was built to last despite a rapidly changing world as well as changes in the dynamics of the relationship. However, just as the listener thinks that the relationship will end, the narrator doubles back to the idea that the relationship was built to last and he is not walking away. Rather, he acknowledges how his changes have affected her, and that they will work it out together.

Echo, released in 1999, contains another of Petty's gems about a woman finding herself and getting out of an abusive relationship. "Free Girl Now" has a catchy, toe-tapping rhythm to it, but more pertinently, details the same sort of struggle that Petty portrayed in a number of other songs. The woman has had a tough time of it, but she is walking away and reclaiming her life. It is easy to picture her walking with another woman who had taken too much, and declared that "These Boots Are Made For Walking," as Nancy Sinatra proclaimed in 1966. Many anthems to finding one's freedom were released by female artists—Gloria Gaynor's mid–1970's recording of "I Will Survive" or "Survivor" by Destiny's Child. Petty's sensitivity to the way women feel and react remained through his recording career and made it possible for a male author to release an anthem of freedom for women.

In 2002, *The Last DJ* was released with the track "You and Me." Like other Petty love songs, the lyrics were straightforward. Petty, as a narrator, never promised impossible things, but, in this song, he was particularly straightforward—you, me, the road ahead. However, like many of his other songs, much more is implied in the simple lyrics—faithfulness, companionship, all the things that make for a good relationship. All of that comes through in the music and in the way he sings. Again, as he did in "American Girl," he encapsulates an entire story in a few simple verses.

In addition to his albums with the Heartbreakers, Petty released four solo albums (although all of them included some back-up from various members of The Heartbreakers). *Full Moon Fever*, released in 1989, included the song "Love Is a Long Road." Once again, his spare writing style tells a full story about the difficulties inherent in trying to maintain a relationship when living a musician' lifestyle. The album also includes another one of his lullabye songs, "Alright For Now," as song deceptively simple in its lyrics. In it, the narrator appears to be addressing his lover who is going to bed as he is leaving for work. It is a song of thankfulness; the story it tells is of his gratitude to her for the support through difficult times. It also implies that there may have been some difficulties between them recently, so he is reassuring her that everything is okay.

Petty's 1994 *Wildflowers* was, according to Petty, the divorce album (Zanes). The title track, "Wildflowers," again showcases the lean yet highly evocative style that worked so well for him; there were never any extraneous words in his writings. Like many of his other love songs, this gives the woman permission to be herself, and although he does say she belongs with him, he neither requires nor compels her choice.

The third solo album, *Highway Companion*, was released in 2006. "Damaged By Love" was another in Petty's lyrical stories about women who have passed through hard times; in this case, she came out rather the worse for the experience. And, true to form, the lyrics tell a story deeper and more complex than the words would suggest. The listener, hearing Petty's light voice and the easy rhythm of the song, can nevertheless understand all that is unsaid—how much this woman means to the songwriter, but she does not realize how deeply he loves her. Is he the cause of the damage, or was she hurt by past love in her young life?

In 1993, Petty and the Heartbreakers released a "Greatest Hits" album, which, contrary to the traditional concept of such a compilation, contained a new song. "Last Dance With Mary Jane" was another of Tom's story-songs, although this time telling the story of both Mary Jane and the narrator. For many listeners, the song is inextricably bound up with the rather eccentric video, featuring Tom as an undertaker's assistant and Kim Basinger played the corpse. However, leaving the video behind and concentrating on the story, it is both a coming of age scenario and a paean to world-weariness. Mary Jane is moving forward as she moves on, but the narrator knows he is stuck in a rut and needs something to pull himself out, yet he keeps returning to his last dance with Mary Jane.

Playback, a six-disc compilation released in 1995, included the track "God's Gift to Man." This cut tells the story of a man who gets in over his head with the woman of the title. During the song, the viewpoint changes from third person to first person, which can leave the listener wondering how many characters there are in this story. It is possible that the narrator knows the story so well because he fell into the same situation as the navy man, and was taken in and discarded in the same way. The title character does not fare as well as other women in Petty's stories, though, and in a rare moment of bitterness, the narrator states she has a heart black as coal and will eventually get her comeuppance—though he implies she will not understand why.

Mudcrutch, a band that Petty originally formed in Gainesville in the early 1970's, was reformed and recorded two albums. One of the songs, "Oh Maria," is a bit of a departure from Petty's usual writing about women; it's about a particular woman at a particular place and time. However, in his usual style, the lyrics are lean and tight, as the narrator laments that he cannot take her out of her life of prostitution and give her all she deserves.

The second album, released in 2016, included a relatively light-hearted sounding track entitled "Trailer." It was very much in Petty's vein of short musical stories. The narrator bought a trailer for his sweetheart and himself, and he gave up other dreams to stay with her there; of course, she ultimately left him. This could sound like a bitter, self-pitying complaint, but Petty keeps the story relatively light—one can almost see his shoulders shrugging and a self-deprecating smile as he sings it. As with other songs he wrote, Petty does not lay blame on the woman; his lyrics imply that is just the way it is.

Tom Petty's unique style and vision permeated both his songwriting and his personal life. Despite a harsh and abusive father, he managed to grow up with an amazing sense of the way women felt and thought. Petty noted that he grew up surrounded by women that he respected, and, perhaps, this influenced the respect for women that he shows in his music. While he brought a unique flavor to each of the albums he recorded, both solo and with two bands, the Heartbreakers and Mudcrutch, his treatment of women remained consistent. He was able to make the point he wanted to make without resorting to crudeness or disrespect. He did not apply a double standard to women, and his songs are full of powerful female characters with clear agency.

The stories Petty told of American women resonated with listeners. "American Girl" became an anthem; during the 40th anniversary tour, images of American women of all races and ethnicities, all walks of life and religion, surged across the large-screen display behind the band. Petty knew what the song had come to mean for his audience, and he embraced it. He made certain that everyone knew who the American Girl was—she was all of us, all across the country. Petty celebrated women and womanhood in his music, capturing the strength and fragility, the toughness, the ability to go on under any conditions, that many of us have faced. Moreover, he did not just sing about it. Though he was a very private person, most of what we know about him indicates that he treated women in life as he did in song. He was not perfect, of course, but his actions are for the most part those of a man who has great respect for everyone around him, female and male. Overall, he left a legacy of amazing, universal images of womanhood that will continue to resonate with listeners for a long time to come.

WORKS CITED

IMDb. Mark Dinning. Retrieved March 31, 2018. IMDb.com.
Mervis, Scott. "Tom Petty Let the Songs Do Most of the Talking." *Pittsburgh Post-Express*, October 3, 2017.
Zanes, Warren. *Petty: The Biography*. New York: Henry Holt and Co., 2015, Kindle edition.
Zollo, Paul. *Conversations with Tom Petty*. London: Omnibus Press, 2012, Kindle edition.

Rebels, Refugees
and American Girls

A Study of Tom Petty's Political Mojo

ALESSANDRA CLAYTON TRINDLE

The year 2015 was a seemingly quiet year in American politics. President Obama was finishing out his second term; there were no major elections being held; we were at war with the same countries that we had been at war with for over a decade. We had marriage equality; we had expanded health care coverage for some; the stock market was going strong, and the economy had bounced back from the disastrous dip in 2008–2009.

However, beneath this surface of calm was a roiling storm that was at least 150 years in the making. Starting in 2014 when Mike Brown, Jr.'s body had been left to bake on the hot asphalt of Ferguson, Missouri after being shot and killed by Ferguson police officer Darren Wilson, a movement started called Black Lives Matter. Activists and protesters flooded into Ferguson and immediately began demanding answers, and the state pushed back by refusing to accept their right to hold a peaceful vigil and request accountability from law enforcement. What ensued was extreme civil unrest, but unlike in years past, the movement did not stall with that one event. It grew. With each person killed by police, the chants grew stronger and louder: "Black Lives Matter!" By 2015, Black Lives Matter had a national organization, multiple branches throughout the country, and the full attention of the world.

Halfway through 2015, an event occurred that was breathtaking in both its audacity and its simplicity. A young activist, Bree Newsome, climbed the flagpole of the South Carolina statehouse on June 27th and removed the Confederate flag, resulting in her immediate arrest and then eventual permanent removal of the flag on July 10, 2015.

It's therefore not a surprise that during a Rolling Stone interview after Ms. Newsome's act of courage, Tom Petty was asked about how The Heart-breakers had flown a Confederate flag during their *Southern Accents* tour to illustrate the character in the song "Rebels." Even though the interview is written, readers can almost *hear* the sincere regret in Petty's voice as he explained the decision to use the flag for the 1982 tour and the moment during the tour when he stopped the concert and told fans, to both boos and cheers from the crowd, that he and The Heartbreakers were not about the Confederate Flag and what it symbolized to so many. Calling his decision to use the flag "downright stupid," Petty discussed the casual meaning of the flag to a Florida native such as himself, but then he went on to explain:

"If you think a bit longer, there's bad connotations to this. They might have it at the football game or whatever, but they also have it at Klan rallies. If that's part of it in any way, it doesn't belong, in any way, representing the United States of America." He added emphatically, "Again, people just need to think about how it looks to a black person. It's just awful. It's like how a swastika looks to a Jewish person. It just shouldn't be on flagpoles" [Greene].

Those statements alone could have been the end of the topic, but then Petty continued to expound on his theme in a way fans would not expect from a millionaire rock star grandpa from Malibu, California. Tying the Confederate flag into a greater discussion about police brutality and the prison-industrial complex, Petty lamented:

"Beyond the flag issue, we're living in a time that I never thought we'd see. The way we're losing black men and citizens in general is horrific. What's going on in society is unforgivable. As a country, we should be more concerned with why the police are getting away with targeting black men and killing them for no reason. That's a bigger issue than the flag. Years from now, people will look back on today and say, 'You mean we privatized the prisons so there's no profit unless the prison is full?' You'd think someone in kindergarten could figure out how stupid that is. We're creating so many of our own problems" [Greene].

The proverbial mic drop was this last quote at the end of the interview. Petty's celebrated ability to cut to the essence of any issue was demonstrated by his ability to tie together historical events and bring them into present relevance. It is rare for a star of Petty's stature to admit that he had made a mistake. It is especially rare for someone who had grappled with fame for four decades to use an example of a thirty-year-old mistake as a way to frame current events. What Bree Newsome did by removing the Confederate Flag from the Capitol Building in South Carolina had nothing to do with Petty, and yet he saw her actions on a continuum of American history and even compared the oppression of the Confederacy to Nazi Germany while bringing everything back to present day America. In this interview, Petty showed a clear political evolution and a better grasp of history than many Americans. The question we must ask is, "How did he arrive at this awareness of the complexity of structural power in the United States?"

Much has been written about the tumultuous nature of Tom Petty's childhood in Gainesville, Florida. Born into the Baby Boom generation in 1950, he was the eldest child of Earl and Kitty Petty, who had his younger brother, Bruce, a few years later. During a time when America prided itself on its easy stability and conventionality, the Petty family showed the cracks in the façade. The household was chaotic due to Earl's abuse of his wife and sons, but instead of bending to his father's will, Petty found ways to rebel. Kitty Petty loved music and shared that love with her sons. Tom quickly discovered that he had a knack for playing the guitar and memorizing songs, which initially made his sports-loving father disappointed until he discovered that his son was talented. What did drive his father bonkers was when Petty let his hair grow long when he was about thirteen or fourteen. This was around 1964, and long hair had not yet become de rigueur, especially in a quiet, conservative college town in Florida. In Paul Zollo's book, *Conversations with Tom Petty*, Petty recalls that time, saying, "My dad and I fought all the time. About having long hair and about dressing the way I did. It looked really bizarre. It looked really freaky, in that time period. This was before the hippies" (Zollo 20).

Recounting the verbal and physical fights he and his father got into over his appearance, in addition to getting in trouble in school and not being served in restaurants, Petty gives us a sense of his core inner strength, determination, and sheer stubbornness. Anti-authoritarianism was the style of the times, but Petty clearly was not mimicking others for attention. One can believe that he wrote and sang a song like "I Won't Back Down" with conviction because from a very young age his actions were entirely his own. Adding in the long haired punk named Spike, who walks into a Gainesville biker bar and lives to tell the tale in fan favorite "Spike," and the drunken bad boy in "Rebels" whose woman kicks him out of the car in disgust, Petty's affinity for outcasts is apparent in many of his songs.

It was not only his long hair and style of dress that had Petty thumbing his nose at the establishment. Later, in 1981, when his career was going strong and he and the Heartbreakers were a popular act, his record label, MCA, attempted to draft off of his music sales by raising the price of his fourth album, *Hard Promises*, to $9.98. Petty was having none of it. Album prices had been $8.98, and Petty felt very strongly that he and the Heartbreakers owed their fans affordable prices for their music. Speaking to Paul Zollo about the situation and his insistence not to raise the album price, Petty said:

> "That was quite a struggle. That caused me a lot of pain. Because I didn't have a line of artists backing me up. It seems to me today that maybe if they had listened to me then, things wouldn't be as bad as they became. I could see then that you couldn't

price this music out of the reach of the common person. That's who your audience is" [Zollo 72].

Petty won his fight with MCA, and album prices remained at $8.98. *Rolling Stone* put him on the cover [March 19, 1981] tearing a dollar in half, which prompted Mick Jagger to let slip that Petty's refusal to raise prices forced The Rolling Stones to also keep their album prices at $8.98 as well. Petty was obviously pleased that his stance had been effective, telling Zollo, "I was proud that I pulled it off" (73.)

What makes Petty's stance about album pricing particularly surprising is that it had come on the heels of a lawsuit he had entered into with his record label, when the distribution of Shelter's records changed from ABC Records to MCA Records. In 1979, Shelter Records was sold back to MCA Records, and Petty was furious at the way the deal was handled. He and The Heartbreakers felt their previous contract was unfair and because their contract with Shelter had a clause that allowed them to void the contract if Shelter was sold to another company without their approval, Petty was able to sue in order to win back publishing rights and a better deal going forward. MCA Records did not take him seriously at first, so Petty put in a half-million dollars of his own money to produce the third album for the band, and then declared bankruptcy. By doing that, all contracts were effectively void. He and MCA Records came to an accord, allowing Petty to stay under the banner of Backstreet Records where Petty would have complete creative control.

The fact that Petty valued his songs and creative content enough to potentially blow up his entire career is telling. Petty was savvy enough to realize that a band with a popular following and successful albums behind them had more leverage than the record companies wanted to admit. His desire for creative control was about more than money, however. His songs were clearly more than just vehicles to success for him when he discussed his legal and financial machinations with Zollo and said, "My songs had really been taking away from me when I didn't even know what publishing was." (71) That is the lament of a parent whose children are no longer part of the family and readers can feel the palpable hurt in his words.

Fortunately for us all, Petty prevailed. His song "Century City" was born from the frustration he felt in having to spend time in glass skyscrapers, wrangling with lawyers, when he could have been in the studio creating. His disdain for the interests of the establishment and corporations is evident in the album, *The Last DJ*. Released in 2002, it held no love for the music industry. In the eponymous song, Petty laments the one disc jockey remaining whose refusal to kowtow to what the corporate brass wants to hear on the radio puts his career in jeopardy. The kicker is that there is not another person waiting in the wings to slide into the last DJ's on-air spot; it's a computer program. Petty is clearly pointing out that what makes art great is the human connection. The following song on the album, "Money Becomes King," does not let up in excoriating the excesses of late-stage capitalism. In "Joe," Petty's narrator pounds out the perspective of a record company CEO in the most blunt and brutal of terms. The listener is left with the conflicting knowledge that Joe loves himself as much as Petty hates him. Many artists have battled with their producers; that's baked into the tension between expression and commerce. With Petty, however, the listener gets the sense that he is mourning the loss of the artist as the driving force in the artistic process. In the age of American Idol and The Voice, camera-friendly singers stand at the ready to climb the charts with already-generated songs that sound just different enough to be considered "new" yet do nothing to push the bounds of already prevailing expectations. In *The Last DJ*, Petty's lamentation is for all of us for failing to know more, demand more, and seek more. We accept the commercial mush we are spoon-fed and think we are on the cutting edge.

While Petty could play rough with corporations, he was often gentle with other musicians. Some recording artists take any possible charge of plagiarism seriously, filing lawsuits with only the slightest of provocation. Tom Petty reacted differently. In many cases, he did nothing except acknowledge the theft with a laugh, as was what happened when the Red Hot Chili Peppers riffed off of "Mary Jane's Last Dance" with their song, "Dani California" or when The Strokes admitted that they had been inspired by Petty's iconic "American Girl" when writing "Last Nite." In fact, in a *Rolling Stone* interview June 28, 2006, when Petty was questioned about The Strokes by interviewer, Andy Greene, he said, "I saw an interview with them where they actually admitted it. That made me laugh out loud. I was like, 'OK, good for you.' It doesn't bother me." This generosity was based in part on his knowledge of the creative process and his own respect for the artists, who influenced him, such as The Beatles and The Byrds. The sense that artists collaborate and build off of each other is a large part of the Petty ethos. In fact, Petty was so obviously not upset by The Strokes' use of "American Girl" that he allowed them on his tour for a few dates in 2006. Throughout his career, Petty showed a deep appreciation for the work of others, and it appears he was generally flattered by those who mimicked him.

However, he was also quick to preserve his rights when he felt the infringing artist had gone too far, as was the case with Sam Smith's "Stay With Me" which mirrors Petty's "I Won't Back Down" in the chorus. While Smith had claimed that he had never heard "I Won't Back Down" before, it was impossible for him to deny the similarities between the two songs. The two artists came to an amicable agreement in October of 2014 that was publicly announced in January of 2015, giving Tom Petty a writer's credit for "Stay With Me."

Petty's ability to collaborate went far beyond his reactions to other artists borrowing his work. Talking about his song-writing process with Paul Zollo, he discussed how Mike Campbell would bring him tapes with just music. Petty would listen and see if he could fashion lyrics and turn Campbell's work into a song. The tapes would be totally instrumental, and according to Petty, he would "just start cold. If something's there that I get a feel for, it starts to happen" (98). The process for the two of them was for Campbell to pass him tapes with a plethora of work, and for Petty to listen and then see if he could get a feel for a song. They never sat together in the same room during this creative brainstorming, yet they had enough trust in each other's talents that they could work together for over forty years in this fashion.

Petty spent most of his career, whether in Mudcrutch or with The Heart-breakers, as a *leader*. The extraordinary thing about this is not that he was in charge; it was how he was capable of being in charge while still giving his band-mates the room to be themselves. It seems that the Tom Petty work ethic dictated that ego was set aside for an end goal of getting the work done. It is not that the band did not experience drama, but Tom's approach to those situations was usually light-handed and relatively even among the group. Whether it was Stan Lynch being temperamental about how he felt about his role within the group or Howie Epstein's long-term drug use, Petty was able to roll with the potential distractions with equanimity. He saw it as his job to bring the best people together and play the best music in the best way possible. That all sounds completely obvious, except that Tom Petty was able to create magic when he did it.

Like most musicians, Petty got a rush from working with other talented people, especially if they were industry icons. He took the experience as an opportunity to learn and grow artistically. However, one of his most famous collaborators, Stevie Nicks, he almost did not work with because he saw her as too corporate, too Top 40, and not a good fit for him musically. Luckily, Nicks was able to winnow her way into Petty's studio and life. As Petty told Paul Zollo:

"Stevie came to me around '78. And she was this absolutely stone-gone *huge* fan. And it was her mission in life that I should write her a song. And we were a little wary of Stevie. We didn't quite know whether to like Stevie or not, because we kind of saw this big corporate rock band, Fleetwood Mac, which was wrong, they were artistic people. But in those days, nobody trusted that sort of thing and we just kept think-ing, 'What does she want from us?' And then, of course, she turned into one of my great, great friends forever. But Stevie was really adamant about me writing her a song" [74].

Fortunately, he wrote "Insider" with Nicks in mind, and it became one of the classic songs in the Petty catalog.

It is interesting to note how Petty worked. For all that he would hide himself away at home pouring over tapes from Mike Campbell, he definitely saw making music as communal. Where it would have been easy for him to simply say, "My way or the highway," he clearly dug what a group of musicians working together could produce. In starting the Traveling Wilburys, where he teamed up with Bob Dylan, George Harrison, Roy Orbison, and Jeff Lynne, it would have been expected for these gods of rock to spar over who took the lead, but as Petty described to Paul Zollo, "Nobody really outranked anybody. It was a group effort" (122). In discussing how he worked with Mike Campbell and Benmont Tench, the two Heartbreakers who were there from beginning to end, he said, "And it's very much a collaboration between the three of us. It's probably the biggest part of the records we make, is those three of us, the collaboration we make in tone, in texture, and in melody. That's what creates that sound" (243).

The emphasis on Petty's ability to collaborate, to step aside and let others shine, to lead yet not hog the spotlight speaks to more than just his artistic temperament. His actions appear to be more in line with the natural and communal ways of socialization. In short, he exemplifies feminist ideology.

That assertion may seem preposterous, given Petty's rock god status. The instruments and postures of a male rock star are not typically known for being anything other than masculine in scope, with the hip gyrating, the exaggerated strumming, the pounding rhythms, and the flexing of muscles. Petty is an exception to the rule. Aside from the laid-back nature of his stage presence, especially as he aged, there is not a single Petty song involving a woman that does not give the woman complete agency, with the possible exception of Mary Jane's Last Dance. This ability to toggle between male desires and female needs is unique in rock. You will not find lyrics in Petty's songs that objectify women or that turn them simply into vessels for male desire.

From "American Girl" where the woman is alone and on the cusp of a decision, to "Good Enough" where the woman cuts a life-long unapologetic swath yet the man still loves her, to "Swingin'" where the woman chases love and then takes her fate into her own hands, to "Rebels" where the woman picks up the man from jail and then ditches him by the roadside, to "Breakdown" where Petty begs yet also acknowledges that it is not his call whether he gets what he wants, all of his songs see women as complete unto themselves. This is rare in one song by a male artist but to have a 40-year catalog worth of songs where women consistently have agency, consistently have their own reason for existing beyond the male gaze, is truly incredible.

Petty's genuine love of women as human beings, not objects, stems in part from his childhood. *In Conversations with Tom Petty*, Paul Zollo states, "Your treatment of women in songs is generally pretty tender. You're not ruthless with them, as are many rockers" (202). Petty's reply is entirely authentic as he said:

"I like women a lot. Always have. I was always the man who loved women. Not in a lascivious way. I grew up surrounded by women more than males. My dad was never around much. And my grandmother, my mother, my aunts, my cousins—-I was in that world a lot. And somehow I came out of it respecting women in kind of an equal way. There's a lot of people in rock'n'roll who don't. I don't know if I've always been that good to them, but I think I have for the most part" [202].

Given the era of music where male singers talked about what they planned to do to their conquests ("Rock You Like a Hurricane," The Scorpions) or what they thought of their conquests ("(She's My) Cherry Pie," Warrant), Petty's position on women as human beings separate from the male gaze is remarkable. Growing up as a teenager in the 1980s, it seemed as if my only value to men was based on the length of my legs and the poutiness of my lips. In music videos, the female form was expected to roll around on the hoods of cars or lounge in a hot tub wearing only a bikini. With Petty, it felt safe to put myself into his songs, knowing that I was loved, even if I was behaving badly or not easily acquiescing to his desires. That feeling was extremely empowering.

It should be no surprise, considering Petty's disdain for the establishment, capitalism, authoritarianism, and commercialism that he spoke out in a *Rolling Stone* interview with David Wild on November 14, 2002. Taking on the need for wealthy people to acquire *more* of everything, he said,

"'I don't think it's a good attitude in your life to feel that you have to be rich to have self-esteem. You know, I saw a billboard in New York I wish I had photographed. It was for the TNN network. It said three words against a patriotic background of red, white and blue—BIGGER, YOUNGER, RICHER. Now, I find that fascinating: 'Bigger, younger, richer.' This whole idea of being wealthy has gone too far.'"

Imagine any of Petty's contemporaries, like Bruce Springsteen or Madonna, saying such a thing. They might criticize the implied patriotism or the commercialism of art, but most people of Petty's generation gave up on egalitarian ideals in order to embrace materialism in all its supposed glory by the end of the 20th century. Whether charging outrageous ticket prices at concert venues or becoming known as a day trader on the stock market or finding younger and younger women to marry, the musical Boomers tend to tout liberal ideals while distancing themselves from the struggles of ordinary people. Bruce Springsteen still sings about the heartland as if it is his soy bean crop that is failing, and Madonna remains stuck in the "Material Girl" 1980s.

What is a surprise within the interview is the strong tone Petty takes in regard to an artist's responsibility to listeners. One might expect him to be laissez-faire or completely oblivious to the role of art, given how he spent his life creating the best possible music he could without considering whether or not it would be popular or commercial, but this assumption would be wrong. Petty said to David Wild:

"When I was a young rock & roll star, I was really fascinated and shocked at times by the power that I had, by the power of my words, and shocked that it can be taken wrong. I don't believe in censorship, but I do believe that an artist has to take some moral responsibility for what he or she is putting out there. And I think a lot of these young kids are going to have to learn the hard way before they realize that you can actually do some damage if you're being careless or frivolous in what you're saying."

This exhortation to younger artists, however, is not just about morality or responsibility to the listener. What Petty is really warning about is the danger of losing oneself for the lure of money. One can make a quick million or so with cheap lyrics and flashy gimmicks, but it seems like what Petty wants to see from younger artists entering the music industry is a love of the craft as an art form more than as a vehicle for monetary success. Commercialism in the arts causes the message to be diluted and prevents the artist from growing, which further tears at the fabric of artistic content. Petty's entire ethos involved a desire to be as true to himself as possible without veering into sheer selfishness. His measured decisions and calculated risks all added up to a solid career of over forty years and a legacy that will live beyond all our generations.

If Petty wanted musical artists to create carefully and with good intent, he did not hold only them responsible for societal ills. Within the same *Rolling Stone* interview with David Wild in 2002, he excoriated the television industry's "for-profit" model that essential eats its own and stated the following:

"I think television's become a downright dangerous thing. It has no moral barometer whatsoever.... The music business looks like, you know, innocent schoolboys compared to the TV business. They care about nothing but profit. They will make a movie about murdering their kids, you know? And they'll put the guy who killed them on TV. And before long, he might even have his own show."

The truth of the "eat your own" model of profit on television is undeniable. Within the quote, he explored the danger to one's health of watching the news on television, and this was long before the era of "fake news" and the media's complicity in supporting lies from elected officials.

When discussing Tom Petty's politics, there are some clear themes: He's anti-authoritarian. He's collaborative. He's highly critical of greed. The question then becomes, does this make Petty a liberal or a Democrat? After carefully studying Petty, the answer appears to be, "Does it matter?" His principled stances and calculated risks could be beneficial parts of a political platform, but in a world where money is king, there is no profit in playing the role of a jester.

While Petty did send cease-and-desist letters to Republican candidates who attempted to use his songs at campaign rallies, and while he did perform at the Clinton White House, there seems to be a strong theme of turning his back on establishment politics, of not wanting to run with the popular kids, of not wanting to lose his everyman roots. His ability to look at the world with clear eyes and to criticize us all, including himself, makes him more of a prophet. Long before it became obvious to many of us, he saw the dangers of capitalism, racism, misogyny, and bigotry. He tied his concerns together in simple and direct songs that used a mix of humor and imagery to make his points. Petty was born into an era where America was far simpler yet not that great. He died in an era where America was far more complex yet still not great. In between, Petty spoke to the promise of us: our humanity, our love, our strength, our foibles, our successes, and our failures. He saw both our potential to be better than we are and the truth that we are our own worst enemies. He was gentle with us, but he was also firm. How we use the gifts he gave us is our choice as individuals and because so many of us heard his words, we are a collective force. He would want us to use our power wisely.

WORKS CITED

Greene, Andy. "Tom Petty on Past Confederate Flag Use: 'It Was Downright Stupid.'" *Rolling Stone,* July 14 2015, https://www.rollingstone.com/music/news/tom-petty-on-past-confederate-flag-use-it-was-downright-stupid-20150714.

Wild, David. "10 Tings That Piss Off Tom Petty." *Rolling Stone,* November 14 2002. https://www.rollingstone.com/music/features/the-ten-things-that-piss-off-tom-petty-20021114.

Zollo, Paul. *Conversations with Tom Petty.* London: Omnibus Press, 2005.

Something Good

An Exploration
of the Issue of Cover Bands

KAREN FRIEND

"You're not strangers if you love the same band"
—Unknown

With album sales topping 80 million and over 40 years of successful serenading, Tom Petty is one of the most successful songwriters of all time. Fans, left wanting since Tom's passing on October 2, 2017, are not only torn up but torn *about* cover and tribute bands and the sudden feast of tribute concerts. Time will tell how Petty's legend will live on, be it through annual Sunday brunch gatherings with friends or a series of all-you-can-eat buffet style covers. A permanent fixture on rock and roll's menu, Petty will never be forgotten, but a proliferation of homages threatens the balance between quality and authenticity. Cover bands and tribute shows ultimately offer fans respite, collusion in their grief, while delivering interpretations that satisfy and get to the point. The explosion of imposters and copy-cats deftly deliver parts of what has been lost, offering skillful caterwauling resuscitation with reverence and respect. No one who loves the same band is a stranger, for you have so much in common.

The name of Tom Petty's favorite musician might ring a bell. It may even swivel a hip. Since the age of ten, Tommy Petty always had a lot to say about "The King," Elvis Aaron Presley. It started in 1962, in Gainesville, Florida, when little Tommy Petty's uncle, Earl Jernigan, got a job as prop-man and assistant set director on the film set of Presley's film *Follow That Dream*. Due to an abundance of Earls in the family, everyone called Tom's uncle "Jernigan." It was a simpler time. Gainesville was a small town. Thomas Earl Petty was just sitting around on a pile of straw (seriously) wondering what he was going to do that day. His Aunt, Evelyn Jernigan, nonchalantly asked her blonde-haired, laid back nephew if he'd like to "go and see Elvis Presley" (Dean). Tommy, as he was then known, was game to see this Elvis character. He knew of Elvis "mostly because Elvis had caused some controversy" with his swiveling hips. Tom told Bill Dean of the Gainesville Sun, "He was known to me as a fellow who wiggled. And I did a little impression with a broom, of wiggling like Elvis." Tommy's aunt Evelyn, known as Ellen, loaded the car with kids and drove 30 miles to the film set in downtown Ocala (Dean).

Elvis was to shoot a scene involving driving up in a car and entering a bank. There was a huge crowd. "The biggest crowd I'd ever seen in the streets of Ocala," Tom said (Dean). The crowd was so huge that it was almost impossible to control, even with fences and barricades. Thousands of people in a town accustomed to dozens.

> "And then, I swear to god, a line of white Cadillacs pulled in. I'd never seen anything like that. He arrived in a fleet of white Cadillacs. I was standing up on a box to see over everyone's head, because a big roar started up when the cars pulled in. Guys in mohair suits and pompadours began bounding out of each car. Every time someone emerged, I would ask 'Is that Elvis?' And my aunt would say 'No. No, that's not Elvis'" [Dean].

But when the real Elvis appeared, Tom knew. Immediately. "He stepped out radiant as an angel." Tom said. "He seemed to glow and walk above the ground. It was like nothing I'd ever seen in my life. At 50 yards, we were stunned by what this guy looked like. And he came walking right towards us" (Dean).

When Elvis walked directly over to Uncle Earl, Aunt Ellen, and little Tom Petty, "we were speechless," Petty recalled. As Uncle Earl introduced Elvis to his nieces and nephews, the King of Rock and Roll smiled and nodded to each open-mouthed youngster. "I don't know what he said because I was just too dumbfounded," Tom said. "And [then] he went into his trailer" (Dean).

In his wake, people were screaming, handing album covers and photos over the chain-link fence hoping Elvis would sign them. One of Elvis's "Memphis Mafia guys," as Tom described him, took [the photos and albums] into the trailer and returned, each bearing authentic Elvis autographs. That proved to be a pivotal moment for Petty, a tow-headed pre-teen who was instantly enamored and off to the races. "And I thought at the time, 'That is one hell of a job to have. That's a great gig—Elvis Presley,'" Tom said (Dean). It's easy to imagine this being delivered with Tom's crooked, knowing grin and starry, blue eyes. Maybe a finger on his chin for good measure.

From then on, Tom Petty could be found doing everything he could think of to get his hands on anything Elvis. "I traded my Wham-O slingshot to this kid for a box of 45s, and in this box there were so many Elvis records, and they were all the greatest ones" (Dean). Tom Petty stayed inside listening to Elvis records (which did not sit well with his father). Tom even sent a dollar all the way to England to order *The Elvis Presley Handbook*. For this, he was ridiculed by his entire family, "for wasting a dollar." Tom remembered that the book took months to arrive, "but the day it came was like Christmas" (Dean).

"I caught the fever that day, and I never got rid of it," Petty later said in Paul Zollo's 2005 book, *Conversations with Tom Petty*. "That's what kicked off my love of music." It was not until two or three years later, when the Beatles came, that Tom's temperature would rise again and he would feel inspired to pick up a guitar. But learning all of those Elvis songs gave him a background in rock and roll. "It became an invaluable thing to have," Petty said, "so for that, I thank him" (Zollo).

We *all* have Elvis to thank for that.

For many, our relationship with Tom Petty remains unique. Much like how Tommy Petty took to Elvis, fans often found themselves enthralled with Tom Petty and the Heartbreakers. It was almost as though it could not be helped. The casual rebelliousness of his music, the chorus causing your fist to pump in the air almost without permission, the promise of fun and freedom. Seeing Tom Petty and the Heartbreakers live provided something much more than entertainment. Waves of familiarity and strangers becoming one collective heartbeat that filled a room of thousands. This is something big. This is something good. Through his music, Tom offered a lifetime of soulful beats, romanticized rock and roll lyrics, blended with a peace and love that you could never be too drunk to follow. His smile was contagious and his style was unprecedented. Who else but Tom and Elvis could pull off wearing silk scarf on stage?

Covering Tom Petty songs and paying him tribute brings something to the table. It offers listeners a magical experience, akin to time travel. Tom Petty music is unique and alters the brain in a manner akin to motherhood, irretrievably and inexplicably. Carl Hiaasen, Journalism professor at the University of Maryland, writer for the *Capital Gazette* and fellow Gainesville native, had this to say of Tom Petty: "What is good music? Good music is the music you put on when you're alone or you don't want to be alone, and either way the music makes you feel something in your day-job guts. And if it ain't love or heartache or defiance or hope, then it's close enough" (Hiaasen).

The very morning after a shooter turned an October 1, 2017, outdoor Las Vegas music festival into a tragedy, Tom Petty was discovered, unresponsive in his bedroom. He had suffered cardiac arrest. Essentially, a broken heart. Petty's hip had been in bad shape for a while. He had been taking painkillers, opioids, to help soldier him through the epic, year-long Heartbreaker's 40th anniversary tour. As the shows progressed, an extensive 53 engagements, so did Petty's hip injury.

"Despite this painful injury he insisted on keeping his commitment to his fans and, as he did, it worsened to a more serious injury," Dana Petty and Adria Petty, Tom's wife and daughter, said in a statement. "On the day he died he was informed his hip had graduated to a full-on break, and it is our feeling that the pain was simply unbearable and was the cause for his over use of medication" (Petty and Petty). Traces of fentanyl, oxycodone, temazepam, loprazolam, citalopram, acetyl fentanyl and despropionyl fentanyl were found to be in Tom Petty's system. Petty's wife and daughter added in their statement, "We knew before the report was shared with us that he was prescribed various pain medications for a multitude of issues including Fentanyl patches and we feel confident that this was, as the coroner found, an unfortunate accident."

Tom Petty provided inherent good throughout all of his music. It is impossibly inoffensive, catchy, honest, and seems almost too simple to be true. Tom was not doing an Elvis impersonation but there was always a bit of Presley present. "It's Good to Be King," Tom sang on Wlidflowers.

There were not a lot of Elvis impersonators before the King was discovered slumped beside his throne. In fact, Elvis was only 42 when he died in August of 1977, found in the upstairs bathroom of his Graceland mansion. By no means ancient even in 1970's standards, Elvis seemed to have beaten the curse of James and Janis by living beyond the age of 27. The official record of death submitted by the coroner attributed Elvis Presley's death to cardiac arrhythmia, an irregular heartbeat, but the underlying cause of his heart problems remains a source of controversy. With many prescription drugs, including codeine, Valium, morphine, and Demerol, reported to be present in his system on that fateful summer day, there may have been additional drugs as well. Vernon Presley, Elvis's father, had the complete autopsy report sealed. Perhaps these are the documents Tom was referring to in his 2006 Highway Companions *Down South* as these documents will remain sealed until 2027, fifty years after The King's death. Petty's "It's Good to be King" (but just for a while), also begs for Elvis-related speculation.

Soon after Elvis died, becoming an impersonator became a career option. There were one or two people covering Elvis songs in the 70's but more and more, no longer able to scream towards the stage in hopes of scoring a sweaty scarf, fans were coming together to mourn the loss of their favorite musician by hiring look-alikes. Elvis impersonators would appear at personal parties and get everyone "all shook up." Conventions attract hundreds, even thousands of Elvis impersonators, who continue to be a world-wide phenomenon (there have been at least three prominent Elvis impersonators of Samoan descent) ("Elvis Impersonators"). Donning a pompadour and a white, beaded jumpsuit in the heat of the Vegas desert takes a special breed of devotion. In the post–Tom Petty era, donning purple kicks, a top hat and shoulder-length blonde hair does as well, but there is disagreement among Tom Petty fans about the place and relevance of Tom Petty cover bands.

"I'd be unlikely to see a cover band because why would I?" says outdoor concert-goer Robyn from New York. "It's like going to see the movie of a book I love. Something is always left out, and never captures the scope of the original, no matter how hard they try" (Hansen-Harple). Petty fans, lost in the wake of his unanticipated departure, are particularly torn about whether or not to attend cover shows. "I have not listened to too much TP since October. I'm just not in the mood," says one fan on the TomPetty.com forums.

The shock and grieving over the loss of Tom Petty continues, and another fan added: "It troubles me when I see the word 'was' instead of the word 'is' when read about Tom. Even about the box set. It troubled me when *Rolling Stone* referred to Mike Campbell and Benmont Tench as 'former' members of the Heartbreakers" (Friend). Some music fans are more open to tribute bands after Petty's death. "Of course I would see a tribute band! I would go see any band that was anywhere near me! Music you love is music you love. [Cover bands] are usually unbelievably talented and they love the same stuff you do. Instant bond," said Lysa Milch from Brooklyn. "I'd totally see a cover band if they were kids from a local School of Rock or something.... Or if enough friends wanted to see a Petty cover band so I can spend time with them, I'd go more so because of that than to hear the Petty-adjacentness of the bad themselves," fan Stan Chan from New Jersey adds.

Katie Moulton writes for *Westworld* and explores the Petty cover band controversy in her article *We Never Needed Tom Petty Cover Bands*, "…For all the current and future Petty impersonators and Heartbreakers cover bands out there, please: The greatest tribute you can pay now to Tom Petty is to make this music your own." (Moulton)

The idea of cover bands and tribute shows strikes a chord as well as a nerve with musicians. There is eye-rolling. There is passion. There is anger that may be misguided. There is more eye-rolling. Petty fans share the passion as well as the eye rolling. Fans, curious and mourning, want to know if these tribute bands are worth the trip, the financial as well as the emotional investment. But fans demonstrate the line in the sand between tribute and mockery simply by showing up to performances. Their sheer presence indicative of what is worthy of support.

Tom Petty himself recreated many songs in his own vein, providing renditions of everything from Thunderclap Newman's "Something In the Air" to Beck's "Asshole," Lucinda Williams' "Change The Locks," Bonnie Raitt's "Louisiana Rain," and Beatles' songs including "Taxman." Tom Petty did fifty-two covers in all; some of these even made it to studio albums and many to Tom Petty and the Heartbreakers' live concert performances.

In addition to these covered songs, Petty contributed to many collaborations and sometimes even gave songs away, as did Mike Campbell who is often credited writing "Boys of Summer" and giving it to Don Henley. It was Mike Campbell's rendition of Chuck Berry's Johnny B. Goode during his audition that prompted Tom to bring him aboard the Heartbreakers. That cover, an impromptu tribute on a "cheapo Japanese guitar," changed the course of music forever.

Petty enjoyed collaborating and often indulged with fellow artists, including working with Del Shannon, Bob Dylan, Johnny Cash, and Roger McGuinn. Petty found working with other musicians to be inspiring. Not only did he not mind sharing, he encouraged the evolution born of layering partnerships. Tom spoke to *Rolling Stone* about being a member of The Traveling Wilburys and said he loved every minute of it. "It was all great," he added, "You're in the best band you've seen, with all your heroes who are also your friends. It's still hard to conceive, just a fabulous thing" (Greene).

But in the discussion of covering other people's music, it is important to note the difference between cover bands and tribute bands. According to musician Scott Milch, the difference between a cover and a tribute band "is simple. Cover bands play a wide variety of other people's music where tribute bands are playing one person's music." Scott cuts to the chase, "I definitely encourage seeing cover bands. What makes me cringe is when you call yourself a tribute band and you don't perform the tribute with respect. For example, you think you're playing the songs correctly but you're not."

Angela Iancannone, a New York City–based singer, disagrees. "I love cover bands, especially when they play a variety of music and make the music their own. If you can no longer see Pink Floyd but you want to hear their music, then go for it. Cover and tribute bands clearly aren't paying for the money, they're playing for the love of music."

Amanda Liptz Kornfield has over 300 rock and roll shows under her belt. "I don't mind [covers] if that's what they are and that's what they set out to be." There's clearly a line between tribute and theft. Are cover bands simply stealing? Are they doing the songs and the writers (and thereby the fans) an injustice when they spin their own evolution of a piece or work? Fans seem to be able to denote the differences. "The look, the sounds, all *heavily* borrowed," Kornfield says. "Who wants to be at a show thinking, 'who the hell does this guy think he is, Freddie Mercury?'"

Jon Scondotto is not heavily into the metal scene anymore, though his full-sleeve tattoos and resting grump face might convince you otherwise. "There is a very big bone of contention between people who have toured playing their own original music and people who do tribute and cover bands," he says. "It's sort of like the Bloods and the Crips, only nobody gets shot."

As lead vocals for bands such as *Lament* and *Few and Far Between* while composing for *Your Water*, Jon Scondotto says he "gets the resentment," between cover bands and artists who play only original pieces, "and I do think it's valid. Because the amount of effort and work it takes to write something original, compose it with other people, get someone involved to release it, and then perform it on a regular basis, is extraordinary. The amount of time it takes to learn "Piano Man," not so much.

Regardless of which camp fans are in, or if their tent is staked firmly somewhere in between, it is true that the future is not what it used to be. Cover bands, tribute concerts, and *The American Treasure* boxset will be the closest fans will get to Tom Petty without a flux capacitor. But in the meantime, there is something good to be found in music, in collaboration, in concert.

While millions of fans continue grieving, a special breed are taking to the stage, just as they do most nights. Bands with clever names that give a nod such as "Damn the Torpedoes," "Southern Accents," "Petty Fever," "Larry Hart and the Hartbreakers," and even "Petty Theft" have been donning their top hats in front of audiences in tribute to Tom Petty and the Heartbreakers. Like the Samoan Elvii, some are new to the game but some have been around for decades. They play where they can—the summer concerts, baseball games, the seedy clubs, the darkened bowels of rock and roll forgotten. And now they play for those who do not wish to forget, for those who could not forget even if they wanted to.

Rich Kubicz has been to every show that "Damn The Torpedoes" has performed since their 2007 inception, and that he rates them "a 6 or 7, tops." Kubicz is a member of the band, and when Kubicz and "Damn The Torpedoes" are onstage, they are, of course, hoping to look out to see a large crowd. But they are also hoping to see fans that share their passion. "I think we have the dedication to play the music as closely to the records as possible. I think we owe it to Tom and we owe it to the people that come to our shows," said Kubicz.

It takes more than a southern twang and a suede top hat to make Tom Petty. Grieving fans may be both the toughest critics and the people that should most give cover bands a chance.

"When I look out into the audience, I see a bunch of music lovers … just like me. I see some people that are out to have a good time … and it's up to us to give them a good time. And I [speak for the entire band when I say we are] inspired to do our part to make that happen" (Kubicz). Surprisingly, Kubicz and "Damn the Torpedoes," who have fans flocking into clubs and outdoor summer concerts on the east coast, also want the fans to pick apart what they are doing on stage. Based on the sideways glances of the crowd, they have come to the right place.

"I'm hoping to see the people watch us … scrutinize us," Kubicz said that he appreciates the attention to detail and that he "hopes that people are looking close" to what they are doing with the music. Kubicz continued:

> I know there are some really diehard Tom Petty fans out there that have negative opinions of us. Either it's that we are ripping off Tom Petty or we will never be like Tom Petty so don't even try. We understand that and we appreciate that. But they don't realize that we are fans just the same. We are musicians and we are fans. So, our purpose is to entertain people who want to have a live Tom Petty experience. We try our best to get as close as possible. You can come and experience that with us. You can come enjoy the night with fellow Petty fans. You can have a place where we all get together to celebrate the life and music of Tom Petty. Or you can stay home. That's it. Simple.

And what perfect timing to find something good in this world, something that brings people together, pointing out something in common, something that we can sing together, fists pumping unapologetically in the air in unison and at all the right parts. I dare a Tom Petty fan to attend a Petty cover band show and not join in during "Free Fallin." It's scientifically impossible.

Still, some Petty fans disagree. Tax season or not, Aaron Olk, a Certified Public Accountant in Philadelphia, is unlikely to spend his time or money seeing a cover band, despite his love of music. "Imitation is not the sincerest form of flattery; the sincerest form of flattery is inspiration," said Olk.

Olk brings up an important point about the evolution of music and the dichotomy of honoring someone via tribute and leaving their art untouched. "When John Lennon started listening to Bob Dylan, he didn't release a Dylan cover album with the aim of sounding like Dylan. He raised his game. He was inspired to new levels of song writing. He recorded Norwegian Wood. Now that, that is the sincerest form of flattery." Olk continued, "The tribute band is diet soda. It's Jim Belushi. It can never replicate what it imitates, nor does it offer anything of value on its own … it merely reminds you of something you like."

Even Brian Friend, a Petty superfan, one who followed the band around on several multi-city tours, and proposed to his wife from the 4th row of a North Carolina Petty show in 2008, agrees on some level. "As much as I love Petty and hearing his music, with cover bands it's hard for me to want to go. It's risky. Purely because, to me, if I like an artist enough to think about going to a cover band show then I hold their music sacred enough to go in with the attitude that the cover band can't possibly satisfy." Still, Friend sees the value of cover bands. "That being said, cover bands are a good thing. There's a comfort there. Something enchanting. I think they should be supported." "However," he added, "Tom is allowed to change the songs. Only Tom."

FreezrBurn is made up of six musicians who can also relate. They have been playing their whole lives, "—and that's a LONG time!" says lead Sally Moscatiello. By day they are professional engineers, mathematicians, small business owners, and civil servants. At night, they play music "for the sheer love of music." Moscatiello says that music brings them all together, "writing songs and playing music that make people feel the way Petty made us feel is truly a unique kind of high. That's what draws us to the stage. Let's face it—a party is just no fun without great music!"

Moscatiello added, "When you hear a song from your teenage years, (such as a Petty song!) you suddenly remember what you were doing and where you were when you heard it. It evokes an emotion. You start singing along, or playing air guitar, or dancing. We call it "The Power of Petty."

Mark Felsot has been holding court at SiriusXM since 2002. Mark has a long production history including being the producer of Tom Petty's "Buried Treasure" show. Mark currently hosts a show of his own on SiriusXM's channel 31, Tom Petty Radio. In a recent conversation, Mark provided a peek into his musical preferences:

> Tribute bands can fill a necessary void for fans. There are a couple of amazing Pink Floyd tribute fans that have invested in the sounds and lights to really recreate a Pink Floyd show as best as possible. I've seen a couple of them and have enjoyed the shows. I'm an old Genesis fan and fortunately for me there are a couple of tribute bands that provide the music and atmosphere for that era of Genesis that I love since I'll never get to see the real band members do that again.

Other important Tom Petty fans have weighed in on the tribute band debate. Keith Eveland is the administrator of the Tom Petty Nation, the largest Facebook group of Tom Petty fans with over 30,000 members. Eveland had this to say about Tom Petty tribute bands:

> I like 'em if they're good and pay proper respect to the material and to Tom. I think they are now the only way to hear a full show of TP music. I've encouraged and supported them. I don't care if they choose to try and look like Tom or not, that's not relevant to me, it makes no difference. I've seen a few really good ones and the guys in the bands have all been really cool. I only seen one that I didn't like. The guy was a good singer, but he messed up the words to every song except 2 the whole night. But that band rarely, if ever, posts in TPN. I've seen 5 tribute bands and was only disappointed one time. A friend who went with me thought it was great but doesn't know all the words like I do and he didn't think that was important. He said he gave them an E for effort. I said, yeah, that's about right cus an E is right between a D and an F! But anyway I wholeheartedly am happy to support the good ones and go see them if they are close enough and I can make it!

Far from a tribute act, Jake Thistle, a teenager from New Jersey, has been playing Tom Petty and the Heartbreakers songs since his dad presented him a guitar for his fifth birthday. He can be found in suburban ice cream shops and bagel stores, with his six-string and his microphone, jamming his high-school heart out. Thistle donates his proceeds (over $10,000 last year) to Rock The Dogs, a charity run by lead guitarist of the Heartbreakers, Mike Campbell and his wife, Marcie. As a "thank you" in 2017, Campbell called Thistle backstage to meet the band. According to Thistle, "it was the highlight of my musical career."

Jake loves to play. He says he is "close to the songs" and that can sometimes interfere with his ability to relax and enjoy other interpretations of the music. "Other people doing covers makes me analyze it. And I'd rather be playing," he said. While Thistle isn't old enough to legally enter some of the places in Jersey where his favorites might be playing, "my personal feeling is that even when I do covers I try to be true to the spirit of the songs without sounding just like the original. To me, I want to bring something new to the songs that feels real to me ... which is different than most tribute bands who dress up and try to sound exactly the same. So, even though I do covers, I do them to learn about music and songwriting."

Just as Elvis inspired a young Tommy Petty that day in 1962, an artist never knows how they may inspire a new generation of artists and musicians. The torch is passed from generation to generation in different ways, and, sometimes, that inspiration comes in the form of tribute and cover bands. Whether Tom Petty bands are for all his fans are not, they clearly bring something to the table for many people. Regardless of how someone chooses to carry the torch that is Tom Petty, it's the right way if it works for that person.

And when asked, "Tom, how do you feel about cover bands out there?" Tom said, with his distinguished, typical grin, "The only thing about cover groups, you know, it's alright as long as they're not better than us." The interviewer assured him that "trust me, Tom, they're not quite there yet." "Then we'll tolerate that," responded Tom (DanHaggertyNews).

Works Cited

Chan, Stan. Personal interview. June 2018.
DanHaggertyNews. "Tom Petty and the Heartbreakers on Their SB Halftime Show." Youtube, 8 February 2008, https://www.youtube.com/watch?V=OG7ea6DB_Ci.
Dean, Bill. "Tom Petty's Love for Rock 'n' Roll Began the Day He Met Elvis in Ocala." *The Gainesville Sun*, as published by Ocala.com, 19 August 2007, http://www.ocala.com/article/LK/20070819/News/604239189/OS/.
"Elvis Impersonators." *Wikipedia*. 2 September 2018, https://en.wikipedia.org/wiki/Elvis_impersonator.
Eveland, Keith. Personal interview. June 2018.
Felsot, Mark. Personal interview. June 2018.
Friend, Brian. Personal interview. June 2018.
Greene, Andy. "Readers' Poll, the 10 Best Super Groups," *Rolling Stone*, 10 August 2016.
Hansen-Harple, Robyn. Personal interview. June 2018.
Harple, Doug. Personal interview. June 2018.
Hiaasen, Carl. "From One Florida Boy to Another—R.I.P Tom Petty." *The Capital Gazette*, 17 March 2013. http://www.capitalgazette.com/lifestyle/ac-cn-hiaasen-column-1008-story.html.
Iancannone, Angela. Personal interview. June 2018.
Kornfield, Amanda. Personal interview. June 2018.
Kubicz, Rich. Personal interview. June 2018.
Laney, Karen. "Tom's Favorite Elvis Songs." *Ultimate Classic Rock*, http://ultimateclassicrock.com/tom-petty-top-ten-elvis-presley-songs/.
McCranor Henderson, William. *I, Elvis: Confessions of a Counterfeit King*. Willowdell Books, 2017.

Milch, Lysa. Personal interview. June 2018.
Milch, Scott. Personal interview. June 2018.
Moscaiello, Sally. Personal interview. June 2018.
Moulton, Katie. "We Never Needed Tom Petty Cover Bands." *Westword*, 6 October 2017, https://www.westword.com/music/tom-petty-cover-bands-take-note-make-the-music-your-own-9562285.
Murray, Frank. Personal interview. June 2018.
Olk, Aaron, Personal interview. June 2018.
Petty, Dana and Adria Petty. "A Statement from the Family." TomPetty.com, 19 January 2018, http://www.tompetty.com/news/statement-petty-family-1764366.
Scondotto, Jon. Personal interview. June 2018.
Scott, Jon. Personal interview. June 2018.
Thistle, Jake. "Live at Salem Roadhouse with Damn the Torpedoes," YouTube, 11 April 2015, https://youtu.be/OvoFtEb6kb0.
_____. Personal interview. June 2018.
Wood, Mikael. "Why Losing Tom Petty Feels Like Losing a Piece of Ourselves." *The Los Angeles Times*, 2 October 2017, http://www.latimes.com/entertainment/music/la-et-ms-tom-petty-appreciation-20171002-story.html.
Zollo, Paul. *Conversations With Tom Petty*. London: Omnibus Press, 2015, Kindle edition.

Fears, Frustrations and Knowing How It Feels

*The Emotional Signifiers
of Tom Petty's Songs*

NATE BAUER *and* SHYE GILAD

We suspect the co-authors here are not the only ones who have heard Tom Petty's songs differently since his death in October 2017. But unlike David Bowie, whose music seems designed to transcend time and mortality through its wide array of persona and artistic planes, or Prince, whose conflation of sex and strangeness meant his songs often experienced dramatic shifts in tone and meaning even during his productive and creative peaks, Petty's work has a new, distinctly memorial, melancholy layer of meaning.

Petty's music demonstrates an ability to simply and directly evoke his listeners' struggles and emotions, and to provide language and lenses for thinking about our latent needs, hopes, and fears that has empowered generations of fans who have felt displaced and disenchanted by an "American Dream" of abundance, prosperity, and social satisfaction. This is because the primary core themes Tom Petty explored in his music—struggle, defiance, interpersonal and social "noise," a subversion of uniform and superficial masculinity, and resilience, all in the context of widespread Reagan and Thatcher-era socioeconomic tumult—depended strongly on the artist's own seeming resilience and life-affirming sneer.

Further, Tom Petty's music is *lasting*, and continues to strongly evoke both individual and communal responses across generations of fans, up through today's most engaged and active cultural participants.

For many original Petty fans, the raw energy of 1978's "I Need to Know" might recall a first childhood crush or the anguish felt from a painful breakup.

Maybe 1981's "The Waiting" reminds early listeners of a long distance relationship from their college days. Or for current Philadelphia Flyers or Wisconsin Badgers fans, the same song can now summon its playful performance during interruptions in games when officials are reviewing a close call. For the MTV generation, Petty was the Mad Hatter, swallowing Alice whole in the time capsule-worthy 1985 music video for "Don't Come Around Here No More."

Some of Petty's most memorable incarnations on screen, in fact, were not made to promote him or his music at all. In an iconic, chilling scene from the 1991 thriller *Silence of the Lambs*, readers may remember abductee Catherine (Brooke Smith), carefree and innocently singing to "American Girl" in her car, just moments before her capture by the film's serial killer Buffalo Bill. Or maybe there are cinematic memories of Tom Cruise as 1996's sports agent Jerry Maguire, frustratingly searching for the right song to capture his feelings after being fired from his job, dumped by his fiancé, betrayed by his co-workers and clients, and then finally (maybe?) sensing a glimmer of hope after a meeting with a valuable prospect.

Like Catherine, Jerry's in the car, listening to the radio in an era before satellite stations, streaming music, and widespread Internet adoption. He is visibly excited, tapping on the steering wheel and first attempting to sing with the Rolling Stones. Fast tempo, but the lyrics not quite right. He searches for something better, landing first on "Angel of the Morning," and then Gram Parsons' "She," both lovely but far too saccharine and sentimental.

Cruise's character finally finds what he's looking for: Tom Petty's "Free Fallin'." Jerry jumps in to sing along with the instantly recognizable chorus and very quickly experiences an emotional transformation, from pent up anxiety to pure unbridled joy. His face breaks into a smile, he taps the steering wheel, and he laughs out loud in relief as he finishes the first chorus. By the second time through, Jerry is shamelessly belting out the song at the top of his lungs, holding the note long after the chorus ends, throwing his head back and shaking back and forth, smiling with his whole body, finally letting out an involuntary "WHOOO!" His is an unlikely feeling of winning exhilaration, a mix of hope and relief that maybe everything will be all right after all.

At the very core of Tom Petty's widespread success and cultural relevance is his ability to channel the primary emotions that many Americans were feeling across the four decades of his remarkable career: loss of safety and security, fear of rejection and loneliness, and frustration from the lack of that winning feeling. Without writing stories about the explicit politics of economic inequality and social injustice, Petty wrote songs that gave language to the emotional outcomes of feeling left behind.

As we explore the socio-economic realities of the Tom Petty era, we also consider the interactions of music cognition and acquisition, psychological theories of human needs, fears, and loss, and the impact of technological innovations that profoundly changed music and media consumption. We attempt to highlight here a few crucial strands of the extraordinary musical DNA that bind the fabric of generational soundtracks exquisitely woven, song by song, by an unassuming yet unforgettable artist.

It is rare for an artist to enjoy such wide appeal as Petty in any genre, across age and class, and for such an extended time period. According to industry auditor *Billboard*, "Petty was a steady presence on the Billboard Hot 100 chart between the late-1970s and mid-'90s, whether solo or with his long-running backing band The Heartbreakers. He charted more than two dozen songs on the tally, led by a trio of top 10s, between 1981 and 1999 ("Tom Petty by the Numbers"), reflected by his cornerstone status on *Billboard*'s Mainstream Rock Songs airplay chart, arguably Petty's home base on those charts.

Petty logged ten Billboard Mainstream Rock Song #1s among twenty-eight top 10s, the latter the most in the chart's thirty-six-year history" ("Tom Petty's Top 20..."). For more perspective, if one includes the five top 10 hits Petty scored with Bob Dylan, George Harrison, Jeff Lynne, and Roy Orbison as supergroup The Traveling Wilburys, his career includes a full thirty-three top ten hits on the Billboard Mainstream Rock charts; only eleven other artists have ever logged even twenty ("Mainstream Rock").

The Traveling Wilburys' debut album won a Grammy Award ("Traveling Wilburys") in 1990 for Best Rock Performance by a Duo or Group with Vocal (beating out U2 and The Rolling Stones; ("32nd Annual Grammy Awards"), adding to Petty's impressive Grammys history, which includes two other wins (Best Long Form Music Video 2008, Best Male Rock Performance (2005; "Tom Petty"; GRAMMY.com) and 18 nominations over 33 years (1981–2014). Tom Petty's success spanned periods of varying predominant popular music formats including FM radio, cassettes, MTV and music videos, CDs, iPods, and the Internet. Few artists, businesses, or even industries could survive this kind of disruptive change, yet with each decade Petty's music endured and his audience grew. What at first listen may seem like a collection of well-crafted (if not simplistic) Pop-Rock songs formed a meaningful connection deep in the hearts and minds of a multi-generational legion of fans.

Petty on Our Brains

The positive influence of music on cognition is an area science is just beginning to validate. Advances in neurobiology and neuroradiology have enabled us to observe the brain's reaction to music, and researchers are eager to measure the power of music as it relates to mental health, cognitive performance, and wellness. *Music & Memory*, for example, a program designed to help people with Alzheimer's, dementia, and other cognitive and physical problems reconnect with the world through music, employs iPods with customized playlists featuring songs popular when the participating individual was under thirty years old.[1]

There appears to be an ideal age, it turns out, for learning your artistic musical tastes, beginning at 14 and peaking at 24 (Holbrook and Schindler 122). Perhaps one of the latent drivers of Tom Petty's widespread appeal is that his music has almost always been "there" for a large part of the population when we needed it—in adolescence, in young adulthood, and in our aimless 20s.

The three major decadal peaks in Petty's career have meant that three generations of Americans were reaching their peak age of musical influence when Tom Petty was topping the charts. If you're an American born between 1952 and 1992, it is extremely likely that Tom Petty's songs were a part of your musical universe. This is especially true for people born between 1953–1967 (1977–1981 albums *Tom Petty and The Heartbreakers, You're Gonna Get It!, Damn the Torpedoes, Hard Promises*), 1965–1975 (*Full Moon Fever* [1990], *Into the Great Wide Open* [1991]) and 1970–1980 (*Greatest Hits* [1993], *Wildflowers* [1994]). For Baby Boomers and Gen-Xers that make up the largest part of this cohort, Tom Petty's music has likely been a part of life for more than thirty years. The overlap with the Millennial generation means their kids probably have memories associated with his music as well ("Tom Petty Top Songs").

While the powerful themes of Petty's music remain timeless and relevant to struggles of youth, it may be difficult for younger generations to imagine the relative scarcity that existed in the music industry (and the entertainment industry en mass) in the decades prior to mainstream Internet adoption in the United States. From the late 1970s through the 1990s, Americans consumed music through the radio, physical record albums (and cassette tapes and compact discs), and music videos. These three delivery channels were complemented by concert tours, which for most consumers meant that they might get to see their favorite artist once or twice a year. Decades before broadband Internet and multimedia streaming platforms such as iTunes and Spotify, if listeners wished to hear or see a specific artist "on-demand," they had to either buy an album/cassette/CD/VHS tape, or call their favorite radio station, put in a "request" for their favorite song, and hope the station obliged.

Radio was the only way to consume music for free, and it was easy to access 24-7. Radio predominated in the car, which was especially important to a growing suburban population spending more and more time driving each year. "From 1940 to 2000 [...] the suburbs continued to grow substantially. By 2000, half of the entire U.S. population lived in the suburbs of metropolitan areas" (Demographic Trends).

The listening did not normally stop with the commute. Radio was an "always on" medium in the workplaces of the middle and working class during this era, especially for construction ("Case Study: DeWalt"), food service, and office workers seeking pleasant accompaniment to liven up the tedium of repetitive work. While some of these jobs become permanent vocations, for many Americans a clerical, construction, or food service position was a ritual "first job" to gain experience at the beginning of their career, coinciding for the majority with their peak age of music acquisition. During these Americans' formative years, Tom Petty's music was a consistent presence, providing language to express emotions, hopes, and needs they were in the process of recognizing and defining.

Jammin' Me

As the dominance of FM Radio gradually gave way to new technologies and on-demand media, socio-economic conditions in the U.S. were also changing. For the majority of the population, the change was not for the better. It is our point here that these shifts, as American workers and consumers shuffled toward a post-industrial technology surge and a resulting divorce from widespread national direction/identity and common social connection, not only prompted Tom Petty's unique catalog of music and message, but at the same time built up his listeners' need for and connection to his work.

In a dramatic way, the income and wealth gap spread and widened out from the first beat of Drummer Stan Lynch's spastic shuffle on "Rockin' Around with You," the first track from Tom Petty's 1976 debut album "Tom Petty and the Heartbreakers," and continued through the last chord of "American Girl," the last song played by Tom Petty and the Heartbreakers on the last night of what would be their last tour, at the Hollywood Bowl on September 25, 2017. These two songs, which bookend Petty's career, create an emblematic charm for his music's extra-emotional and extra-linguistic resonance during most of the late 20th century in America.

America had gotten to where it was in 1970, and since economists began keeping track in that year, each decade has ended with fewer people in the middle class than at the start (NPR). The innocence and thrill of "Rockin' Around with You" matched perfectly with the hopeful mood of the United States' bicentennial anniversary. On the other hand, the marked dissonance of the jangly major riff that props up "American Girl" against a dark narrative of phallogocentric failures foreshadowed economic, social, and emotional losses for generations to come.

In 1976, American radio and record sales trended toward exuberant songs like "Rockin' Around with You" and away from more pensive, reflective offerings. This is also an era when pop music was distinguishing itself from harder edged and sometimes less accessible punk and rock. There were many who wanted less to reflect on an era defined by the Vietnam conflict and civil rights battles than on forms of music that offered a pleasant pop escape. For many, that kind of escapism from harsh realities is the reason they sought out upbeat pop music in the first place.

And yet, with a superficial, syrupy whimsy from Disco and Easy Listening (since reclassified as "Yacht Rock") around the corner, it is no wonder that "American Girl" would not chart until 1994, eighteen years after its original recording. In 1994 the country was staring into the expanse of the internet, and in the face of this uncertainty, listeners were eager for reflection. "American Girl" went on to become perhaps Tom Petty's most iconic hit. By 1994 in America, chances were that if you or your family were a part of the working or middle class, the American dream was a fiction. Incomes were decreasing, and so was individual wealth. According to the Center on Budget and Policy Priorities, beginning in the 1970s, American economic growth slowed, and the income gap widened.

Since 1970:

- Income growth for households in the middle and lower parts of the distribution slowed sharply, while incomes at the top continued to grow rapidly.
- The concentrations of income at the very top of the distribution have risen to levels last seen over eighty years prior (during the "Roaring Twenties").

  Wealth—the value of a household's property and financial assets, minus the value of its debts—became more highly concentrated than income. The best survey data show that the share of wealth held by the top 1 percent rose from just under 30 percent in 1989 to nearly 49 percent in 2016, while the share held by the bottom 90 percent fell from just over 33 percent to less than 23 percent over the same period [Stone et al.].

In a 2015 analysis for *Washington Monthly*, economist Phillip Longman described dynamic conditions that tracked Tom Petty's career and central emotional themes thusly:

These vastly different economic trajectories experienced by today's living generations are basically unprecedented. Throughout most of our history, inequality between generations was large and usually increasing, to be sure, but for the happy reason that most members of each new generation far surpassed their parents' material standard of living. [...]

The aggregate downward mobility of Americans born since roughly 1950 has been their exposure to the massive growth of payday loans, subprime mortgage lending, and other wealth-destroying consumer finance products. Americans who came of age before the 1970s were largely protected from predatory lending by usury laws, for example, which capped fees and interest costs on loans. But starting in the 1980s, these consumer finance protections largely disappeared. At the same time, financial engineering, including securitization, led to the growth of financial institutions with business models that allowed them to prosper—at least in the short term—by lending money to people who could not afford to repay.

These trends, combined with generally lagging or falling individual and household incomes and rapidly expanding access to credit, often on predatory terms, lead to an explosion of borrowing. When this was followed, in turn, by a collapse in home prices, the result was devastation to the balance sheets of most Americans under fifty. By 2010, the average family headed by a person twenty-five to forty-nine had a net worth that was 32 percent below that of their counterparts in 1989. [...]

Today's [2010s] fiftysomethings may be part of the first generation in American history to experience this kind of lifetime downward mobility, in which at every stage of adult life, they have had less income and less net wealth than did people who were their age ten years before [Longman 52–57].

Petty himself transcended these tiers of the socio-economic ladder, yet somehow he retained a deep emotional connection to this broad slice of American culture even as he achieved extraordinary wealth and fame. Born into a poor family, he slowly worked his way through the working class and beyond (Zanes). Because his early life experience was so true to the frustrations and aspirations of lower and middle class Americans, his songs deliver a powerful degree of authenticity and pure emotion. He spoke directly to this population's deepest hopes and fears, and the timing of his career perfectly positioned his music to forge significant and lasting neural connections within the minds of the listeners. Nonetheless, the widening gap of income inequality and slow economic growth throughout the arc of Tom Petty's career left a large part of the U.S. population trenched in the middle or lower class, searching for identity, belonging, and security—and flirting treacherously with the very real possibility of having their primary needs unmet and threatened

These late 20th Century dynamics of mature and post–Industrial First World Capitalism—of social class, income, and wealth inequality—provide lenses through which to view and understand Tom Petty's message(s) and connection with his audience. And some of the most prominent frameworks from 20th century psychology and behavioral economics serve to shape and polish these views.

In 1943, for example, Abraham Maslow's "pyramid-shape hierarchy of needs captured the world's imagination by suggesting that humans are driven by innate needs for survival, safety, love and belonging, esteem, and self-realization, in that order" (Abulof 508). Though Freud and Jung had suggested similar ideas of powerful, innate, semiconscious human drives governing much of how we behave and communicate, Maslow's resonance came

Income Gains Widely Shared in Early Postwar Decades — But Not Since Then

Real family income between 1947 and 2016, as a percentage of 1973 level

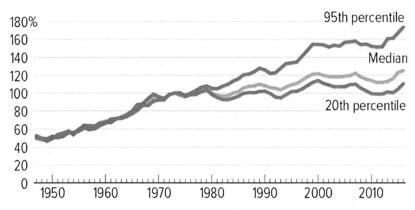

Note: In 2014 Census split its sample of survey respondents into two groups to test a set of redesigned income questions. In 2015 (reporting on 2014 income using the new questions), Census released two estimates of 2013 incomes, one based on the old questions and one on the new. The chart uses the estimate based on the old questions, based on CBPP's judgment that, due in part to sample size, it is likely more accurate for 2013.

Source: CBPP calculations based on U.S. Census Bureau Data

Income gains between 1947 and 2016 (Center on Budget and Policy Priorities).

from his ability to more precisely define and structure human priorities and trajectory toward affluence. According to Maslow, "Human needs arrange themselves in hierarchies of pre-potency. That is to say, the appearance of one need usually rests on the prior satisfaction of another, more pre-potent need. Man is a perpetually wanting animal. Also no need or drive can be treated as if it were isolated or discrete; every drive is related to the state of satisfaction or dissatisfaction of other drives" (370).

The point here is one of sequence and precedence. According to Maslow there are "Higher and Lower Needs." And though it's fundamental and perhaps self-evident that we must meet and achieve at least some of these basic needs to survive, the idea is that some come first on the list, and are in fact *pre-requisites* before meeting (and, as we and Roland Barthes suggest, even *perceiving of*, in a semiotic sense) others. And on up.

Petty's songs reflect fundamental needs in the middle of Maslow's pyramid, specifically Belonging and Esteem. These drives captivate a large (middle class + working class) and frequently marginalized audience. Petty's signature

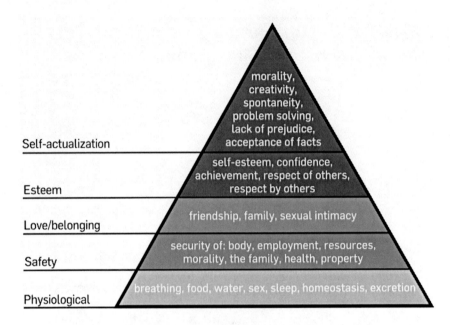

Maslows's hierarchy of needs (Wikipedia Commons).

songs are direct and efficient capsules, full of the same perspectives as those of his audience. He often addressed his antagonist or declared a manifesto, even in his titles: "I Won't Back Down," "Don't Do Me Like That," and "You're Jammin' Me" strummed a primal chord with these listeners and provided basic articulate language for naming and expressing feelings that we as American residents, thinkers, and consumers have never before been able to recognize and understand.

During the decades Petty charted the most top 10 Billboard Hot 100 songs in history (1970–2000), between 82 and 86% of the U.S. population could be defined as Middle, Lower Middle, or Lower Class ("The American Middle Class…"). The 1980 study by Lynda C. Gratton "Analysis of Maslow's Need Hierarchy with Three Social Class Groups" considered a sample of two hundred forty adults across three social class groups. Those findings "provided evidence that individuals of a similar social class share similar notions of which needs are most important to them, and these notions differ across social class" (Gratton 463), and they also showed that the need for Belonging is of great importance to the lower and working class groups, while a strong desire for Esteem is shared between the working class and middle class.

The Self-Actualization need was primarily a middle class desire. Also, "[c]ertain aspects of a need appear to be more important to most people than other aspects. For instance [the following three aspects] are all more important to most of the respondents than the general needs of which they are items.

- Having a sense of humor (Self-Actualization)
- Being respected (Esteem)
- Having someone who is very close (Belonging)." (Gratton 471)

An analysis of "Tom Petty's Top 20 Billboard Hot 100 Hits" shows how the focus of these themes speak directly to our majority population.

Tom Petty's Top 20 Billboard Hot 100 Hits, as categorized by themes from Abraham Maslow (hierarchy of needs) and Karl Albrecht (loss aversion)

Rank	Title	Year	Theme	Maslow	Albrecht
1	Stop Draggin' My Heart Around	1981	Loss	Social Belonging	separation (empowering)
2	Free Fallin'	1990	Breakup	Social Belonging	separation (empowering)
3	Don't Do Me Like That	1979	Pain	Esteem	ego/death (empowering)
4	I Won't Back Down	1989	Inspiration	Esteem	ego/death (empowering)
5	Don't Come Around Here No More	1985	Pain	Esteem	ego/death (empowering)
6	You Don't Know How It Feels	1995	Nostalgia	Social Belonging	separation (empowering)
7	You Got Lucky	1982	Breakup	Social Belonging	separation (empowering)
8	Refugee	1980	Desire	Social Belonging	separation (empowering)
9	Mary Jane's Last Dance	1994	Loss	Social Belonging	separation
10	Runnin' Down a Dream	1989	Aspiration	Self-Actualization	ego/death (empowering)
11	Jammin' Me	1987	Inspiration	Social Belonging	Loss of autonomy/ Smothered
12	The Waiting	1981	Desire	Social Belonging	separation (empowering)
13	Change of Heart	1983	Loss	Social Belonging	separation
14	Learning to Fly	1991	Aspiration	Self-Actualization	ego/death (empowering)
15	Breakdown	1976	Desire	Social Belonging	ego/death (empowering)
16	Needles and Pins	1986	Loss	Social Belonging	separation
17	I Need to Know	1978	Breakup	Social Belonging	ego/death (empowering)

Rank	Title	Year	Theme	Maslow	Albrecht
18	A Face in the Crowd	1990	Nostalgia	Social Belonging	separation (empowering)
19	Make It Better (Forget About Me)	1985	Breakup	Social Belonging	separation (empowering)
20	Here Comes My Girl	1980	Inspiration	Esteem	ego/death (empowering)

A full fourteen of these biggest Tom Petty songs address Maslow's *Belonging* theme, four address *Esteem*, and two address *Self-Actualization*. Further, it is interesting to note that the Self-Actualization themed songs do not appear until 1989–91, suggesting the artist's own development and progress, and satisfaction of some components of more basic emotional needs.

Breakdown	1976	Desire	Social Belonging
I Need to Know	1978	Breakup	Social Belonging
Don't Do Me Like That	1979	Pain	Esteem
Refugee	1980	Desire	Social Belonging
Here Comes My Girl	1980	Inspiration	Esteem

In brief: 1976–1980 brought first major hit, "Breakdown," a shuffling and jazzy declaration of nonchalance whose intensity betrays a mild panic underneath, as well as many radio listeners' introduction to Petty's common search for belonging. This was followed by "I Need to Know," a punk-infused yelp of frustration and vulnerability, seeking affirmation or at least respect. "Don't Do Me Like That" was soulful and hooky in its straightforward desperation, and serves as an emblem of Petty's early focus on personal confidence and esteem. "Refugee" was an efficient and sneering plea for a casual partner to commit, and "Here Comes My Girl" was a polished, thrilling celebration of the relief that comes from deep and true romantic connection, evoking both the Byrds and the Kinks.

The Waiting	1981	Desire	Social Belonging
Stop Draggin My Heart Around	1981	Loss	Social Belonging
You Got Lucky	1982	Breakup	Social Belonging
Change of Heart	1983	Loss	Social Belonging
Don't Come Around Here No More	1985	Pain	Esteem
Make It Better (Forget About Me)	1985	Breakup	Social Belonging

From 1981 to 1985 came "The Waiting," a catchy cross-pollinated lesson in patience and desire. "Stop Draggin My Heart Around" was a two-sided appeal for control and resolution in a challenged relationship. "You Got Lucky" vamps and swaggers as a way to mask a post-breakup sadness, and "Change of Heart" is a big-guitared throwback and a justification for walking away from a superficial pairing. "Don't Come Around Here No More" is a newly strange and vibrant attempt at empowerment that re-energized and complicated Petty's entire body of work, and "Make It Better (Forget About Me)" was another funky, complex look at Petty's style, his speakers' emotional needs, and the places they could go.

Needles & Pins	1986	Loss	Social Belonging
Jammin' Me	1987	Inspiration	Social Belonging
I Won't Back Down	1989	Inspiration	Esteem
Runnin' Down a Dream	1989	Aspiration	Self-Actualization
Free Fallin'	1990	Breakup	Social Belonging
A Face in the Crowd	1990	Nostalgia	Social Belonging

Through the end of the 1980s, Petty made "Needles & Pins," a smart and sweet cover (with Stevie Nicks) of The Searchers' British Invasion pop. "Jammin' Me" was an oddly topical exploration of social strain and media saturation, rooted in Bob Dylan's mischievous side. "I Won't Back Down" was a measured and confident attempt at finding strength in a personal code, and "Runnin Down a Dream" was breathless in its energy and determination. Lasting trademark "Free Fallin'" is a three-chord miracle of a song whose vocals evoke just enough energy to sell the tension between the two words in its title, and "A Face in the Crowd" is an understated portrait set against unspoken depth and, perhaps, regret.

Learning to Fly	1991	Aspiration	Self-Actualization
Mary Jane's Last Dance	1994	Loss	Social Belonging
You Don't Know How It Feels	1995	Nostalgia	Social Belonging

Though his recording and live performance career continued until his death in 2017, Tom Petty's last major period of Billboard chart appearances was during 1991–1995, which included "Learning to Fly," a bird's eye epic that still finds genuine connection with its speaker's struggle and achievement; "Mary Jane's Last Dance," a Twin Peaks–era gothic drama based in sex, loss, and confinement; and "You Don't Know How It Feels," a full-on musical mission statement for Petty's mid–90s mellowed out stoicism, as well as some of the finest and most eclectic sounds he and his band ever put on record.

Petty's Songwriting DNA

A 2014 study by David H. Henard and Christian L. Rossetti of North Carolina State University "analyzed popular music's most successful songs over a 50-year period (1960–2009), utilizing a combination of quantitative and qualitative approaches to uncover communication themes from nearly 1,000 songs that best resonated with mass audiences. The study identifies 12 communication themes and finds that they are used repeatedly over time; are largely emotional in nature; appear congruent with contemporary societal and environmental influences; and help predict a song's chances of commercial success" (Henard 178).

Henard and Rossetti's work "validates insights across several academic disciplines by highlighting the fact that commercially successful communication themes in popular music are those that resonate with core human experiences." Their study uses "a relatively narrow range of themes that evoke emotional reactions, have a historical context, and complement the audience's contemporary social environment." Further:

> The communication themes identified resonate with a diverse and large population of consumers and extend beyond the field of music. These themes are universal in the sense that most individuals have experienced them at some point and can relate to the message presented. They transcend geography and time and are themes that are replete across classical literature and art, thus demonstrating their rigor [Henard 187].

When we distill the "communication themes" of Tom Petty's Top 20 Billboard Hot 100 Hits in accordance with the methodologies of Henard and Rossetti's study, we can observe strong alignment with the seven primary themes that resonate across a large group of listeners:

> Each of us experiences pain, loss, and confusion. At some point in our lives, we—as consumers—each seek inspiration, aspire to greater things, or reflect nostalgically on the conjured idealism of the past. Likewise, we can become jaded, desire something different, and rebel against our current situation. These themes are universal. They are classic. They speak directly to our core humanity. They are communication themes with broad applicability and have stood the test of time ... [Henard 187].

We can see from these studies that while Petty's songs may seem basic and immediate in language and chord structure, they resonate within the listener at a much deeper, subconscious level. Petty's music speaks to our primal needs and employs communication themes that are deeply emotional and universal to a large population of Americans.

Perhaps an even more powerful connection is the relationship of Petty's work to our primal fears, which scientists understand as a root cause of many behaviors and biases. One example of this scientific recognition is the Prospect Theory principle of Loss Aversion, as outlined by Behavioral Economists Daniel Kahneman and Amos Tversky. "When directly compared or weighted against each other, losses loom larger than gains," Kahneman observes. "This asymmetry between the power of positive and negative expectations or experiences has an evolutionary history. Organisms that treat threats as more urgent than opportunities have a better chance to survive and reproduce" (Kahneman 282).

Karl Albrecht's "Feararchy" framework, meanwhile, posits there are five basic fears that all humans demonstrate:

1. Extinction—the fear of annihilation, of ceasing to exist. This is a more fundamental way to express it than just calling it "fear of death." The idea of no longer being arouses a primary existential anxiety in all

normal humans. Consider that panicky feeling you get when you look over the edge of a high building.

2. Mutilation—the fear of losing any part of our precious bodily structure; the thought of having our body's boundaries invaded, or of losing the integrity of any organ, body part, or natural function. Anxiety about animals, such as bugs, spiders, snakes, and other creepy things arises from fear of mutilation.

3. Loss of Autonomy—the fear of being immobilized, paralyzed, restricted, enveloped, overwhelmed, entrapped, imprisoned, smothered, or otherwise controlled by circumstances beyond our control. In physical form, it's commonly known as claustrophobia, but it also extends to our social interactions and relationships.

4. Separation—the fear of abandonment, rejection, and loss of connectedness; of becoming a non-person—not wanted, respected, or valued by anyone else. The "silent treatment," when imposed by a group, can have a devastating psychological effect on its target.

5. Ego-death—the fear of humiliation, shame, or any other mechanism of profound self-disapproval that threatens the loss of integrity of the Self; the fear of the shattering or disintegration of one's constructed sense of lovability, capability, and worthiness [Albrecht].

Applying these basic fears to our analysis of Tom Petty's Top 20 Billboard Hot 100 Hits, we can observe his most popular songs speak to our fears of Separation, Ego-death, and Loss of Autonomy. Some songs (i.e., American Girl, Free Fallin') encompass multiple fears, and give us a safe, shared, social space to vicariously address our concerns. Kahneman and Albrecht's theories propose that our fears are a stronger motivator than our potential gains. Petty's ability to connect with our universal fears through his music is a primary reason for his widespread appeal and listeners' strong emotional connections to his music.

It is the shared and common nature, however, across a culture and listenership, that may yield further understanding about Tom Petty's social semiotic impacts on a wider cultural subconscious. With the deep psychological connections to his music in mind, through the modern lenses of Maslow, Kahneman, and Albrecht, some next questions include: What real and demonstrable transitions, if any, did Petty's messages and meaning undergo during his lengthy and eventful popular music career and what do these changes suggest? How should we read the emotional themes and signifiers in Petty's work in contrast to his peers in time and genre, including Bowie, Nicks, Bruce Springsteen, and John Mellencamp? And what can we determine about the real-world socioeconomic conditions that precede and correspond to Petty's recording career, as well as workers' emotional responses to them (as demonstrated here) when viewing Petty's lyrical content through a Barthesian/Lacanian linguistic lens?

NOTE

1. "People who were just sitting there, not engaged in anything, light up when they start hearing music from when they were 25."—Jonathan Burdette, M.D., a neuroradiologist at Wake Forest Baptist Medical Center. "Music Has Powerful (and Visible) Effects on the Brain." ScienceDaily. April 12, 2017. Accessed April 01, 2018. https://www.sciencedaily.com/releases/2017/04/170412181341.htm.

WORKS CITED

Abulof, Uriel. "Introduction: Why We Need Maslow in the Twenty-First Century." *Society*, vol. 54, no. 6, 2017, pp. 508–09, doi:10.1007/s12115-017-0198-6.
Albrecht, Karl. "The (Only) 5 Fears We All Share." *Psychology Today*, 22 March 2012, https://www.psychologytoday.com/blog/brainsnacks/201203/the-only-5-fears-we-all-share.
"The American Middle Class Is Losing Ground." Pew Research Center's Social & Demographic Trends Project. 9 December 2015, http://www.pewsocialtrends.org/2015/12/09/the-american-middle-class-is-losing-ground/.
"Case Study: Dewalt Jobsite Radio Product Design." Altitude. 2018. https://www.altitudeinc.com/casestudy/dewalt-worksite-radio/.
Demographic Trends in the 20th Century: Census 2000 Special Reports. Bibliography, 2012.
Gratton, Lynda C. "Analysis of Maslow's Need Hierarchy with Three Social Class Groups." *Social Indicators Research*, vol. 7, no. 1–4, 1980, pp. 463–76, doi:10.1007/bf00305612.
Henard, David H., and Christian L. Rossetti. "All You Need Is Love?" *Journal of Advertising Research*, vol. 54, no. 2, 2014, pp. 178–191, doi:10.2501/jar-54-2-178-191.
Holbrook, Morris B., and Robert M. Schindler. "Some Exploratory Findings on the Development of Musical Tastes." *Journal of Consumer Research*, vol. 16, no. 1, 1989, pp. 119, doi:10.1086/209200.
Kahneman, Daniel. *Thinking, Fast and Slow*. New York: Farrar, Straus and Giroux, 2015.
Longman, Phillip. "Wealth and Generations." *Washington Monthly*, June–Aug. 2015, https://washingtonmonthly.com/magazine/junejulyaug-2015/wealth-and-generations/.
"Mainstream Rock (Chart)." *Wikipedia*, https://en.wikipedia.org/wiki/Mainstream_Rock_(chart).
Maslow, A. H. A Theory of Human Motivation. *Psychological Review*, vol. 50, no. 4, 1943, pp. 370–396, http://dx.doi.org/10.1037/h0054346.
"Maslow's Hierarchy of Needs." Wikimedia Commons, 29 June 2009, https://commons.wikimedia.org/wiki/File:Maslow's_Hierarchy_of_Needs.svg.
NPR Staff. "A Portrait of America's Middle Class, by the Numbers." NPR. 7 July 2016, https://www.npr.org/2016/07/07/484941939/a-portrait-of-americas-middle-class-by-the-numbers.
Stone, Chad, et al. "A Guide to Statistics on Historical Trends in Income Inequality." Center on Budget and Policy Priorities, 29 August 2018, www.cbpp.org/research/poverty-and-inequality/a-guide-to-statistics-on-historical-trends-in-income-inequality#_ftn1.
"32nd Annual GRAMMY Awards." GRAMMY.com. 28 November 2017, https://www.grammy.com/grammys/awards/32nd-annual-grammy-awards.
"Tom Petty." GRAMMY.com. 28 November 2017, https://www.grammy.com/grammys/artists/tom-petty.
"Tom Petty by the Numbers: A 'Breakdown' of 40 Years of Hits." *Billboard*, 3 October 2017, https://www.billboard.com/articles/columns/chart-beat/7988674/tom-petty-heartbreakers-40-years-hits-breakdown.
"Tom Petty Top Songs." Music VF.com, http://www.musicvf.com/Tom Petty.art.
"Tom Petty's Top 20 Billboard Hot 100 Hits." *Billboard*, 2 October 2017, https://www.billboard.com/articles/list/6165346/tom-petty-top-20-billboard-hot-100-hits-heartbreakers-stevie-nicks.
"Traveling Wilburys." Recording Academy Grammy Awards. 2018, https://www.grammy.com/grammys/artists/traveling-wilburys.
Zanes, Warren. *Petty: The Biography*. New York: St. Martins Griffin, 2016.

Peace and Petty

Music's Healing Power

Shawn W. Murphy

"Tom's music saved my life," says Jessica Aiken-Hall, who overcame an abusive childhood, abusive relationships, and depression with the help of music by the late Tom Petty.

"I was born into chaos.... For many years, I existed in a toxic environment mere inches from death. As a child, I didn't know any different. I assumed all parents plotted to kill their children. All mothers had their kids keep a lookout for their father while they had sex at a strange man's house," Aiken-Hall writes in her 2017 memoir, *The Monster That Ate My Mommy*. "The chaos was so comfortable anything else looked frightening. I was scared to leave it" (8).

Then, at age 14, she heard "You Don't Know How It Feels." "For the first time in my life I felt like someone understood me. It was this song that helped me see that I was not alone," she reflects. "The song found the words I had been unable to find. Tom Petty was right—no one knew how it felt to be me. And with that, my love for Tom Petty was born. His music gave me peace. It was the knowledge of not being as different as I had thought that kept me from committing suicide. If I felt sad or depressed, or angry or alone, I listened to his songs. I was never alone when I had Tom's music."

Tom Petty became the soundtrack to her life. "Free Fallin'" inspired her to leave an emotionally abusive boyfriend. "Don't Fade On Me" eased pain from the death of her grandmother, who raised her. After her family lost their house to fire, "Square One" helped her see that since there was no human toll, starting over was possible. "Something Good Coming" gave hope and strength to get out of an abusive marriage. Then, there's Mudcrutch's "I Forgive It All." The last words she said to her mom before her death were "I forgive you." She says, "I find a great deal of comfort in knowing, or assuming, that Tom had forgiven his (abusive) father, and it helped me forgive my mom." She says "Keeping Me Alive" sums up the impact of Petty on her: "Tom's music really helped push me through the hard parts of life."

Aiken-Hall is not the only one who has been healed by the music by Tom Petty, which was the soundtrack to the lives of many fans. Following his October 2, 2017, death, these stories emerged on Tom Petty Nation (TPN), a Facebook group with more than 30,000 members worldwide, among them Aiken-Hall. For days, then weeks, then months, these fans grieved the loss by consoling one another online. As part of this communal healing process, many of the troubled fans talked about which songs were helping them through the mourning process for Petty. Then, they disclosed which songs helped them through troubling times in their lives. Many of them were interviewed for this essay. They said his songs empowered them to survive physical and emotional trauma; his music helped get them through medical crises, abuse, addiction, divorce, and death. And for Petty himself, music helped him in much the same way. This is an essay about the healing cycle in which music healed Petty throughout his life, his music healed his fans, and how the communal concerts healed both Petty and his fans. In other words, music can be therapeutic.

While Tom Petty's fans talked about how listening to his songs was therapeutic for them, they were perhaps unaware that music as a healing mechanism is an established field with demonstrated benefits: music therapy. "Music therapy has been shown to have a significant effect on an individual's relaxation, respiration rate, self-reported pain reduction, and behaviorally observed and self-reported anxiety levels," according to the American Music Therapy Association (AMTA), the largest professional association of its type, representing more than 5,000 music therapists. The AMTA states these benefits of one of their approved programs: "non-verbal outlets for emotions associated with traumatic experiences; anxiety and stress reduction; positive changes in mood and emotional states; active and positive participant involvement in treatment; enhanced feelings of control, confidence, and empowerment; (and) positive physiological changes, such as lower blood pressure, reduced heart rate, and relaxed muscle tension."

Research has revealed that music helps one cope with emotional and physical trauma. In various clinical trials, it has been shown that music can reduce depression and anxiety, while improving social resilience, at all ages; decrease the need for pain medication for those undergoing invasive medical procedures; improve one's ability to speak after a stroke or traumatic brain injury; music can help those suffering from Parkinson's disease to initiate movement of their rigid and trembling limbs; positively affect cardiac and respiratory functions in premature and full-term babies; and for Alzheimer's disease and dementia sufferers improve symptoms, such as rekindling memories, lowering agitation, enhancing concentration, increasing communication, and helping with physical coordination, which was the basis for a 2014 documentary, "Alive Inside."

The notion that music is a powerful elixir is nothing new. "The idea of music as a healing influence which could affect health and behavior is as least as old as the writings of Aristotle and Plato," according to the AMTA. The first known reference to "music therapy" is in an un-bylined article in a 1789 edition of *Columbian Magazine* titled "Music Physically Considered" (90–93). By the early 1800s, the first formalized recorded music therapy treatment was conducted. After World Wars I and II, music therapy was used to help heal soldiers. Volunteer musicians went to veterans' hospitals to play for those who had suffered physical injuries and/or emotional trauma from what they had experienced on the battlefields. "The patients' notable physical and emotional responses to music led the doctors and nurses to request the hiring of musicians by the hospitals," according to the AMTA. "It was soon evident that the hospital musicians needed some prior training before entering the facility and so the demand grew for a college curriculum." In the early 1900s, various associations were formed with the goal of formally teaching music therapy. Today, there are 72 AMTA-approved college programs nationwide, and there are a number of academic journals that publish research into music therapy, among them the *Journal of Music Therapy*. Today, music therapy is defined as the use of music "to address physical, emotional, cognitive, and social needs of individuals," according to the AMTA. Music therapy can involve listening to, playing, singing, creating, moving to, or teaching music. The American Psychiatric Association recognizes music therapy as beneficial. It notes the connection between music, the mind, and our ability to heal.

Arts-based therapy—using reading, creative writing, and music—has been shown in various clinical studies to help heal not just those suffering from physical trauma, but also its psychological aftereffects. "Music can … play a role in helping individuals and communities to cope with trauma, whether it be through the intervention of music therapists, community music making programs or individual music listening," according to a 2015 study published in a *Frontiers in Psychology* titled "Music and Trauma: The Relationship Between Music, Personality, and Coping Style." In various case studies, music therapy has been used as a coping mechanism for trauma survivors. For example, music helped children who were traumatized after tornadoes destroyed their homes and community in the southeastern United States. Elementary school teachers helped the children compose songs that allowed them to "acknowledge and process their emotions in a healthy and healing way," state the researchers. In another example, music was used in Australia to help children cope with the aftermath of massive bushfires that claimed

173 lives and a wide swath of land and property. These fire survivors wrote songs and performed them with their peers. "The musical experiences were reported to have helped people to 'hear one another,' bond with others also experiencing loss, and regain confidence." And following the crisis in New York City when airplanes took down the World Trade Center, more than 7,000 programs were conducted by 33 music therapists to help survivors—children, adults and families. "The programs were designed to reduce stress, improve coping, and process the trauma associated with the crisis by drawing on a range of techniques including musical improvisation, songwriting, singing, sharing stories, and relaxing with music" (Garrido et al.). These intervention programs, referred to as the New York City Music Therapy Relief Project, were sponsored by the AMTA. In all of these studies, the participants, who were experiencing trauma following a crisis, were helped by music to develop coping strategies. They were able to better understand and express their anxiety and helplessness, to boost their self-confidence and feeling of safety, and to relax in a secure place.

While the AMTA prescribes a formal intervention program run by a licensed music therapist, most of us laymen use music therapy in an informal way. TPN members say they used Petty's music to get through physical trauma or life-threatening illness, and also the emotional trauma that typically comes with it.

One such person is Sherri Lindstrom, who in 2010 suffered a spiral break on a femur and endured surgery, rehabilitation and physical therapy. With the goal of being well enough to make it to a Heartbreakers concert for which she had already purchased a ticket, she made her physical therapist play "Last Time You're Gonna Hurt Me" during months of treatments, and she played "I Won't Back Down" while fighting pain and gaining strength to stand on two feet again.

Petty's music gave strength to another fan, Sheila Spencer, many times in her life. Among these times was the death of her newborn baby in 1999. She had given birth to extremely premature twin boys: the smaller baby weighed 22 ounces, the larger baby weighed 28 ounces. Among a list of health concerns, both suffered from brain bleeds and had lungs too immature to breathe on their own. Doctors told her they had a 30 to 40 percent chance of survival. Both underwent serious surgeries within a week of their birth. The smallest baby lived five weeks before his lungs failed. The larger baby spent 101 days in the neonatal intensive care unit, and had multiple surgeries before and after discharge. Grieving the loss of a son, caring for an ill newborn, and struggling to pay for medical expenses not covered by her insurance, Spencer listened to Petty's music to lift her spirits and empower her to push on.

By 2002, she had saved up enough money so that she could partake in some additional Tom Petty music therapy. Spencer took in a live Heartbreakers show, of which she had seen seven during her lifetime. "It was magical, and after that experience," she says, "I began calling Tom Petty concerts my 'spiritual revivals.'"

In 2015, Spencer was diagnosed with breast cancer. "During each of the 25 radiation treatments, I listened to Tom Petty," she says. "Tom Petty saved my life. I am now cancer-free." The radiation oncology staff, who seemed cognizant of the therapeutic value of listening to music, asked before her first treatment if there was any particular music that she wanted to hear while undergoing radiation. "Without hesitation, I said, 'Tom Petty!'" Spencer recalls. "They called up some Tom Petty on their iPod for me. Only after hearing his music was I able to be okay with the treatment. The staff there knew I needed it and it would be playing before I arrived in the treatment room."

Another TPN member, Deb Kartzoff, says her life was saved by Tom Petty's songs and concerts. Devastated by the loss of her husband and mother, she flew from her Australian home to see three concerts on the Heartbreakers 2017 tour. The trip marked her first time in America and seeing Petty in person. She says this was the therapy she needed: "Tom was certainly my mental savior in the worst time of my life."

Petty's music gave her the strength to get through her worst years. In 2011 and 2012, her father underwent cancer treatments, her mother was diagnosed with terminal cancer, doctors gave Deb her own cancer diagnosis, and then her husband was diagnosed with rampant melanoma. Within three months her husband was dead. Not long after her mother was dead. While her father and she continued their cancer treatments, their physical health slowly improved, yet Deb's mental health slipped. "This nearly killed me," she recalls about simultaneously grieving these deaths, organizing funerals, overseeing estate paperwork, undergoing cancer treatments, caring for her sick father, and continuing to raise two young children. "I remember weeping and wailing. Screaming into the void. My life was gone."

It was at that moment that she rediscovered Petty's songs. "Tom, his music, his philosophy—him—he saved me when I needed it," she says. "Looking at Tom kept me from wanting to die. And then I really started listening to his songs. His words resonated and gave me strength to keep on top. I was a mess. Seriously, I was." She flew halfway around the world for some more music therapy, in the form of a communal Petty concert.

TPN member Mitzi Edge and her youngest son also knew about the sense of community that came from being at a Petty concert; together they saw five of them. "Through the years he was my concert buddy," she says. "We both were huge fans, and he was asked one time why he would go with his mom to the concert. His reply was, 'There was no one (I) would rather go with.' We listened to Tom *all* the time together."

Yet, when Mitzi's son was 21, he sustained a head injury when skate-boarding, and ended up in a coma. "I sang Tom Petty songs to him constantly," she recalls about sitting bedside in the hospital's intensive care unit. "I would look the words up on my iPhone to make sure I didn't sing the same verses over and over." She sang "Wake Up Time," the song she used to sing to wake him up for elementary school. "Finally, on day three he came out of his coma. The first thing he said to me was, 'Mom, I have Tom Petty songs in my head.' I just died laughing and crying at once. I told him, 'no wonder—I sang them for three days.' The power of prayer and music!"

For most of us, we *know* music helps us, particularly when faced with emotional trauma, so we regularly administer music therapy. We feel better when we listen to the songs and see the shows. We self-medicate with lyrics that speak to us. Music is ever-present; it helps us celebrate the good times and consoles us during the bad times.

"Whenever humans come together for any reason, music is there: weddings, funerals, graduation from college, men marching off to war, stadium sporting events, a night on the town, prayer, a romantic dinner, mothers rocking their infants to sleep, and college students studying with music as a background," Daniel J. Levitin wrote in his 2006 book, *This Is Your Brain On Music: The Science of a Human Obsession* (6).

For Tom Petty, music was ever-present, and it proved to be therapeutic for him throughout his lifetime. He listened to and wrote songs that helped him celebrate the joyful times and get through the disturbing times. "Music has always been my passport to a better place," Petty told Peter Bogdanovich for the 2007 documentary *Runnin' Down a Dream.*

From an early age, Petty, who suffered through child abuse by his father, longed for that better place. Petty recounted to Warren Zanes for his 2015 book, *Petty: The Biography,* that his father, Earl, was emotionally distant, verbally aggressive, and physically violent. He recalled a scene in which the 5-year-old tested the ability of a toy slingshot, a gift from his father, and the skill of his marksmanship by hitting a Cadillac driving by his yard. After the car was hit, its angry driver reported the incident to Tom's mother, Katherine, or "Kitty." Later, when Earl arrived home, the boy was on the receiving end of his wrath and rage. In was then that the verbal abuse escalated to physical abuse, which became a pattern throughout his childhood. "I felt kind of weird, not knowing what was coming next," Petty remembered. "But when my father got home later, he came in, took a belt, and beat the living shit out of me. He beat me so bad that I was covered in raised welts, from my head to my toes. I mean, you can't imagine someone hitting a child like that. Five years old, I remember it so well. My mother and grandmother laid me in my bed, stripped me, and they took cotton and alcohol, cleaning these big welts all over my body" (qtd. in Zanes 20). Kitty would try to become the buffer between Earl and Tom. Despite her affectionate efforts, though, Earl continued to get his hands on Tom. "My mother's rap was, 'You gotta be a better boy. You just can't do that. You can't make him that mad.' But I was fucking *five*. She learned, for her part, that you'd better not mention it to Earl. That was one of the first ones. But there were many, many more" (20).

One of the ways that Tom Petty sought to escape the abuse was to find consolation in music. At age 10, Petty and some cousins got to meet Elvis Presley during filming of *Follow That Dream* in Ocala, Florida. Elvis shook the little hand of Tom, who stood still, stunned and speechless, yet smiling. "Within days, Petty says, he traded his slingshot for a box of 45s, many of them Presley classics. Elvis became a symbol of a place Tom Petty wanted to go" (Zanes 27). Later, Tom would see Presley, then the Beatles, and later the British Invasion bands on the Ed Sullivan TV show, triggering a yearning to be them. By age 12 Petty got his first guitar, quickly learned chords and songs, and soon thereafter played with Gainesville bands throughout his pre-teen and teen years. His quest for a better place came from performing music, with the Epics and the Sundowners, and eventually Mudcrutch and the Heartbreakers. His escape to a better place also came from seeing live music. But it was primarily the songs Petty penned that brought him the most solace. Petty generally did not explain the story behind the story of his songs, but, Zanes notes: "There's little question that songwriting has been the thing that has made it all more livable. The songs have been his safe house. In them you can hear a man wanting a little more freedom and a little more peace" (305).

Petty's songs became the safe house for TPN member Marissia Garrett, who also suffered from child abuse. For her, and for many other Petty fans, the song "Refugee" became a wake-up moment. "I've been kicked around in my life. That song is an anthem for me because I grew up struggling and fighting for my freedom in a very abusive household. It made me feel like I wasn't the only person who had to get past some hard times and battles. I grew up with an adoptive mother who suffered badly from narcotic addiction and she was physically violent," Garrett says. "She made me feel like I could never live up to her standards and that made me feel like an underdog. I can remember her leaving welts from a belt on me and leaving for days at a time and me having to stay at whoever was available while she left. Nothing was ever good enough."

Later, Petty's music helped her get through an abusive marriage and a divorce. While in "a physically and mentally abusive marriage" in which she "was pushed around, slapped, mentally beaten down, controlled, the whole nine yards," Petty's songs were her "escape." Says Garrett, "[The songs] gave me the will to better myself…. I found him to be the soundtrack of my life. His music has always made me happy."

TPN member Donna Michelle Harris Eggers had the same soundtrack.

With Petty's musical guidance, she maneuvered through childhood sexual abuse, and later her parents' divorce and their deaths. Starting at age 4, she says a relative repeatedly "preyed" on her with flattery, surmising that because she came from a domestic home in disarray that she "was desperate for love and attention." Later, at age 11, Eggers says she was sexually abused by a family friend. At age 12 she heard "Refugee" coming from the radio on her nightstand and thought Petty was singing directly to her. "'Refugee' made me feel like I didn't have to be frightened and victimized all the time. I didn't have to live like a refugee," she says.

"He kept me sane all these years," Eggers says. "His music has been my religion, my therapy and the soundtrack to my life, the good and the bad parts. I had been through trauma in my childhood and his music helped me escape. It has become such a welcome coping mechanism my entire life—like he wrote the songs just to make me feel better, like he got me, like we were great friends." Five months before Petty's death, Eggers saw the Heartbreakers in concert. "I swear, every song got to me. I got teary eyed when he sang 'Refugee,' 'American Girl,' 'You Wreck Me,' and 'Wildflowers.' My friend asked me why and I couldn't explain it to her. I didn't really know. I just knew that he and I were kindred spirits through his music."

"Refugee" also spoke to Vivian Morris, who first heard the song from a small radio in her basement bedroom. The song was her refuge when, in fifth grade, she was placed into foster care. "I didn't know what a refugee was, but I knew that I was one. I couldn't have articulated it at the time, but that song made me realize that lyrics have meaning and that music was something like alchemy, creating understanding (and) fortification," Morris explains. "It seemed Petty was talking to me and my experience at the time, wanting me to feel better and somehow offering hope that things would get better. That song was the first time I realized I could have a personal relationship with a song, a conversation of sorts, and that personal connection could be healing because I felt heard and understood."

Later, as a young adult, Morris also began seeing Petty in concert and experiencing the impromptu "Refugee" sing-along with thousands of fans. "I never made it through hearing that song live without crying and being healed a tiny bit," she recalls. "It just hit me hard that I'll never have that experience again. Ever since that initial emotional connection with a song, I've turned to music to understand myself. It mostly happens in the communal live music experience."

Petty's songs and concerts provided sanctuary to those whose childhood was a domestic maelstrom, and they also helped others get through the loss of a loved one. TPN member Bob Keppler, who lost his sister, was helped by Petty's music. Bob's sister, Candy, and he were united by their love for Tom Petty. "I got my sister hooked on the Heartbreakers," he remembers, noting that Petty's music helped cement the bond between the siblings. They would buy and listen together to all the albums, and they would see four concerts together from 1981 to 1989. They would even buy each other Petty-themed gifts for birthdays and holidays.

During this time, though, Candy suffered with mental illness. At age 13, in 1974, she was diagnosed as bipolar. She suffered with the illness through her teens and into adulthood. "I often didn't understand what was happening with her or why she was doing the things she was, but no matter how crazy things got, we could always find common ground when it came to Tom Petty and the Heartbreakers," Bob says. Candy needed periodic treatment over the years at mental health facilities, which Bob remembers as "scary places" that "very much had an asylum feel to them." He vividly remembers one time, at age 16, when he needed to drive Candy, then 18, to an in-patient facility and check her in by himself. "It pained me to the depths of my soul to look over and see her curled up in the passenger seat, sobbing, knowing there was nothing I could do but take her to 'the dungeon,'" he says. "I'll never forget the moment on the drive when she looked up at me and said, 'I'm so scared' through the sobs." During that ride, Bob played Tom Petty's music to help calm Candy, and to help calm himself. "*Hard Promises* was in the cassette deck and '*I Got a Thing About You*' was playing," he says. "I think of that moment every time I hear that song."

As it naturally happens, the Keppler siblings as adults were off living their separate lives, separated by distance. Bob focused on his career, and he and Candy "drifted apart over the years." Bob says, "She'd grown desperate, cried wolf many times before, so I completely missed it when her demons took over, and one day she was gone." In 1999, when she was 38, Candy overdosed on prescription medication and alcohol; the official cause of death was an *accidental overdose, although Bob notes that she was* "in some drug house surrounded by addicts," adding, "I'm certain she had just had enough of the struggle with her demons and took her own life."

Afflicted with guilt, Bob questioned himself: "'Why wasn't I more concerned? Why did I ignore all the signals? Why didn't I do more?' Those were questions best not answered, so I dealt with them the way I dealt with most 'unpleasant' things: push it to the back and move on, life goes on. Not really the best way to mourn a sister."

Years passed before Bob finally came to grips with his sister's death and found the words to express how he felt. This turning point came after he saw a Heartbreakers concert on the *Mojo* tour. Loving the new songs he heard performed live, he purchased the CD in order to hear the other material. In the liner notes, he noticed something that stopped him cold in his tracks— track 5, "Candy," and track 6, "No Reason to Cry." Bob's sister's name was a Tom Petty song title, followed by a song about loss and sorrow. He cried "like a baby" as he listened to those songs, which conjured up his sister's memory. "It instantly opened my heart to grieve for my sister and restore the bond we once shared," he says. "Only Tom Petty and the Heartbreakers could do that.... I know she would've been ecstatic to have seen her name on a Heartbreakers album. It awoke something in me and I knew I had to address issues I'd long pushed aside. After which, and for the first time, I truly mourned for Candy, came to terms with a lot of things about our relationship, and feel connected to her once again. My life will never be the same."

After seeing one of the concerts on the Heartbreakers' 2017 tour, Bob came up with "the bright idea of sharing the joy of the tour with Candy." He assembled the CD covers from the four tours that the two of them had seen together in the 1980s, plus the *Mojo* cover because it contains the namesake "Candy," put them into Ziploc bags, and used melted wax to adhere them to the family headstone, where are spread some of Candy's ashes.

For Tom Petty, music helped him through a loss of a different kind. On May 17, 1987, when Petty's Encino, California, house burned to the ground as his family stood in the driveway watching flames devour their home and all of its contents. Later, Los Angeles fire inspectors would conclude this was the work of an arsonist—never to be identified. Twenty years later, Petty recalled the event in the Bogdanovich documentary: "It was a nightmare. Just a few feet from where one of my daughters was sleeping the fire started. We all survived, but the house didn't." Recalled Petty's daughter, Adria: "I remember my dad coming over and putting his arm around me. I started to cry, and he went, 'Don't do that. This is no time for that. We need to be tough. We'll get through this together. We're all safe and that's all that matters'" (*Runnin'*).

Just over a month after the fire, I saw the Rock and Roll Caravan—Tom Petty and the Heartbreakers, Georgia Satellites, and Del Fuegos (in which Warren Zanes played guitar)—perform at Great Woods in Mansfield, Massachusetts, on June 27, 1987. Petty never let on that night what was likely in his head, saving it for "I Won't Back Down," which he penned for 1989's "Full Moon Fever" album. In what was surely music therapy for Petty, the song was defiant, telling us—perhaps speaking directly to the arsonist—that he will not cave in or budge, regardless of what is thrown at him. In a 2009 interview with *Rolling Stone*, Petty acknowledged to David Fricke that the song stemmed from the arson, even though it does not speak about it directly. About the song, he said: "It's so bare, without any ambiguity. There was nothing there but truth." About the fire, he said: "I took that personally. Surviving something like that makes you feel alive. That was the mindset: I will survive, I will move on" (qtd. in Fricke 75).

Music helped Tom survive another loss in his life: his marriage. "Songs were a safe place to be," Petty told Zanes for the *Petty* biography. He spoke about the therapeutic role of music during the trauma in his life, which included an abusive wife and divorce. "I needed a safe place. So I went there a lot" (258). Tom and Jane Benyo Petty's marriage had been on the rocks years before *Wildflowers*—"the divorce album," as Tom calls it (qtd. in Zanes 253). Tom loved Jane, but couldn't live with her anymore; as Tom told Zanes, he had lived too long in "an abusive marriage" (258) where Jane, who suffered from mental illness, abused him.

Throughout the 1994 *Wildflowers* album, a song's narrator speaks to a loved one that the end of the line has been reached. The lyrics convincingly convey his ambivalence about the marriage, yet conclude it must end. The title track marks the relationship's end by saying she should move on and be free to find a mate who's better suited for her; "Time to Move On" predicts an uncertain future, yet concludes it's a road worth taking because it would end anxious and confrontational times; "Hard On Me" questions his marital faith as he endures a spouse who makes things difficult and wonders about sheltering in the arms of someone who will believe in him; "A Higher Place" has him trying to remain optimistic and positive about a relationship that is stuck in a lower place, yet acknowledges that the only way out of this rut is to leave; and "Wake Up Time" reconciles the relationship's demise as an opportunity for both spouses to move on and find peace and happiness.

As Zanes wrote in Petty's biography, *Wildflowers* is "one man's open journal of love's demise and the dream of more" (251). Zanes said Petty's lyrics sent a clear message to Jane, delivering a message that he couldn't seem to verbalize at home. About the album, Petty himself said: "That's me getting ready to leave. I do not even know how conscious I was of it when I was writing it.... It just took me getting up the guts to leave." He laments the impact that separation and divorce might have on their children. "I knew this would be devastating to the whole family.... But staying there was finishing me off. I'd become a different person" (qtd. in Zanes 253).

After the 1996 divorce, Tom was living alone in a secluded cabin in the woods of Pacific Palisades, California. Deep in a post-divorce funk, Petty was suffering from clinical depression. "It was just a lot of pain. My personal life had blown up," Petty disclosed on camera for the Bogdanovich documentary. "Here I was, I got everything I wanted and it fell apart. My career was always fine, but it was quite a blow to realize that my personal life has gone to hell.... Really, I just fell down. It was the only time I remember in my life when I just fell down. The load was too much. I was always the one, no matter what happened, who would soldier on. But not this time" (*Runnin'*).

Loss in the form of an ended marriage also impacted TPN members, including Jeanne Moulton Cashman, who used Petty's music to help her through a divorce, and then to heal from it. When she discovered her husband was with another woman, she felt as if the briars had pricked her, and the fire had burned her, so the song "Insider" struck a chord. She rediscovered the Tom Petty and the Heartbreakers music she had listened to prior to her marriage. "I started to revisit music of my choice," she says. "It was very healing for me."

TPN member Annette Chapligin from Sweden was healed by the song "Wildflowers" during her separation and divorce. The song's message about letting go and embracing freedom resonated with her. Post-divorce, she garnered strength from listening to "Hard On Me," "Wake Up Time," "Alright For Now," and "Time To Move On." After Petty's death, she set up in a corner of her home a makeshift shrine to Tom Petty with candles and wildflowers.

Also healed by Petty's music after a failed relationship was TPN member Jennifer Oates. In her mid–20s she found herself far from home, adrift in "a horribly dysfunctional relationship" and unemployed after losing her job. So, she packed up her Petty CDs, hit the road, and headed for home. As she crossed the border from the state she was leaving, "Change Of Heart" came on. Its indomitable spirit spoke to her. She cranked it up and yelled out the defiant lyrics about being unwanted, yet strong enough to move on. "That song helped me go from really torn down to pissed and determined," she says. "His music has always helped me pick myself back up, dust myself off and keep taking on the world."

For TPN member Shannon Nicole Kringen, her loss came in the form of her parents' divorce and relocation to another state when she was age 11. Living with her mother, she was far from her father, grandparents, and friends. "Refugee" boomed from a juke box in a pizza parlor. "It was love at first listen," she says, then reels off many Petty songs that have helped her at different times in life, both good and bad times. Petty's music has helped her through soured relationships, anxiety, and depression.

Known as "Goddess Kring" on her radio show broadcast in Seattle and online, she is known to play Petty songs and talk about the healing power of music. "Maybe music is my drug. I don't drink or smoke anything, but I listen to music every day," she says to me. "I sing along, I dance, I walk, I exercise— music is my constant companion. [It] makes me feel better, energizes me, grounds me, balances me, helps me channel my emotions, process my feelings. Sometimes songs satisfy me in ways that personal contact with humans I know does not. I feel closer to songs I love than to people sometimes." But it is Petty's music that she especially loves. "Tom Petty music became a symbol to me for being able to handle whatever mood I was in and whatever relationship issues I am going through … [I feel] validated, reinforced, grounded, stabilized when I listen and sing along with Tom Petty lyrics. The truth of his soul comes through his music."

For TPN member Kathleen Connors, the Petty soundtrack helped her through the physical trauma of miscarriages and surgeries, as well as the emotional trauma from her abusive marriage and divorce, and her father's death. She says "You and I Will Meet Again" soothed the anguish of "many miscarriages" because she knew she'd "see her babies in Heaven"; "I Won't Back Down" uplifted her during a health scare and three surgeries in a year; "Learning To Fly" licensed her to grow wings and flee from an abusive marriage; and "Room At the Top" and "I Forgive It All" comforted her while caring for her ailing father who suffered from dementia, and consoled her while she held his hand as he took his last breath. "Tom's music was like medicine for me. I always felt better while listening to it…. He traveled with me down every road I've been on. He *was* my 'Highway Companion,' I *was* his 'American Girl,' and ever since he went to that 'Room At the Top,' I haven't been the same. I grew up with him. Every song represents a memory of my life, especially tough times that challenged me."

Since Petty's death, "Keeping Me Alive" provides Connors comfort. "The light comes back when I listen to him sing. The bright beacon that is Tom's soul shines again and it calms me and reminds me that his physical presence may be absent but his spirit is still very much with us. Every lesson I took from Tom is still learned, every feeling he ever gave me is still present, every lifeline he threw is still in the water."

At one point in his life, Tom Petty was in need of his own lifeline when the powerful grips of depression and drug addiction ravaged him. Emotionally traumatized by his divorce, he created physical trauma for himself when he walled himself into the cabin and self-medicated with heroin. "I probably spent a month not getting out of bed, just waking up and going, 'Oh, fuck.' Lying there, the only thing that stopped the pain was drugs. But it was stupid. I'd never come up against anything bigger than me, something that I couldn't control. But it starts ruining your life," Petty told Zanes in the biography. Petty managed to get out of bed long enough to pay a visit to his therapist, who he had been seeing over time. "My therapist said something to me that, in that moment, cut through all the clutter: 'People with your level of depression don't live. They kill themselves or someone else.' I said, 'You're kidding.' 'No,' he tells me, 'with this level of depression, people *can't* live.' Maybe that was when I realized that in fact I *wasn't* living, that I was heading in the other direction" (qtd. in Zanes 260).

A glimpse into his mind at that time are the lyrics on the 1999 *Echo* album, which was recorded during his time of addiction. "Room at the Top," "Echo," and "No More" all have the narrator talking about isolation, sadness, loneliness, regret, remorse and angst while he tries to numb the pain. Yet there's hope that he can overcome this, he can keep things real, and he can change for the better. This is seen foremost in "Lonesome Sundown" as it toggles between how hard it is for him being lonely (without Jane) while love, promise and redemption await him (with then-girlfriend Dana York).

Bogdanovich had documentary footage of Petty disclosing his heroin use and subsequent addiction, but that was left out of the film at Petty's insistence. What was not on the cutting room floor was Petty on film saying: "I wasn't in good shape. I just wasn't. I was in deep shit. I had cut myself off from most of the world and become something of a hermit" (*Runnin'*). It was not until Zanes' biography that the world learned about Petty's darkest days, when he was holed up in the cabin shooting heroin into his veins in an attempt to ward off his deep depression and inner demons. Thinking that heroin would mask his depressive state, Petty found it made it only worse. "You start losing your soul. It's an ugly fucking thing. Really ugly" (qtd. in Zanes 269).

After getting detoxed from heroin and counseled for depression, Petty said he felt "reborn" (qtd. in Zanes 271). That sensation of rebirth quite likely intensified a few years later when he married Dana York in 2001 and Tom Petty and the Heartbreakers were inducted into the Rock and Roll Hall of Fame in 2002. This new lease on life was channeled into the 2002's *The Last DJ*. In this loosely structured anti-corporate-music-business concept album, Petty counters his analysis of a shady industry run by greedy and lecherous businessmen with some poignant songs about love, past and present. Undoubtedly the most therapeutic song for Petty to write and sing was "Dreamville," which is a nostalgic look back at his Gainesville childhood in the 1950s and 60s. It is filled with memories of innocence, simplicity, and his loving mother.

While Petty found some relief through music to help him through an abusive childhood, an abusive marriage, divorce, clinical depression, and drug addiction, so did TPN member Nancy Wilson, whose life of physical and emotional trauma somewhat parallels Petty's. "Tom's music limped me through many phases," Wilson says, "helped me through many difficulties in life."

During her younger years, Wilson "had suffered childhood trauma and abuse" that ultimately led her to "a failed suicide attempt." From 1994 to 2002 Wilson battled depression and "a horrible" meth addiction. Through these times she says there were relevant Petty songs that "ministered to" her, such as "A Wasted Life," "Insider," and "Don't Fade On Me." "Refugee," in particular, helped her. About the song, she says that it "spoke to (her) as a light and life in the midst of (her) darkness and dying," explaining, "I had given up to the point it never even occurred to me I could still fight." She channeled Petty's lyrics. "I began to try again. I could sit there, wallowing in my abusive past, or fight to be free. It was a real long fight."

Later in life, after she escaped from an abusive marriage, Petty "continued to speak to" her with certain topical songs, such as "Echo" and "Wildflowers." By 2011, when she was divorced, continuing her education, and working at a veterinary clinic, the on-topic songs "Free Girl Now" and "Walls" were her "saving grace." She is now 15 years clean from drug addiction and "almost fully recovered" from depression.

Nearly all of Petty's fans interviewed for this story recall fondly the communal feel of a Tom Petty concert. They talk about Petty's warmth of spirit on stage and the ad-hoc community in the audience. And they talk about singing along together, as a shared experience. Having seen 13 Petty shows myself, I can attest to this. Tom Petty was cognizant of this. In the Bogdanovich documentary, Petty noted the importance of his music to his fans—and to himself. "It's my place of peace as much as it's something to bring to others," he said. Petty recounted a post-dark-days conversation he had with Johnny Cash, a longtime friend, who told him, "This is noble work." Petty questioned, "Noble work?" To which Cash answered, "Yeah, it makes a lot of people happy." Petty reflected: "That hit me like a bolt to the brain. Why didn't I ever have that thought before? … Then I went and played some shows and looked out and as far as you can see people are jumping up and down. They're happy. It helped me to see the value of it and what it meant in these people's lives, because, really, what it means to them is exactly what it meant to me" (*Runnin'*).

Like other Petty fans, TPN member Kathleen Connors speaks about the therapeutic value of his songs and of his concerts, and is saddened that there will be no more of either: "And to know I'll never stand in an arena and sing along with thousands of other voices and watch as Tom spreads his arms and soaks up all that love is heartbreaking. Tom Petty and the Heartbreakers concerts were lovefests. It was a time to fill up your soul-tank … so you could go back to the world renewed and refreshed."

Music therapists are aware of this therapeutic, almost medicinal, quality of live concerts. "There's just something about music—particularly live music—that excites and activates the body. Music very much has a way of enhancing quality of life and can, in addition, promote recovery," said Joanne Loewy, director of the Armstrong Center for Music and Medicine at Mount Sinai Beth Israel Medical Center in New York City and co-editor of the *Music and Medicine* journal (qtd. in Novotney 46).

Is music medicinal? And what lies ahead in the field of music therapy? These are the driving questions posed by The Sync Project, a Boston-based company that launched in 2015. The company intends to create smartphone app technology that predicts the songs people need to hear in order to maintain focus or lower their heart rate. Moreover, by building on what is already known about the positive impact of music therapy and combining the latest technology in the health and music industries, the company hopes the app will be capable of playing music that improves overall physical and mental health. The Sync Project—that has among its advisors Peter Gabriel and Annie Clark, known musically as St. Vincent—was profiled in a May 7, 2015, *The Atlantic* magazine article, "Can Music Be Used as Medicine?" by Chau Tu.

The question of whether music is medicinal was also considered on

April 24, 2015, in Boston when Harvard Medical School hosted a seminar called "Music as Medicine: The impact of healing harmonies," at which the implications—and applications—of music therapy were discussed by experts on the panels and in the audience. Among the topics discussed was why people get certain songs stuck in the head and whether concert-going has a positive impact on one's health; the scientific jury is still out on both.

Nevertheless, we know from our own experiences that music, recorded and live, has the power to uplift or ground us during times of anguish, grief, and loss—including Petty's death. Just as Tom Petty's music heals us, music healed Tom Petty. It is unknown whether Petty was an armchair scholar in the therapeutic use of music during times of crisis and trauma, but it is clear that music served this purpose for him. Throughout his life, listening to music consoled and inspired him, and creating it did the same.

Petty talked about aging during a 2006 *Rolling Stone* interview with Neil Strauss. "You realize you have a limited amount of time left," said Petty, noting the importance of focusing on what's important: family, friends, and music. "You realize this music is going to be here a long time after I am gone. So I really put everything I can into it and make it as good as I can and get everything in me out" (qtd. in Strauss 74).

With news of his passing, Bruce Springsteen said this to *Rolling Stone's* David Fricke about Petty's legacy: "Good songs stay written. Good records stay made. They are always filled with the promise and hope and life essence of their creator. Tom made a lot of great music, enough to carry people forward" (qtd. in Fricke 18 Oct. 2017).

And it will be Tom Petty's music that will help empower us all to carry forward, heal ourselves, and find that inner peace.

WORKS CITED

Aiken-Hall, Jessica. *The Monster That Ate My Mommy*. Moonlit Madness Press, 2017.
_____. Personal interview. 18 November to 21 December 2017.
Alive Inside. Directed by Michael Rossato-Bennett, Projector Media, 2014.
AMTA (American Music Therapy Association) website, https://www.musictherapy.org.
Cashman, Jeanne Moulton. Personal interview. 18 November to 21 December 2017.
Chapligin, Annette. Personal interview. 18 November to 21 December 2017.
Connors, Kathleen. Personal interview. 18 November to 21 December 2017.
Edge, Mitzi. Personal interview. 18 November to 21 December 2017.
Eggers, Donna Michelle Harris. Personal interview. 18 November to 21 December 2017.
Fricke, David. "Bruce Springsteen Remembers Tom Petty." https://www.rollingstone.com. 18 October 2017, https://www.rollingstone.com/music/features/bruce-springsteen-remembers-tom-petty-w508746.
_____. "It's Good to Be King." *Rolling Stone*. Issue No. 1093, 10 Dec. 2009, p. 75, https://www.thepettyarchives.com/archives/magazines/2000s/2009-12-10-rollingstone.
Garrett, Marissia. Personal interview. 18 November to 21 December 2017.
Garrido, Sandra, et al. "Music and Trauma: The Relationship Between Music, Personality, and Coping Style." *Frontiers in Psychology*, vol. 6, 10 July 2015, https://doi.org/10.3389/fpsyg.2015.00977.
Kartzoff, Deb. Personal interview. 18 November to 21 December 2017.

Keppler, Bob. Personal interview. 18 November to 21 December 2017.
Kringen, Shannon Nicole. Personal interview. 18 November to 21 December 2017.
Levitin, Daniel J. *This Is Your Brain on Music: The Science of a Human Obsession.* New York: Plume, 2006.
Lindstrom, Sherri. Personal interview. 18 November to 21 December 2017.
Morris, Vivian. Personal interview. 18 November to 21 December 2017.
"Music Physically Considered." *Columbian Magazine. Feb. 1789, Pp. 90–93,* https://dspace.library.colostate.edu/bitstream/handle/10217/184634/MMTA01507.pdf?sequence=4.
Novotney, Amy. "Music as Medicine." *Monitor on Psychology,* vol. 44, no. 10, November 2013, p. 46, http://www.apa.org/monitor/2013/11/music.aspx.
Oates, Jennifer. Personal interview. 18 November to 21 December 2017.
Petty, Tom. *Runnin' Down a Dream.* Edited by Warren Zanes, Chronicle Books, 2007.
Spencer, Sheila. Personal interview. 18 November to 21 December 2017.
Strauss, Neil. "Tom Petty's Last Dance." *Rolling Stone,* no. 1004, July 2006, p. 74, https://www.thepettyarchives.com/pdfs/magazines/2000s/2006-07-13_RollingStone1004.pdf. https://www.thepettyarchives.com/archives/magazines/2000s/2006-07-13-rollingstone.
Tom Petty and the Heartbreakers: Runnin' Down a Dream. Directed by Peter Bogdanovich, Warner Brothers, 2007.
Wilson, Nancy. Personal interview. 18 November to 21 December 2017.
Zanes, Warren. *Petty: The Biography.* New York: Henry Holt, 2015.

About the Contributors

Nate **Bauer** is the director and acquisitions editor for the University of Alaska Press. Prior to his work there, he was lead science communicator at the International Arctic Research Center. He has also worked at Pearson's Evaluation Systems, designing teacher certification tests, and has written response letters to passionate constituents in a U.S. Congressional office.

Rebecca A. **Caton** is a health sciences library administrator. Her background in teaching, business, and reference librarianship has provided a broad base from which she approaches many writing topics. She enjoys exploring generational differences, separating fact from fiction in her literature research, and sharing these findings with others through writing. Her strong, left-brain sense of logic is colorfully complemented by right-brain creativity brought to life through Tom Petty's music.

Karen **Friend** is a writer from Brooklyn, New York, who works in information technology. Her boyfriend proposed at a summer 2008 Tom Petty concert in North Carolina. They now live together in suburban Maryland with their two young boys and an extensive ticket stub collection.

Shye **Gilad** is an adjunct professor and entrepreneur-in-residence at Georgetown University's McDonough School of Business. He earned an MBA in international business, and a Professional Certified Coach (PCC), with a certificate in Leadership Coaching from the Georgetown Institute for Transformational Leadership. He is passionate about music, motorcycles, and random acts of comedy.

Mara Lee **Grayson** is an assistant professor of English at California State University, Dominguez Hills. Her research focuses on racial literacy in composition studies. She holds a Ph.D. from Columbia University and is the recipient of the 2018 Mark Reynolds *TETYC* Best Article Award. She is the author of *Teaching Racial Literacy*.

Shawn W. **Murphy** is a professor of journalism at State University of New York at Plattsburgh. He also has taught at Midland Lutheran College (Nebraska) and Oklahoma Panhandle State University. Prior to pursuing a career in academia, he worked as a reporter, editor, and photographer for several community newspapers and a magazine.

Stephen **Newton** is a professor of English at William Paterson University in Wayne, New Jersey. As a young man, he had a variety of work experiences, including pumping gas, working on cars, washing dishes and flipping burgers, being a nightshift janitor at the Grand Ole Opry, and was Santa Claus at a shopping mall outside of Nashville, Tennessee.

Lauren Alex **O'Hagan** is a Ph.D. student within the School of English, Communication and Philosophy at Cardiff University. Her research project uses a dataset of 3,000 Edwardian book inscriptions to explore social class in early 20th century Britain. She is also a translator and proofreader, as well as an avid bass player and self-confessed addict of classic rock and '80s pop culture.

Pamela P. **O'Sullivan** has been a librarian at the College at Brockport, New York, for 10 years; her duties include events coordinator and copyright guru. Prior to that, she was a public librarian. She has a long-standing love affair with the music of Tom Petty and is developing a project that would include the recording of some of her own songs.

Spencer **Rowland** is a second-year graduate student and teaching assistant at Wright State University. His field of study is writing and rhetoric and through the guidance of the English Department, he has found a way to combine his two passions of English and music via the subfield of sound studies. He has been a drummer for over a decade and a multi-instrumentalist for the last four years.

Crystal D. **Sands** is an adjunct writing professor at Walden University and freelance author. She is a former writing center director and has taught writing at the college level for more than two decades. She is an award-winning online educator and has published several reference books and textbooks, as well as numerous articles, including "All I Need to Know in Life, I Learned from Tom Petty's Music."

Alessandra Clayton **Trindle** lives in the Midwest with her partner, two children, and four adult rescue cats. She has loved Tom Petty and the Heartbreakers for nearly four decades and can readily admit how Tom Petty shaped her own worldview. Her other political essays can be found on her blog at Feminactivist.

Megan **Volpert** has been teaching high school English in Atlanta for many years and was 2014 Teacher of the Year. She edited the American Library Association–honored anthology *This Assignment Is So Gay*. She has published two books on Tom Petty: *Straight Into Darkness*, and as editor, *Tom Petty and Philosophy*. She writes regularly for *PopMatters* and has also published seven other books on communication and popular culture, including two Lambda Literary Award finalists.

Tom **Zlabinger** is an assistant professor of music at York College in New York, where he directs the York College Big Band and the York College Summer Jazz Program. He completed a Ph.D. in ethnomusicology at the Graduate Center and has written primarily about the depiction of musicians and music making in and around various media franchises.

Index

193